BiR -2087212

AN A TO Z OF ANCIENT EGYPT

COMING SOON . . .

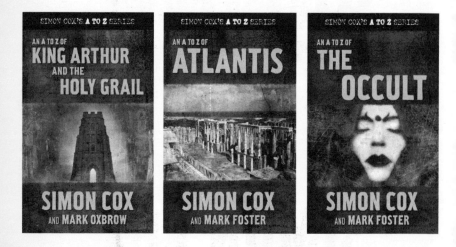

SIMON COX'S **A TO Z** SERIES

SIMON COX'S A TO Z SERIES

AN A TO Z OF
ANCIENT EGYPT

SIMON COX
AND SUSAN DAVIES

with extra material by

Ed ~~Davies, Mark Foster and Jacqueline Harvey~~

MAINSTREAM
PUBLISHING
EDINBURGH AND LONDON

First published in Great Britain in 2006 by
MAINSTREAM PUBLISHING COMPANY (EDINBURGH) LTD
7 Albany Street
Edinburgh EH1 3UG

ISBN 1 84596 077 7

A catalogue record for this book is available from the British Library

Typeset in Baskerville and Gill Sans

Printed and bound in Great Britain by
William Clowes Ltd, Beccles, Suffolk

ACKNOWLEDGEMENTS

This is always one of the most difficult sections to write; there is a fear of leaving out somebody who played a crucial role in the book's development. We hereby apologise to anybody we might have left out of our list and want to state that our appreciation knows no bounds. So here it is, our acknowledgements to the good and the great, the people who have helped in any way to bring this book to fruition.

First, three people who contributed research and material for this *A to Z* and without whom progress would have been considerably slower: Jacqueline Harvey deserves our appreciation and respect for her Egyptian insights and knowledge; Ed Davies of Ancient World Research, who as usual proved prolific – here's to you PP; Mark Foster, who once again stepped in to fill a void and whose cover artwork is as awesome as ever.

Thanks also to Caroline Davies for the great cover image and for being a brilliant photographer; Robert Kirby, the greatest living literary agent, and Catherine Cameron, who enables him to be so; Bill Campbell at Mainstream; Fiona Brownlee for telling Simon to get a haircut, though he is still not sure about that one; Ailsa Bathgate, who is still in recovery from the previous book; and Claire Rose – the bubbly is on its way!

In Egypt, we would like to thank: Abdallah Homouda for the introduction and kindness shown – you are truly TGLE; Salah Tawfik and Ahmed Abo el Ela – two fine historians and great friends whose research, knowledge and friendship we have appreciated immensely.

We would also like to thank Mark Oxbrow and Ian Robertson for continued friendship and support, and for being the best Fringe co-hosts anyone could ask for.

Susan would like to thank: Marcus Davies for Amsterdam entertainment – one day the kilogram steak is yours. For being true friends: Patricia Legan, Jane and Alexander, Alison, Neil, Joe and Baby Roberts, Georgina and Alan Gammon, Cameron Macleod, for the ichats, Stewart Medhurst, Mother for being Mother, Gran for being remarkable and Uncle Alfred for being amusing.

Simon would like to thank: the US crew – Jennifer Clymer for still being brilliant; M.J. Miller (it's still all about me, baby!); Jason Melton (thanks for the Mercer – I owe you one). On the home front: Mark and Claire Cox; Mum and Dad on their island retreat; Gemma Smith and Samwise the troublesome pooch; Richard Belfield and Marcus Mazure for the Lost Leo; Andy Gough (altogether now, Krasnopolsky); Mark Freitag for making my music sound better; the Marina Court mob; for once more providing the brain food and nourishment needed, the boys in Kempton's best restaurant, Blue Ginger; a continuous musical backdrop provided by Epica, Kamelot, Nightwish, After Forever and a whole host of symphonic metal.

CONTENTS

INTRODUCTION

Welcome to the first in a series of A to Z books that I will be bringing out over the next couple of years. The A to Z series is intended to bring you an insight into enduring mysteries, alternative history and ancient cultures. What this series is not intended to be is the ultimate reference guide; for that, you should look elsewhere, and I will include in each of the books a brief bibliography listing some of the books that in my opinion will give you the best head start on each subject. What I have tried to do is bring together information and research from both the orthodox and alternative camps, so enabling you, the reader, to take a balanced approach to some of the material and theories, old and new, that are out there.

I am undertaking the A to Z series with a number of different co-authors and also with the input and help of other researchers and writers, in what is truly a team effort. By executing the work in this way, I hope to bring a much broader view to the table. The A to Z series kicks off with this, *An A to Z of Ancient Egypt*, and will continue with *An A to Z of Atlantis*, *An A to Z of King Arthur and the Holy Grail* and *An A to Z of the Occult*. Not only do these subjects and areas fascinate me – and they always have – but I have also researched and written about them in the past. I hope to bring even more subjects into the series in the future.

In this, my first effort, I, along with my co-author Susan Davies, have tried to make the beautiful and mysterious world of Ancient Egypt more accessible and understandable without restricting ourselves to straight facts and figures. The aim was to stay in a narrative frame of mind and not to fall back on simply reciting dates, measurements and lists ad infinitum. What you will find here are opinions, hints at new theories and research, and questions about the orthodox history that we have been taught. I make no apologies for this; indeed, it was the intention from the start.

For the facts and figures we have used in this book, our reference has been *The Oxford Encyclopaedia of Ancient Egypt*, edited by Donald Redford – a veritable bible of Egyptology. And though I might disagree with some of the absolute assertions within the *Encyclopaedia*, it has proven to be a solid foundation on which to rest and an arbiter between divergent chronologies and linguistic variations.

Egyptology as a science is barely 150 years old and has in the past been the domain of an elite. Indeed, when I myself studied Egyptology at University College, London, there was only a handful of other students on my course. This state of affairs stands in stark contrast to the general interest in all things Egyptian. Whenever an image from Ancient Egypt appears on the cover of a magazine or book, sales rocket; whenever a new documentary or movie is released with an Egyptian theme, box-office figures soar. Egypt and its ancient history are a perennial source of fascination; there is a romance and a mystical quality to the study of this ancient culture that is timeless.

Egypt provides wonderful opportunities for travellers to visit some of the monuments left to us by this most brilliant and enigmatic of cultures. Indeed, at Giza there is the opportunity to gaze in awe at the last remaining wonder of the ancient world – the Great Pyramid – following in the footsteps of generations of visitors to this vast monument. It would be a shame, however, to ignore the attractions of contemporary Egypt, with its bustling markets, marvellous landscape and truly unique approach to traffic management. With every taxi driver thinking he is a Formula One competitor, even the most routine journey becomes an adventure. Whether the country is viewed from the deck of a Nile cruiser as the riverbank slips by or enjoyed from the back of a camel courtesy of the enterprising traders at Giza, the memories are guaranteed to last a lifetime.

I love Egypt, it is in my blood, and I hope that in reading this

A to Z of Ancient Egypt some of you will also fall in love with that incredible country. If only one reader does, then the entire exercise has been worthwhile.

Simon Cox,
May 2006

ABYDOS

The main visitor attraction at Abydos is the 19th-Dynasty temple of Seti I, which contains not only some of the most exquisite artwork in Egypt (in the form of the wall decorations of the chapels and the hypostyle halls) but also the mysterious structure known as the Osireion. It is located 165 km north of Luxor, about a three-hour drive – a journey that is currently undertaken in a convoy due to security concerns. Abydos is on the west bank of the Nile, about 15 km from the river, on the edge of the desert. In the Arabic name of the town, Arabah el-Madfunah, 'Arabah the Buried', there is an indication of just how much still lies beneath the sands. The history of the site pre-dates Seti I's temple by over 1,500 years, and to understand the importance of the location, we need to delve deep into the beginnings of Egyptian culture.

The earliest temple in the area is dedicated to Osiris-Khentyamentiu and is situated at modern Kom es-Sultan (which means 'Mound of the Ruler' in Arabic). The renowned Egyptologist Sir William Flinders Petrie excavated here in 1902–3 and deduced that a temple to the canine god Khentyamentiu, 'Foremost of the Westerners' ('the Westerners' in this context meaning 'the dead'), was the focus of rituals there in the Predynastic era. As Osiris rose to prominence, the two gods became syncretised, and the temple to this dual god is referred to on many stelae (stone or wooden slabs bearing inscriptions or paintings) and offering inscriptions from the Old Kingdom onwards. As an aside, it was near Kom es-Sultan that the only statue of Khufu – the builder of the Great

Pyramid of Giza – inscribed with his name was found, a minute, 7-cm, ivory, seated statue now in the Cairo Museum.

Excavations in the nineteenth century revealed large tombs for the kings of the 1st and 2nd dynasties, and shortly afterwards mastabas for the same rulers were discovered at North Saqqara. This led to the theory that the Abydos structures were cenotaphs: in other words, they contained no burials. However, since the early-dynasty rulers were from the Thinite nome (the area around Abydos), it is more likely to have been the Saqqara mastabas that were 'empty tombs'. The area in which the tombs were found is called Umm el-Qa'ab ('Mother of Pots') because of all the pottery finds there. Early excavators included Auguste Mariette, in 1858, and Émile Amélineau, from 1895–8. The methods used by Amélineau attract particular criticism from contemporary archaeologists, and considerable evidence is presumed lost as a result of what amounted to 'treasure hunting' on his part.

At Umm el-Qa'ab, in 1898, Amélineau found what he believed to be the tomb of Osiris, a series of mud-brick chambers and a central structure with storerooms on three sides. In one corner of the tomb, a black basalt artefact was found that was discovered to be a bier on which lay an effigy of the god Osiris. The 'body' was protected at the four corners of the bed by statues of hawks, representing Horus, and the sides of the bed were decorated with guardian lions. In a recreation of the story of Horus's conception Isis, in the form of a bird, is being impregnated on the loins of her husband Osiris. Amélineau found a skull in the tomb and declared it to be the actual skull of Osiris, even after examination showed it to be from a female skeleton. Convinced that the gods had actual burial sites, Amélineau also identified a nearby tomb as the burial place of Horus and Seth. When Anthony Leahy re-examined the basalt bed in the latter half of the twentieth century, it was identified as an artefact dedicated by the 13th-Dynasty pharaoh Khendjer, showing that by this time the Egyptians believed the site to be the burial place of Osiris.

Amélineau's 'tomb of Horus and Seth' was in fact the tomb of the 2nd-Dynasty king Khasekhemwy, as confirmed by Flinders Petrie in 1899–1900, and it was Petrie, too, who identified the 'tomb of Osiris' as that of Djer, a 1st-Dynasty king. Petrie's workers also found a mummified arm that had been overlooked in Djer's tomb, which still had a number of items of turquoise and gold jewellery on it when found. While the jewellery is now in the Egyptian

Museum in Cairo, the arm itself has been lost – leading Petrie to comment, 'A museum is a dangerous place.'

The tomb of Djer, then, became associated with Osiris from the late Middle Kingdom, and from the 12th Dynasty, people from other parts of Egypt wished to be buried at Abydos. There is a temple dedicated to the pharaoh Senusret III at South Abydos, as well as a cenotaph for him. Large numbers of cenotaphs for private individuals were also built, and excavations have so far revealed over 2,000 stelae and numerous offering tablets. Since the tomb of Djer was regarded as the tomb of Osiris, it became a place of pilgrimage, and devout worshippers left tribute to him. In New Kingdom tombs, the inscriptions often show the deceased person making a symbolic pilgrimage to Abydos after death, determined to become associated with Osiris.

Originally, Iunu (Heliopolis) had been the centre of worship of Osiris, but this later moved to two locations: Djedu (modern Busiris) in the Delta, where the *djed* pillar was particularly revered; and Abdjw (Abydos), further south. In one version of the myth of Osiris, his head was buried at Abydos after his jealous brother Seth had cut the god's body into various pieces. There was a yearly festival centred on the temple of Osiris-Khentyamentiu, with an image of the god making a procession to Umm el Qa'ab on a sacred barque shrine. The 13th-Dynasty official Ikhernofret describes the Osiris festival, detailing the preparation of the statue and the purification rituals involved.

Flinders Petrie also discovered the tomb of Queen Merneith at Umm el-Qa'ab, a large structure with many subsidiary burials that had features suggesting she had reigned as a pharaoh. A large number of subsidiary burials – as many as 580 – were also found around the tomb of Djer and around his funerary enclosure, which was excavated by Petrie in 1921–2. The tombs built for the early rulers of Egypt were monumental in scale: Khasekhemwy's tomb at Umm el-Qa'ab, for example, had 58 chambers. Two skeletons were found in the tomb by Amélineau, but it is impossible to know if either belonged to the king.

In the 1960s, Barry Kemp found a row of funerary enclosures to the east of the burial site, reminiscent of the mortuary temples associated with later pyramid complexes. These enclosures consist of large mud-brick walls, constructed in the so-called 'palace-façade' style of architecture that was copied in stone at Saqqara in the Step Pyramid enclosure. Khasekhemwy's enclosure is still visible, and when it was examined by David O'Connor between 1986 and 1991, he found 12 boats buried on the eastern side of the complex. The Khasekhemwy enclosure was vast, 54 m by 113 m in dimension, and even today the walls are 11 m high in some places and over 5 m thick. The enclosure of Qaa also survives and today surrounds a Coptic (Egyptian Christian) village.

Also near the southern end of the Abydos site was a pyramid, in fact the last royal pyramid built in Egypt, along with a cenotaph and temple, constructed for Ahmose I, as well as a temple for his wife, Ahmose-Nefertari. Dr Stephen Harvey re-examined these in 1993 and identified painted fragments possibly showing the struggle against the Hyksos at the start of the 18th Dynasty. A chapel dedicated by the 18th-Dynasty pharaoh Tuthmosis III has been found, and building continued throughout later dynasties. As late as the 26th Dynasty, a shrine at Umm el-Qa'ab was built by Wahibre (also known as Apries, the Greek version of his name), and it was only gradually, following the Persian invasion of 525 BC and the steady decline in Egyptian religion which ensued, that the popularity of Abydos faded. A few artefacts from the Roman period show that the area around Abydos was held sacred for as long as the Egyptian gods were worshipped.

To return to the temples of Seti I and Ramesses II in Middle Abydos, one famous feature of the Seti I temple is the king list on one of the walls. In one of the scenes, the future Ramesses II is shown reading out a list of his predecessors. There are some notable omissions from the list, including the Amarna-period rulers Akhenaten, Smenkhkare and Tutankhamun, who were considered heretics and had been 'tidied' out of the official history. In the Sokar chapel at the Seti I temple there is a relief showing Isis as a bird hovering over the body of Osiris in order to conceive. This scene is a two-dimensional version of the myth of Horus's conception as depicted on the bier found in the 'tomb of Osiris'.

At the rear of the temple is the structure known as the Osireion. It has a long, descending gallery on which extracts from the Book of Gates, the Book of Caverns and the Book of Going Forth by Day (more commonly known as the Book of the Dead) are carved. Margaret Murray and Flinders Petrie excavated the Osireion in 1902–3. They found a central granite hall containing a sarcophagus-shaped island surrounded by water, in a scene that resembles the Egyptian concept of the mound of creation. There is considerable debate over the age of the Osireion: the cartouches carved onto the walls date it to the 19th Dynasty and to Merenptah, the son of Ramesses II; but the style of masonry resembles Old Kingdom buildings such as the Valley Temple of Khafre, next to the Sphinx at Giza. Several anomalies exist: for example, the entrance to the Osireion begins outside the wall of the Seti I temple. Also, when archaeological pits were dug near the walls, pottery dating to the Archaic period was discovered; in a structure supposed to be of 19th-Dynasty origin, any deposits around the base would be expected to be no older than that dynasty.

It is also apparent on visiting the site that either a huge amount of earth was removed to create the Osireion or the ground level was much lower when it was created. If the second of these hypotheses was true, it would mean that the Osireion was built at a much earlier date than the Temple of Seti constructed around it. The Roman writer Strabo visited Abydos and described the Osireion as covered with a great mound that was planted with trees. The once-subterranean chambers are now exposed to the sky, as many of the granite roof blocks are now missing. The god Osiris is sometimes referred to as 'He who sleeps surrounded by water', and this does make the Osireion, with its watery central chamber, seem a likely candidate for the burial place of the god. Also, a Late Period stela refers to 'the hill of Thinis, which conceals its Lord', which could be an oblique reference to Osiris and the mound that Strabo saw covering the Osireion. Perhaps the pilgrims who travelled to the tomb of King Djer believing it to be the tomb of Osiris were in fact visiting a decoy.

In the twentieth century, Abydos became the home of an Englishwoman who was known both to the local villagers and tourists as Omm Seti. Dorothy Eady was born in 1904 in Blackheath, near London, and developed a fascination for Ancient Egypt in general, and the pharaoh Seti I in particular, from an early age. It seems that she suffered a fall at the age of three and was knocked unconscious. When she recovered from the accident, she began to dream about Egypt and considered it to be her home. It became her belief that the spirit of an Egyptian priestess had entered her at the time of her fall and that much of her knowledge came from this former life. She spent a lot of her time at the Egyptian Department of the British Museum and learnt to read hieroglyphs with the help of tuition from Sir Wallis Budge, who was then Keeper of Egyptian and Assyrian Antiquities at the museum.

In 1933, she went to Egypt to marry an Egyptian, and she

spent the rest of her life in the land of her beloved Seti I. When she had a son, he was, naturally, called Seti, and, in keeping with local tradition, she became known as Omm Seti – 'Mother of Seti'. Working with the great Egyptian archaeologists Selim Hassan and Ahmed Fakhry, Omm Seti studied the area around Giza, putting to good use her knowledge of hieroglyphs and her skills at drawing and recording the artefacts found. After visiting Abydos, she became convinced that she had lived there in her previous existence, and in 1956 the Egyptian Antiquities Service transferred her there, where she remained until her death in 1981.

Omm Seti observed the festivals of the Ancient Egyptian calendar, and especially the feast of Osiris. She believed that Osiris was buried in the mound in the Osireion, and she left instructions that after her death she was to receive neither a Christian nor a Muslim burial. Her wishes were to be interred close to the temple, to be with the people she considered to be her own – the ancient priests and priestesses of Osiris and of Seti I.

SEE ALSO: Boat Burials, Osiris, Funerary Books, Khufu, Queens Reigning as Pharaoh

AKHENATEN

Akhenaten has been described as one of history's first individuals because of the unusual and sometimes grotesque manner in which he chose to be portrayed, particularly in the early years of his reign, and his break with the traditional religious ideas of that time. The famous Egyptologist Sir Flinders Petrie called him 'the most original thinker that ever lived in Egypt and one of the great idealists of the world'. He has also been called a philosopher, a religious reformer and a pacifist. Others, though, have been less than complimentary, calling him a 'misshapen individual' and 'effete'. To his successors, he was a 'heretic' and 'the criminal'. Akhenaten's name was not to be spoken or written, and because of this he was excluded from the king lists, his name erased from monuments and his buildings torn down, the stone used in other pharaohs' building projects. The thinking behind this was not just to expunge Akhenaten from history but also to ensure he had a permanent death, with no hope of rebirth in the afterlife. His fate was to be one of obliteration and oblivion. So what do we know of Akhenaten that could explain such hatred?

Born a younger son of Amenhotep III and his chief wife, Tiye, Akhenaten became King on his father's death in c.1372 BC, although there is speculation that he shared a brief coregency with his father. As Pharaoh, he enjoyed a seventeen-year reign, with the first five years, during which he was known by his birth name, Amenhotep IV, based at Thebes. Within Thebes, Akhenaten soon began building a large temple complex called the Gempaaten

('The Aten is found'). Not only was this temple not dedicated to Amun, the predominant god of the Egyptian state at this time, but its architecture departed radically from the traditional temple form, being open to the elements and hence reflecting the visible, physical form of the Aten – the sun disc. In Year 5 of his reign, Akhenaten changed his name and moved the capital to Akhetaten ('Horizon of the Aten'), modern-day Amarna. From this time a softening in representations of the royal family can be seen, with a greater emphasis on domesticity and an increasing naturalism. Nefertiti's role also changed from that presented at Thebes; at Akhetaten she was represented less as a powerful and active queen regnant and more as a loving partner to the pharaoh. This suggests that Akhenaten put all his energy into promoting the cult at an early stage and then relaxed the rules once he was at Akhetaten and the main concepts of the Aten cult had been accepted by the people. Accordingly, although the four elder daughters' names all contain the element 'Aten', those of the younger two do not, using instead the name Ra, which may indicate a less radical form of worship as Akhenaten's reign progressed.

The supremacy of Akhenaten was pivotal in the Aten cult, a cult which had not been devised by Akhenaten but which was the culmination of a process that had been going on for some time whereby the physical form of the sun – the Aten – became an increasingly important aspect of the sun-god Ra, with an increased emphasis on the relationship of the sun to the King. The unique way in which the Aten was emphasised by Akhenaten was totally different, however, and represented a radical departure from what had gone before. The focus now was solely on the Aten and no longer on its association with Ra. The Aten was the creator of all – the source of life itself – it was the only potent deity and the worship of other gods was prohibited. Unusually, under Akhenaten the sun disc remained non-anthropomorphic, attained royal attributes, such as its names written within cartouches, celebrated its own jubilees and wore the uraeus symbol of kingship. Akhenaten was the Aten's earthly incarnation. In many representations of the Aten, it's rays end in tiny hands that hold the *ankh* symbol of life to the nostrils of the king and his Great Wife, Nefertiti. The king was the only intermediary between Aten and the people, being the chief celebrant, with all prayers to the god being addressed through Akhenaten.

But what was the reason behind Akhenaten's desire to promote the Aten as the sole deity? The concept of Akhenaten's monotheistic religion has led some to suggest that he either inspired Moses and the Exodus (Sigmund Freud) or, going one step further, that he actually was Moses (Ahmed Osman). In his reforms, Akhenaten was certainly revolutionary and, whatever the truth behind the Moses connection, it is clear that the religious reforms benefited Akhenaten, with the reasons behind the reforms not necessarily being totally pious in intent. If his dominance and importance to the cult had not been stressed so utterly, it would be easier to believe in Akhenaten's devotion and religious fervour.

It has been stated that Akhenaten's obsession with religious matters marked him out as a pacifist, ignoring the needs of his country and allowing Egypt's standing to diminish. However, the evidence of reliefs and stelae present Akhenaten in the traditional pharaonic role of smiting his enemies, in the form of bound Nubian and Asiatic captives – Nefertiti, too, was depicted carrying out this ritual. In the south, Akhenaten's policy towards Nubia continued to uphold Egypt's interests there, with campaigns undertaken to put down a number of Nubian insurrections. Despite apparent problems in the Levant, there was no loss of territory and even Tyre and Byblos on the outer reaches of the empire stayed within the Egyptian sphere of influence, which must attest to action being taken by Akhenaten whenever it was needed.

One of the main mysteries surrounding Akhenaten relates to the depiction of the human form, which went through a revolutionary change during Akhenaten's reign. In particular, the king was portrayed with a protruding belly, rounded shoulders, full hips, long neck, large chin and elongated skull. This style was not only limited to the king but was used on all who surrounded him. Nefertiti and the small princesses are shown in this peculiar and sometimes bizarre manner, which was more exaggerated in the earlier years and never more so than in the colossal statues of Akhenaten found at Thebes. The question then arises of why Akhenaten wanted to show himself in this way. There are various theories on this point, including suggestions that he was a eunuch (based on a statue of the king without genitalia) or that he was actually a woman. Others have looked to a medical reason for his unusual physique, putting forward the view that Akhenaten suffered from Frölich syndrome, a glandular disorder with symptoms that correspond with how Akhenaten was represented but which also produces impotency – an unlikelihood given that Akhenaten had at least six daughters. A recent proposal is that he suffered from Marfan syndrome, a genetic condition that affects the connective tissues, causing problems with eyesight, the skeleton and internal organs. Outwardly, sufferers of this syndrome are very tall, have long faces, some deformity of the chest and long fingers – all traits that are displayed on the statues and reliefs of the king.

However, it is unlikely that Akhenaten had such an unusual physical appearance, and a more probable reason for the curious representation is that it was directly linked to the Aten cult. It has been advanced that such a portrayal was intended to stress the difference between the king and ordinary people, emphasising his unique position in relation to the Aten. Hence the king portrayed himself as both mother and father of his people, as is seen in the androgynous Nile god Hapy, who shares some of the characteristics associated with Akhenaten. With the Aten always depicted as a sun disc, it has been speculated that, as the Aten was 'the one who built himself by himself, with his own hands', no craftsman was permitted to make an image of him other than the disc, in contrast with the other, anthropomorphic deities. The form taken by the disc had the advantageous effect of allowing the king to take centre stage. The colossal statues of the king that had been set up in Thebes show him with extremely thin and elongated features, especially his face. Again, this has been equated with his desire to impress and overshadow the observer. Originally set up high, these statues would have towered over the onlooker, but staring straight up at the king's depiction, the harsh features would in fact appear more in proportion due to the angle of sight.

While there is little substantive evidence about the intricacies of Akhenaten's life, even less is known about his whereabouts in death. The boundary stela set up to mark the extent of the city of Akhetaten states that if he died outside the city, Akhenaten was to be brought back there for burial. Although the royal tomb at Amarna was unfinished, some funerary fragments relating to Akhenaten have been found inside, leading to the conclusion that he was originally buried within but was probably moved during the reign of Tutankhamun when Akhetaten was abandoned. Where he was moved to, however, is again uncertain, but Tomb 55 in the Valley of the Kings has been suggested, although this is not at all conclusive.

A number of Amarna individuals have been proposed as the

possible occupant of the coffin found in 1907 in the tomb referred to as KV55. Unfortunately, the bad state of the tomb due to water seepage, its chaotic state and the appalling recording and analysis by the archaeologists who found it have not helped in the identification of the occupant. Added to this, the tomb included a number of funerary objects that clearly belonged to different people: Queen Tiye's dismantled shrine, magic bricks inscribed with Akhenaten's name, Canopic jars thought to belong to Kiya, the secondary wife of Akhenaten, and a variety of faience jars, amulets and statuettes. The coffin was badly rotted because of the water damage and a fall from the bier it had originally rested upon. First made for a woman (Kiya?) and adapted for a royal male by the addition of the crook and flail and uraeus, the coffin is very similar in design to the second coffin of Tutankhamun. However, the names inscribed upon it had been excised, the gold mask ripped and the skull damaged, further obscuring the identity of the individual. The initial assessment of the mummy led to the conclusion that it was a woman, later identified as Tiye, but subsequent analysis has suggested a 20-year-old male with facial similarities to Tutankhamun, implying that the occupant of the coffin is Smenkhkare, a shadowy figure reigning briefly before Tutankhamun.

However, textual analysis of the coffin's inscriptions implies that it held none other than Akhenaten himself, a view underlined by the presence of his magic bricks, a prerequisite for any burial. It is thought that two or more coffins and related equipment had been moved here from Akhetaten, but when the tomb was accidentally found by workers cutting another royal tomb, they believed the body within the coffin was that of Akhenaten and thus destroyed all evidence of the heretic king. Whilst we have no conclusive proof as to the identity of the person in the coffin, it is evident that whoever the despoilers thought was in the coffin provoked such feelings of hatred and condemnation that they took the actions they did.

Akhenaten's sexuality has also come under the microscope, with theories ranging from an Oedipus complex to homosexual tendencies. The idea that Akhenaten was gay is based upon a limestone stela showing Akhenaten caressing another individual, possibly male. Unfortunately, the cartouches cannot be read, so it is impossible to know who the other person is. Due to the artistic conventions of the time, it is even hard to see if a male or female depiction was intended. Originally thought to be the enigmatic Smenkhkare, the figure is now considered to be either Akhenaten's father Amenhotep III or even Nefertiti.

This one stela underlines the problems in deciphering Akhenaten's reign, the individuals involved with him and the events that surrounded his life and death. The short period of Akhenaten's rule in the middle of the fourteenth century BC will continue to be the centre of much conjecture due to the difficulty in understanding and interpreting the motives behind the actions of Akhenaten. Thus the many diverse and contrary opinions will continue to abound.

SEE ALSO: Amun, Exodus, Nefertiti, Tutankhamun

AMUN

The name of Amun first appears as one of the Ogdoad, the eight gods of the Creation according to Hermopolitan cosmology. In this aspect as a male frog entity, Amun had a feminine counterpart called Amaunet. They represented air and were regarded as hidden or invisible – Amun means 'the hidden one'. He was most often represented in human form with a blue face, wearing a headdress decorated with two long feathers, possibly reflecting the wind. The ram, a symbol of virility, was sacred to Amun, and the downturned horns of the ram became one of the god's symbols. Reference to Amun is made in the Pyramid Texts in the 5th Dynasty, although early in his development he was worshipped mainly in the area around modern Luxor, known as Waset to the Ancient Egyptians.

Amun assimilated the characteristics of other gods, and by the Middle Kingdom, as a war-god in Waset, he was associated with Montu, another martial deity. When the throne of Egypt was assumed by a dynasty of rulers from this area, Amun became fused with the sun-god Ra, as Amun-Ra, and became a national god. The importance and power of Amun continued to grow and a temple called Ipt-swt ('The Most Select of Places'), now known as Karnak, was established.

Karnak Temple today covers a huge site of 247 acres, and is a complex of structures that was added to for hundreds of years, resulting in numerous chapels and precincts. In addition to temples to Amun, the site contains shrines dedicated to Montu, and also to Amun's consort, the goddess Mut, and their son Khonsu. The priesthood of Amun was very powerful as a result of both the esteem in which the god was held and the wealth of the estates owned by the temples. During the reign of Akhenaten, this power base was dismantled as the pharaoh overthrew the old gods and established Aten as the new state god. At this time, inscriptions of the name of Amun were defaced in an attempt to destroy the previous divine order and leave Aten supreme. This religious reformation did not outlive the king who instigated it, however, and after Akhenaten's death, the priesthood of Amun flourished again. Estimates vary as to the exact wealth of this temple complex, but it is thought that in the 19th Dynasty, 81,000 people were employed by the priests of Amun at Karnak.

At another time of political upheaval in Egypt, during the Third Intermediary Period, the high priests of Amun founded a dynasty that ruled the territory around their stronghold at Karnak. While pharaohs were crowned in the northern capital, Tanis, the priest-kings controlled the south of the country, a situation that lasted for over 100 years. That the authority of the Pharaoh could be challenged by non-royal people, albeit high priests, demonstrates the awesome power of the priesthood of Amun.

One important role that became attached to Amun was that of being a father to the Pharaoh: 'son of Ra' was one of the King's titles. It was suggested that the god could divinely impregnate the Queen, a concept that is reminiscent of the Virgin Birth of Christ. On the walls of her temple at Deir el-Bahri, the female pharaoh Hatshepsut was very careful to show her mother, Queen Ahmose, being visited by Amun in this way, to legitimise her rule. The god has assumed the appearance of Tuthmosis I, the husband of Ahmose, and, after using his divine breath to make her pregnant, he announces that the queen will give birth to a daughter who will rule Egypt.

Hatshepsut's successor was her nephew Tuthmosis III, whose mother had not been a queen of Egypt. To explain his selection as Crown Prince, he recounted how as a boy he had been attending a procession at which the god Amun chose him, and he recorded this story in a chapel at Karnak. The belief was that a statue of the god, carried by priests, could indicate its wishes by guiding the barque on which it was borne.

Another example of the critical importance of divine approval can be seen in the behaviour of Alexander the Great. In 332 BC,

Alexander took control of Egypt, expelling the Persian rulers who had been much resented by their subjects. Alexander's policy for dealing with territory he added to his empire was to leave local people to worship their own gods, and to try to respect the traditions and customs of his new subjects. His place on the Egyptian throne was secure and he could have proceeded with his campaigns of military conquest and prodigious city-building. However, he chose to visit the oracle at Siwa, becoming the first pharaoh to do so. The Temple of Amun (known as Ammon to the Greeks and associated with Zeus) possessed an oracle that was held in high esteem. To visit it required an arduous journey across the desert, but Alexander was determined to ask questions of this oracle. Tantalisingly, he never revealed the exact questions he asked or the answers he received, although he promised in a letter to his mother that he would tell her what had happened when he returned to Macedonia – something he never did. It was popularly believed, however, that the priests at Siwa told Alexander that Ammon/Zeus was his father, no doubt exactly what he was hoping to hear. Coins were struck featuring the head of Alexander wearing ram's horns, to represent Amun.

During the New Kingdom, an important female role in the worship of Amun started to emerge, as 'God's wife of Amun'. The function of this priestess was to represent the wife of Amun in religious ceremonies, helping to emphasise the process of the King's divine birth. The title 'God's hand' was also used, referring to the act of masturbation by Atum during the Creation. The priestess was thus a symbol for the hand which provided the feminine counterpart to the penis during the first 'copulation'. The post was very important, and it became customary for a daughter of the reigning pharaoh to be chosen for 'God's wife'. Once appointed, the lady was required to remain a virgin, so she would adopt as her successor a daughter of the next king. This ensured that the ruling pharaoh always had his interests represented in the heart of the religious cult of Amun. At Medinet Habu, a great temple complex on the west bank of the Nile at Luxor, there are mortuary chapels dedicated to some of the women who had been God's wife of Amun and they clearly were given a lavish burial.

Two important festivals were linked to Amun and celebrated each year. At the Festival of Opet, the statues of Amun, Mut and Khonsu left their sanctuaries at Karnak and went in procession to Luxor temple. The Pharaoh played an important part in the ritual, and in the union between Amun and Mut that mirrored his own divine conception. The procession was an opportunity for people to approach the statues and seek the answers to questions, as described above. As during all festivals, there was also great enthusiasm for feasting and enjoying beer distributed by temple officials. The Beautiful Festival of the Valley enabled Egyptians to accompany the statue of Amun across the River Nile to the west bank, where offerings were dedicated to deceased relatives.

Although as a state god Amun was inextricably linked to the Pharaoh, the ordinary people, as we have seen, could occasionally participate, albeit in a minor way, in the life of the god. At Karnak, there is a small temple built to receive prayers and entreaties carved on stelae; it is dedicated to 'Amun who hears prayers'.

SEE ALSO: Akhenaten, Atum, Ennead, Queens Reigning as Pharaoh

ANKH

This mysterious symbol is seen everywhere in Egyptian art and literature, yet its origins and precise meaning are extremely hard to pin down, and there has been much speculation as to what exactly it was intended to represent. One thing we do know for sure is that the *ankh* is the hieroglyphic character for life. Aside from this, everything else is conjecture.

The ankh was often used as an amulet. The word comes from the Latin *'amuletem'* and translates as 'means of defence'. Amongst the living, it was worn as a means to prolong life, whilst the dead wore an ankh to lend power to their everlasting spirit.

Many avenues have been explored in an effort to identify the true nature of the ankh and its full meaning. Here are some of the ideas that have been put forward as answers to the riddle:

- that it represents a sandal strap. The word for this in Egyptian was *'nkh'*, a very similar word to *'ankh'*.
- that it resembles a stylised human form, with the loop as the head.
- that it depicts the sun rising on the horizon, thus symbolising the themes of rebirth and renewal, central to Egyptian theology. The loop would be the sun itself, the horizontal crossbar the horizon, and the vertical the path of the rising sun.
- that it represents a sacred knot, the *tyet* symbol, or 'knot of Isis'.
- that it is a key that will unlock the gates of death.

- that it is based on a penis sheath
- that it is a physical manifestation of the royal cartouche in which the Pharaoh's name is written.

As well as the above possibilities, it has also been pointed out by scholars that the symbol of the ankh could symbolise the union of man and woman, representing in this way the intertwined lives of Osiris and Isis. The oval would represent Isis, and the cross below Osiris. Understood in this way, the ankh is a simplistic depiction of the human reproductive organs, but it symbolises not just the union of male and female energies but also the marriage between heaven and earth, the interconnection of the living and the dead.

If the ankh does represent the human sexual organs, then it embodies very clearly the symbol's literal meaning, 'life'. As well as being a figure for life itself, it was also used to signify the power to give and sustain life and was associated with life-giving substances and forces such as water, air, the sun and even the gods. There are numerous depictions of Egyptian gods wearing or carrying the ankh, and in this context it is thought to have symbolised immortality. Other images show gods or goddesses with ankhs at their fingertips, almost seeming to administer the life force represented by the ankh.

Interestingly, even when the pharaoh Akhenaten moved away from the traditional polytheistic Egyptian religion to worship the Aten, he took with him the belief in the ankh as a powerful symbol. Reliefs from the period show the sun disc Aten shining down on Akhenaten. Some of the rays of the sun end in hands, several of which are holding ankhs. In one particular carving, these ankhs point towards the nostrils of Akhenaten and his wife, Nefertiti, and it has been suggested that here the ankhs symbolised the breath of life. There is a similar scene present on one of the chairs of Tutankhamun – whose name was originally Tutankhaten – found in the young king's tomb. The scene shows Tutankhamun and his wife Ankhesenamun (note the use of the word 'ankh' in the royal couple's names), and, again, the ankhs are being held by the hands of the sun's rays under the noses of the king and queen.

It would seem, then, that what is being signified by the physical shape of the ankh is something unseen and magical – that quality which makes life possible but which is impossible to quantify. If so, the Egyptians seem to have endeavoured to give this invisible force a name and a shape, attempted to bring it into the realm of the tangible.

An intriguing area for discussion is how the ankh lent its shape to the symbol of the later Christian Church, the Cross. It is known that early Christians in Egypt, and eventually the Coptic Church, adopted the ankh as the symbol of their religion. Because the ankh was known to symbolise life and rebirth in Dynastic Egypt, it was thought a fitting symbol for the burgeoning Christian Church in that country. To the Coptic Church, the loop of the ankh signified the eternal love of God, particularly as embodied in the sacrifice of Christ. It was also understood as a symbol of Christ's resurrection, resembling his halo over the Cross. The ankh adopted by the Coptic Church was modified somewhat: the loop was more circular than that of the traditional Egyptian ankh. Their version was called a *crux ansata* – Latin for 'cross with a handle'.

It is said that during the early days of the Christian Church, those followers who believed that the Cross should become a symbol of their religion were denounced. It was deemed shameful and offensive to use the image of Christ's pain and suffering as the religion's emblem. However, the deep-rooted positive associations surrounding the ankh made the symbol more acceptable in Egypt, and so it was that the Coptic Church embraced the *crux ansata*. Over time, its use spread, and eventually the Cross become *the* insignia of Christ's followers, even to the extent that many churches and cathedrals have a footprint in the shape of the ankh.

So the symbol of life, the very essence of vitality itself, found a new home at the heart of the Christian religion. The Cross does not represent only the vehicle of Christ's death. Deep beneath the veneer of the Cross's darker symbolism lies a much deeper and profound meaning, one that has had significance to mankind for more than 5,000 years.

SEE ALSO: Akhenaten, Nefertiti, Tutankhamun

APIS BULLS

The worship of bulls in Ancient Egypt can be traced back as far as 3100 BC, prior to the unification of Upper and Lower Egypt. Bull cults appear in Egyptian writings of the 1st Dynasty and records of the worship of the Apis bull in particular can be identified as far back as the 2nd Dynasty, although it is from the later Middle and New kingdoms that a greater wealth of information regarding this cult dates.

The Apis bull was originally thought to be the manifestation of the god Apis, a deity from the time of the earliest dynasties associated with fertility, who would later become intertwined with the god Ptah. Rather than being considered a herald, or an animal that could be used to intercede with the gods on behalf of man, the Apis bull was believed to be the *ka*, or life force, of the god Ptah himself, manifest and walking amongst the living. Interestingly, ka was also the word for 'bull'. After the death of the Apis bull, the ka of Ptah was said to reincarnate in the form of a new bull, and so the succession of Ptah's life force was continuous.

When, later in the development of Egyptian religion, Osiris assumed Ptah's identity to become Ptah-Sokar-Osiris, the Apis bull also became associated with Osiris. However, from then on, instead of living a full life and dying naturally, if the Apis bull lived to 28 – the age at which Osiris was believed to have been killed by his brother Seth – the bull was ritually killed with great ceremony. Pliny the Elder and other commentators mention that the bull was drowned, clearly an echo of the legend that Osiris had died in a similar fashion. After the death of the Apis bull, the search for his successor would begin.

The Greek historian Herodotus wrote in Book Three of his *Histories* about how an Apis bull could be identified:

> The Apis is the calf of a cow which is never afterwards able to have another. The Egyptian belief is that a flash of light descends upon the cow from heaven, and this causes her to receive Apis. The Apis-calf has distinctive marks: it is black, with a white diamond on its forehead, the image of an eagle on its back, the hairs of its tail double and a scarab under its tongue.

The Apis bull was treated with great reverence and kept in a special enclosure in Memphis. It was considered to be an oracle, and the future could be divined by the way the bull moved or whether or not he would take certain foods.

There was a yearly festival in honour of the Apis bull that lasted seven days, during which time many people gathered in Memphis. Processions were held throughout the festival, and the sacred bull was led through the crowds, covered with flowers and jewellery. Children who got close enough and smelled the bull's breath were thought to be blessed with the power of prescience ever after.

Upon the death of an Apis bull, its body was embalmed and placed in a tomb with all the ceremonial pomp afforded to pharaohs and members of the royal family. After preparation of the carcass and removal of the internal organs for preservation, the bull's body was mummified, usually in a seated position similar to that in which a sphinx is generally depicted. Artificial eyes were inserted and the horns were decorated with gold leaf.

The mummified bull was then transported to the Serapeum at Saqqara. This impressive underground complex of catacombs and chambers was used exclusively to entomb Apis bulls, and to date 67 burials have been found, although more are thought to have taken place. From the 26th Dynasty onwards, the Apis bull was placed inside a massive granite sarcophagus weighing between 60 and 80 tons. Huge Canopic jars have been found, indicating that the bulls were buried with their viscera, just like the pharaohs themselves. Often the name of the mother cow (which was referred to as the Isis cow and also revered) and the place of the Apis bull's birth were recorded in the tomb.

The cult of the Apis bull lasted right up until AD 398, when Emperor Honorius banned it, ordering that the Serapeum be sealed for ever.

The Serapeum was excavated in 1851 by the French archaeologist Auguste Mariette. As he penetrated the entrance to the Serapeum using explosives, he found the mummy of a man he believed to be Prince Khaemwaset, a son of Ramesses II who had been governor of Memphis and a high priest of Ptah. According to Mariette, Khaemwaset had requested that after his death he be placed in the Serapeum so that he would be buried with the sacred bulls of Ptah rather than in his own tomb. Such was the allure and power of these sacred animals, each said to be the incarnation of a god, that even the son of a king would choose to spend his eternal rest in their sacred company.

SEE ALSO: Osiris

ASTRONOMY

The Ancient Egyptians achieved amazing advances in the field of astronomy, notably the calculation of time, the development of the calendar and extraordinarily accurate astronomical alignment for building construction. The importance of astronomy to the Ancient Egyptians can be clearly seen in their funerary texts and depictions, particularly in the Pyramid Texts found inscribed on the walls of the corridors and burial chambers of nine Old Kingdom pyramids. In these, the deceased king is said to become an 'Imperishable Star' and thus obtain everlasting life. From the Pyramid Texts, it can be seen that the Egyptians knew about the Milky Way, which they called *mespet shedu*, 'beaten path of stars'. Accordingly, the Pyramid Texts put these at the sky's upper limit: 'The King has reached the sky's height: the Great Ones of the Mace Chamber cannot bar him from the beaten path of stars.'

Later periods saw charts of the night sky drawn on the ceilings of temples and the inner lids of Middle Kingdom coffins. These 'star clocks' divided the night sky into 36 decans, with each decan represented by a specific star, or guardian, that could be seen above the horizon at dawn for 10 days. At the end of this period, another star would rise and it would then act as guardian for 10 days. These charts can be found on the astronomical ceiling in the 18th-Dynasty tomb of Senenmut, the Osireion of Seti I at Abydos (1290 BC) and the tomb of Ramesses IV (1150 BC).

What can be stated with certainty is that the Ancient Egyptians had made a prolonged and detailed study of the stars, enabling them to identify astral movement and even retrograde patterns. Herodotus noted in his *Histories* that:

> the Egyptians were the first to discover the solar year, and to portion out its course into twelve parts both the space of time and the seasons which they delimit. It was observation of the course of the stars which led them to adopt this division.

The later Greek writer Diodorus Siculus stated that Egyptian priests knew that the sun's orbit was elliptical and 'traces a retrograde path opposite to that of the other stars'. He also observed that 'they have preserved to this day the records concerning each of these stars over an incredible number of years'. This indicates that the tradition of Ancient Egyptian astronomy went way back.

Astronomy was important to the Ancient Egyptians because it was essential for the priests to know the correct time for the accurate celebration of their daily ceremonies. The hour priests were astronomers who calculated the time so that religious ceremonies were performed on the right day and at the correct hour. For this, they needed to know the order in which the stars and planets would rise, their position in the sky, the moon's movement, and eclipses of the sun and moon. From observations made at night, the hour priests would draw up charts detailing all this information. These charts covered a 15-day period, and the priests' careful observation and recording meant that it was possible to determine the time of the night just by looking at the position of the stars and referring to the charts. To observe constellations, the priests used an 'instrument of knowing' (*merkhet*), as well as a tool for sighting the stars made from the central rib of a palm leaf.

It would appear that two people were involved in these observations. Situating themselves on a north–south axis, one of the priests squatted and stayed perfectly still so that the second priest could observe the stars as they passed by, using his assistant as a reference. Hourly charts have been found on the ceilings of the 20th-Dynasty tombs of Ramesses VI, Ramesses VII and Ramesses IX and stated such things as: 'When the star Orion is above the left eye [of the squatting priest], it is the seventh hour. When the star that follows Sothis is above the left eye, it is the eighth hour.'

The Egyptians called the five planets that are always visible 'stars that know no rest'. These are Jupiter (Horus who limits the two lands), Mars (Horus of the horizon), Mercury (Sebegu – a god linked to Seth), Saturn (Horus, bull of the sky) and Venus (the one who crosses). To the Egyptians, the constellation we know as the Big Dipper was called the Bull's Leg, Orion was 'man running while looking over his shoulder', whilst Cassiopeia was 'person with extended arms'. Sirius was a very important star to the Ancient Egyptians, not only because of its association with the goddess Isis but also because it heralded the inundation of the Nile, essential to the agricultural and economic well-being of Egypt. It was also used to calculate the Sothic year of 365.25 days, which corresponds to the actual length of the solar year and thus was in step with the natural cycle of Egypt's seasons and solstices.

The Egyptians were the first ancient culture to establish such a precise year-length. The use of Sirius as a calendrical indicator signifies the great knowledge and understanding the Ancient Egyptians possessed relating to astronomy and the true length of the year. In the words of René Schwaller de Lubicz, who studied the Temple of Luxor for 15 years: 'We cannot but admire the greatness of a science capable of discovering such a coincidence, because Sirius is the only star among the "fixed stars" which allows this cycle.' He concludes that to know this fact would have necessitated an astonishingly lengthy study of the heavens. The hour priests observed that Sirius was the only star amongst the 'fixed' stars – those visible throughout the year – that shifted its position each night as the earth orbited the sun.

Otto Neugebauer, who made a detailed study of the Egyptian calendar, concluded that it was the only 'intelligent calendar' that existed. Alongside the regnal year, which was calculated from the date of accession of the current ruler, the Egyptians had a civil year, based on the solar year of 360 days plus 5 extra days (known as epagomenal days) that were stated to be the birthdays of the 5 great deities – Osiris, Isis, Horus, Seth and Nephthys. This, though, did not account for the fact that a solar year actually consists of 365.2422 days, thus leading to the odd situation that the Egyptian civil calendar very rarely corresponded correctly to the seasons, causing great problems with the dating of agricultural festivals. However, the Sothic calendar, which was based upon the heliacal rising of Sirius and thus in sync with the solar year, was also used, although solely for religious purposes. With great precision, the priests of Heliopolis were able to calculate when the rising of Sirius – and hence the New Year – would occur and announce to all Egypt this great event.

Every 1,460 years, the civil and Sothic calendars aligned with each other. This coincidence is known to have occurred in AD 140, when there was a great celebration. Therefore, working backwards, we know that past coincidences happened in 1320 BC, 2780 BC and 4240 BC. This has been seen as a clue as to when the calendar was first established. E. Meyer, who made a study of the Egyptian calendar in 1902, concluded that it must have been introduced in 4240 BC. This conclusion was based on the fact that mention is made in the Pyramid Texts of Sirius and its connection to the year, as well as five extra days in relation to the solar year. Although the earliest written evidence is contained in the Pyramid Texts, dating from the 5th Dynasty (c.2600 BC), it is acknowledged by Egyptologists that they were the result of an oral tradition dating back to a time before the unification of Egypt in 3100 BC. This being the case, 2780 BC is too late a date for the introduction of the calendar, and the only other date that it could then be is 4240 BC – much too early for most Egyptologists to accept. Most believe instead that the calendar derived from the lunar year, linked to the agricultural cycles of the Nile. This would have required a comparatively short period of observation.

Astronomy also meant that the Ancient Egyptians were able to ascertain the four cardinal points of the compass for the orientation of religious buildings. The establishment of a temple's four angles was achieved by what the Egyptians referred to as 'stretching the cord', *pedj shes*. This was done by sighting certain stars to find a precise orientation and is first mentioned in the 2nd Dynasty at the time of King Khasekhemwy around 2714 BC. By using such basic tools as a plumb line and square when laying the foundations of buildings, the Egyptians were able to achieve a high degree of accuracy. The pyramids of Giza, for example, were oriented to the cardinal points, as well as being almost precisely on the 30th parallel north. Indeed, authors Bauval and Gilbert have suggested that the Giza Plateau was patterned on the Orion constellation and that the pyramids' airshafts were intended to take the soul of the Pharaoh directly up to Orion/Osiris and Sirius/Isis.

The Temple of Denderah contains two zodiacs, a rectangular one on the ceiling of the Hypostyle Hall and a circular one on the ceiling of the chapel. This portrays the night sky as seen from Denderah and shows that, at the time of the temple's construction,

Sirius was rising between Gemini and Cancer. From this we can see that the axis of the temple corresponds to the position of Sirius in the sky at that time – 18 degrees east of true north. With Sirius also shown near Cancer, the zodiac marks the star's rising at the time of the summer solstice, which was then in Cancer. Interestingly, the Temple of Esna, which has a rectangular zodiac, is aligned in a corresponding angle with Denderah.

How far the astronomical tradition of Egypt seeped into other areas of life is hard to ascertain, but it is interesting to note that a Middle Kingdom tomb (c.2061–1786 BC) stated that the owner 'danced like the planets of the sky'. Does this indicate that the tomb's occupant paced out the paths of the planets in some kind of cosmic dance? If so, what was its purpose? It has even been suggested that the royal crowns of Lower and Upper Egypt correspond to certain constellations, with the red crown of Lower Egypt taking its form from the Little Bear and Draco, while the white crown of Upper Egypt derived from the upper part of Draco. If this is so, the appearance of both crowns on the Narmer Palette and Mace Head, which date to 3000 BC, surely indicates that astronomy as a science was well established in Egypt even at this early date.

SEE ALSO: Giza, Pyramids

ATUM

Atum was a creator god, the centre of a cult at Heliopolis, and he was the main figure in a group of nine gods known as the Ennead. The Ancient Egyptians imagined the original state of the universe as chaos, with only primeval waters and darkness existing. From this arose Atum, as described in the Pyramid Texts, Utterance 600: 'O Atum-Khoprer, you became high on the height, you rose up as the *bnbn*-stone in the Mansion of the "Phoenix" in On [Heliopolis] . . .'. The god Atum is here being likened to the Benben, the mound which was the first land to emerge above the waters. This was symbolised by a conical or pyramidal stone and was also depicted in the form of the obelisks erected to reach up to the heavens. Atum was alone in the world at first, and there are two versions of how he came to create the next generation of gods.

In one version of the myth, Atum masturbated and created his daughter Tefnut and his son Shu from his semen. The hand that he used to pleasure himself was regarded as the feminine counterpart to his penis (technically making it an act of copulation rather than masturbation) and was later reflected in the title of the priestess of Amun referred to as 'God's hand'. The alternative version had Atum spitting his children into existence, with Tefnut as the goddess of moisture and Shu as the god of air, both elements of breath.

Shu and Tefnut in their turn had a daughter, Nut, who was the sky, and a son, Geb, associated with the earth. The Egyptians believed that the physical world came into existence once these four elements – earth, sky, air and moisture – had been created. The planets and stars were thought to be the offspring of Nut and Geb, who then rested on their mother's belly. Many tomb ceilings show an image of Nut, often wearing a dress covered in stars to represent this situation. Nut also swallowed the setting sun each evening. It then passed through her body during the night to be reborn each morning.

Plutarch, the Greek writer, recounts a legend in which Nut was cursed by Ra, preventing her from bearing children on the 360 days of the year. However, the god Thoth provided five extra days in which Nut gave birth to Osiris, Isis, Horus the Elder (not to be confused with Horus the son of Isis and Osiris), Seth and Nephthys. The group of nine gods became known as the Ennead, and the five extra days, known as epagomenal days, were an important part of the Egyptian calendar.

Atum was known as 'the Lord of Heliopolis' in recognition of the centre of his cult, and also as 'the Lord of the Two Lands', linking the god closely with the Pharaoh, who bore the same title. Artists portrayed Atum in human form, wearing the crowns of Upper and Lower Egypt. As a solar deity, Atum was regarded as an aspect of the setting sun, and in later eras, particularly the Third Intermediate Period, he was syncretised with Ra to form Atum-Ra. Various animals were linked with Atum, for example the Egyptian mongoose, renowned for its ability to devour snakes.

SEE ALSO: Amun, Astronomy, Benben, Benu Bird, Ennead, Heliopolis, Isis, Obelisks, Osiris

BENBEN

In Ancient Egyptian myth, the Benben was the first hill to emerge from the waters of the universe. It is the primeval hill or mound of creation upon which all life was created and its appearance became associated with that of the god Atum.

This is one of the earliest and arguably the most important of the Egyptian myths. It is known as the Heliopolitan cosmogony because it was developed by priests of the cult of the sun-god Ra in the city of Heliopolis. According to the Heliopolitan cosmogony, in the beginning of time there was only the primeval ocean, Nun; nothing else existed, not even the gods. Then the myth tells of the emergence of the mound of creation, the Benben, possibly representing the earth itself rising from the empty waters of the universe. Another element of the myth is the god Atum, who is sometimes seen as being formed from the mound and at other times seen as the mound itself. It is Atum who created the Great Ennead of Gods. Again in the Pyramid Texts, we find Utterance 600, which tells of this event:

> O Atum-Khoprer, you became high on the height, you rose up as the *bnbn*-stone in the Mansion of the 'Phoenix' in On [Heliopolis], you spat out Shu, you expectorated Tefenet, and you set your arms about them as the arms of a *ka*-symbol, that your essence might be in them . . . O you Great Ennead which is on On, (namely) Atum, Shu, Tefenet, Geb, Nut, Osiris, Isis, Seth, Nephthys; O you children of

Atum, extend his goodwill to his child in your name of
Nine Bows.

Atum also became intertwined with the sun-god Ra, and in
the form of Atum-Ra the sun was reborn each morning and the
creation myth described in the Heliopolitan cosmogony was
played out each and every day, ending in the destruction of the
sun as evening fell; and so the cycle of death and rebirth revolved
every 24 hours.

A sacred pointed stone, the Benben stone, which symbolised
the primeval mound, was held in Heliopolis. It seems to have
been of great importance and was kept in its own shrine, called,
amongst other names, the Mansion of the Benben and the Mansion
of the Phoenix. E.A. Wallis Budge describes the Benben stone in
his 1926 book *Cleopatra's Needles and Other Obelisks*:

> At a period which is so remote that no date can be
> assigned to it, the people of Anu (the On of the Hebrews
> and the Heliopolis of the Greeks) had as the object of their
> cult a stone, which was thick at the base and tapered to a
> point at the top . . . This stone was called Ben and in the
> texts of the VIth Dynasty its determinative [hieroglyphic
> symbol] resembles a small obelisk, i.e. a short thick shaft
> surmounted by a little pyramid.

I.E.S. Edwards, in his seminal work, *The Pyramids of Egypt*,
describes the importance of this object and reveals more about its
appearance: 'The most sacred object within the temple was the
Benben, probably a conically shaped stone which was thought
to symbolize the first phenomenon in the creation of this earth.'
Budge seems to have been the first to notice that this conical Benben
stone was likely to have been a meteor: 'It may have been a stone
of volcanic or meteoric origin, like the Black Stone of Mekka.'

In *The Orion Mystery*, Robert Bauval and Adrian Gilbert point
out that iron meteors often take on a conical shape when they
fall through the earth's atmosphere, resulting in an object which
matches the description of the Benben stone. The pyramidions
(pyramid-shaped stones) that sat at the summits of pyramids
and on top of obelisks are thought to be representations of the
Benben.

The Egyptian form of Benben was *bnbn*. The root, *bn*, means
'to swell forth' as well as 'virility' and 'reproduction', so it is

an appropriate name for the primeval mound that rose from the waters of Nun. Furthermore, the Egyptian word for the rising sun is *wbn*, and it is likely that this similarity is no coincidence, as in the ancient myth the sun first rose from the mound of creation.

That the pyramidion on top of a pyramid represented the Benben stone is interesting in itself, but, taking this iconography a step further, we can see that the whole pyramid could be seen as a replica of the Benben stone and thus the primeval mound of creation. This is intriguing because, as we have seen, the etymology of the word *bnbn*, as well as its role in myth, shows that the Benben stone was closely connected to the concept of rising, of rebirth and regeneration. The Egyptians seem to have taken the idea of the Benben and incorporated this into the design of their funerary monuments – not only the pyramids but also the earlier mastaba tombs, which were seen as representations of the primeval mound. The conical, pyramid-like shape of the Benben stone represented the idea that life could rise again after being dormant for a long period of time. Incorporating it into the funerary monument itself provided the means for spiritual rebirth to take place. What better symbol could they have used to represent their belief in a life after death than that of the Benben? J.H. Breasted, in *Development of Religion and Thought in Ancient Egypt*, wrote:

> The pyramidal form of the king's tomb was of the most sacred significance. The king was buried under the very symbol of the sun-god which stood in the holy of holies in the sun-temple at Heliopolis, a symbol upon which, from the day when he created the gods, he was accustomed to manifest himself in the form of a phoenix.

If the Benben stone was a meteor, then it is clear that the Egyptians held such objects in extreme reverence. Wallis Budge says, 'When [a] stone happened to be a meteorite, or part of one, special sanctity was attached to it, and virtues of every kind were attributed to it.' Furthermore, in their writings, we see some tantalising glimpses of what the Benben stone symbolised to the Ancient Egyptians. Spell 77 of the Coffin Texts has this to say:

> I am this soul of Shu which is in the flame of the fiery blast which Atum kindled with his own hand. He created orgasm and fluid [?] fell from his mouth. He spat me out

as Shu together with Tefnut, who came forth after me as
the great Ennead, the daughter of Atum, who shines on
the gods.

Here we see associated with the creation of Atum on the Benben a
fiery blast. Could this perhaps be such a blast as is created when
a meteorite screams through the atmosphere and impacts with the
earth?

The connection between the two, between the fiery meteor and
the mound that was the Benben, is intriguing. Why are the two
so closely linked? The association with the Benu bird, or phoenix,
also reinforces this idea of creation through fire. Could a meteor
have been responsible for the emergence of the mound of creation
and the beginning of life on earth? Or was the mound itself in
fact a meteor? Does the Heliopolitan myth describe a fiery meteor
falling into the waters of our planet, or striking the land? Is that
the moment of creation?

The Benben stone was considered a fire-stone and a sun-stone
– it was even thought that the sun had once resided inside the
Benben and had emerged from the mound itself to rise for the first
time above the earth. It was also heavily connected with seeding,
reproduction and the emergence of life itself. Gary Osborn and
Philip Gardiner emphasise this point in their article 'The Great
Pyramid: Seed-Stone of Creation':

> The meteorites that fell to earth were believed to be semen
> droplets of the Creator; deposits from Atum-Ra's own
> creation of the universe. It is said that the meteorites that
> were observed falling, and the ones discovered – some
> of which were conically shaped (pyramidion) due to the
> friction caused by the earth's atmosphere – provided
> evidence for this belief.

These days, many people have begun to consider the possibility
that life may have first arrived on earth on meteorites, that life
could have hitched a ride on such bodies falling to the earth. The
concept is called panspermia, and it theorises that life began on
earth after a meteorite carrying bacteria landed on the planet's
surface long ago, in antiquity. What is incredible is that this
sounds very similar to the concepts present in the story of the
Benben stone and in the Heliopolitan cosmogony as a whole. Did

the Ancient Egyptians know about the idea of panspermia? Is that what they were attempting to record for posterity in their creation myths? We can only wonder.

However, the fact that Heliopolis itself, the place where the Benben stone was kept, is known to have been an observatory is surely no coincidence. The High Priest of Heliopolis was known as 'Chief of the Observers', and I.E.S. Edwards suggested that the occupation of the priest was astral rather than solar observation. Was the study of the stars so sacred an occupation because of this core belief at the heart of the creation myth that life was seeded throughout the universe by meteors? We will leave you with the thoughts of R.T. Rundle Clark, who, in his book *Myth and Symbol in Ancient Egypt*, reveals:

> The Egyptians had two ideas about the origins of life. The first was that it emerged in God out of the Primeval Waters; the other was that the vital essence – Heka – was brought hither from a distant magical source. The latter was the 'Isle of Fire', the place of everlasting light beyond the limits of the world, where the gods were born and revived and whence they were sent into the world.

SEE ALSO: Atum, Benu Bird, Heliopolis

BENU BIRD

The Benu bird is tied intrinsically to the Benben stone and the Ancient Egyptian story of the Creation. In a variant of the creation myth detailed in the Heliopolitan cosmogony, Atum is said to have first flown over the primeval waters as a bird, before coming to rest on a rock, or primeval mound (the Benben), that rose from the waters. The cry of this bird was said to have heralded the beginning of all of creation. The Egyptians identified this bird as the Benu bird, and their images of it resemble a heron or, in the Pyramid Texts, a yellow wagtail.

Atum was closely associated with the sun and was often seen as the sun itself as it progressed throughout the day. So perhaps we should not be surprised to find that the Benu bird also had intimate ties with the sun.

E.A. Wallis Budge described the Benu bird and the Egyptians' belief in it thus:

> In early dynastic times they thought that it [the Benben stone] was the abode of the spirit of the sun, which made itself visible at the Creation by emerging from the top of the stone in the form of a bird. The bird was called the 'Benu'. It was regarded as the incarnation of the soul of Ra and the heart of Osiris. A temple called He-t Benu, was dedicated to it in very early times. The Greeks identified the Benu with the Phoenix.

The *Encyclopaedia Britannica* of 1911 describes further the links between the sun and the Benu bird:

> All the mystic symbolism of the morning sun, especially in connection with the doctrine of the future life, could thus be transferred to the benu, and the language of the hymns in which the Egyptians praised the luminary of the dawn as he drew near from Arabia, delighting the gods with his fragrance and rising from the sinking flames of the morning glow, was enough to suggest most of the traits materialized in the classical pictures of the phoenix.

Because the Benu bird sat on the Benben at the moment the world came into being, the Egyptians also formed a connection between the Benu bird and the Benben stone that was kept at Heliopolis. The bird was often depicted standing on a stylised Benben stone as a symbol of the great sun-god Ra. The early priests of Heliopolis believed that their Mansion of the Benben stood where the original mound of creation had actually risen. In that case, it would have been the precise spot where the Benu bird had alighted on the Benben for the very first time.

It was the Greeks who associated the Benu bird with the phoenix, although the Benu's appearance changes in their account of the bird. Herodotus, the Greek historian who visited Egypt, wrote:

> They have also another sacred bird called the phoenix which I myself have never seen, except in pictures. Indeed it is a great rarity, even in Egypt, only coming there (according to the accounts of the people of Heliopolis) once in five hundred years, when the old phoenix dies. Its size and appearance, if it is like the pictures, are as follows: the plumage is partly red, partly golden, while the general make and size are almost exactly that of the eagle. They tell a story of what this bird does, which does not seem to me to be credible: that he comes all the way from Arabia, and brings the parent bird, all plastered over with myrrh, to the temple of the Sun, and there buries the body. In order to bring him, they say, he first forms a ball of myrrh as big as he finds that he can carry; then he hollows out the ball, and puts his parent inside, after

which he covers over the opening with fresh myrrh, and
the ball is then of exactly the same weight as at first; so
he brings it to Egypt, plastered over as I have said, and
deposits it in the temple of the Sun. Such is the story they
tell of the doings of this bird.

Some scholars have pointed out that the Egyptian creation myth
– the rising of the primeval mound – probably came into being
due to the yearly flooding of the Nile and the importance that
this event had for the inhabitants of Egypt. Without the flood
and the accompanying fertile silt deposited by it, life could not
have continued in the region. The presence of the Benu bird in
this story of the Creation – and its depiction as a heron – makes
perfect sense when the myth is understood in this way, because
herons would have stood alone on isolated islets and rocks in the
swollen Nile as the inundation spread. It is not hard to see why
there might have been a connection between the yearly flood and
the beginning of time in the Egyptian imagination. The annual
inundation would have been seen as literally the start of life – or
at least its rebirth. That the Benu bird, the heron, was seen as the
harbinger of this event is also not unexpected given its presence
throughout the annual flood.

Staying with this idea of the Benu as the heron, archaeologists
have found remains of an especially large type of heron that lived
around the Persian Gulf some 5,000 years ago. It has therefore been
suggested that the myth of the Benu bird – which would later
become the phoenix – might have originated from rare sightings
of this large species, leading to the legend that this unusual bird
turned up in Egypt at regular intervals such as every 500 years.

The Benu bird was also called the 'ba of Ra'. The ba is a part
of the soul, the part most associated with the personality of the
individual, so this can be translated as the 'soul of Ra'. By the
time of the Middle Kingdom, it was said that the Benu bird in its
form as the ba of Ra was responsible for the creation of Atum in
the primeval waters at the beginning of time. Like Atum, the Benu
was described as being self-generated, or 'the one who came into
being by himself', according to a 21st-Dynasty papyrus.

In later times, the Benu bird was seen as a symbol of the
resurrected Osiris and was often depicted wearing the *atef* crown
of Osiris, the white crown of Upper Egypt, with two red plumes
added on either side. The Benu bird is sometimes depicted sitting

in a willow tree, a tree sacred to Osiris. Furthermore, scenes survive which portray the Benu bird sitting in a willow tree on the mound of creation, neatly uniting the myths of Atum and Osiris.

Just like Osiris, the Benu is featured in the Book of the Dead and acts as a potent symbol of rebirth. The creature was often inscribed on the reverse of a heart-scarab, an amulet placed over the heart of the mummified king, to ensure that the heart of a dead pharaoh did not fail the test during the weighing-of-the-heart ceremony which, if passed, would grant entry into the afterlife.

Finally, there are statements in the Papyrus of Ani from 1250 BC, a transcription of the Book of the Dead, highlighting the Benu bird's importance to the Ancient Egyptians:

> I am the Benu bird which is in Anu. I am the keeper of the volume of the book (the Tablet of Destiny) of the things which have been made, and of the things which shall be made.

> I am the Benu bird, the Heart-soul of Ra, the guide of the gods to the Duat [underworld].

SEE ALSO: Atum, Benben, Duat, Heliopolis, Osiris, Ra

BOAT BURIALS

The practice of burying full-size boats alongside their owners seems to have been widespread in Ancient Egypt, as numerous boat burials have been discovered scattered throughout the funerary complexes. They are found beside pyramids, as well as more modest tombs, and to date boat pits have been discovered at Abydos, Giza, Saqqara, Dahshur and Abu Roash.

The oldest boat burials found so far in Egypt are almost 5,000 years old and were uncovered recently at Abydos. They have been attributed to the 1st-Dynasty pharaoh Djer. The numerous 1st-Dynasty tombs at Abydos indicate that the site was a very early Egyptian necropolis. The presence of boats beside some of these tombs proves that the practice of boat burials was as old as Dynastic Egypt and very probably dated back to the Predynastic era.

Boat burials were probably meant to help the dead pharaoh to navigate the underworld and to transport the soul of the departed king to its final resting place. Models of boats were found in the tomb of the New Kingdom pharaoh Tutankhamun, and we know that these were intended to be used in the afterlife by the king. However, the earlier custom of burying full-size boats seems to indicate that, at this stage, the real article rather than a model was required.

The presence of boat burials in Egypt is all the more remarkable when we consider that wood was a scarce commodity for the Ancient Egyptians. Local woods could be used, but for larger and longer planks, cedar wood had to be imported from Lebanon.

The largest boat burials found to date were discovered beside the Great Pyramid at Giza. There are actually seven boat pits surrounding the funerary complex (including the subsidiary pyramids) of Khufu's pyramid, although not all of these share the same characteristics. Five of the boat pits, all discovered empty, are themselves boat-shaped. They are thought to have contained boats, but whether these were intact or disassembled we are not sure. Only a few fragments of gilded wood and rope have been recovered from these pits. However, the two remaining boat pits, on the southern side of the Great Pyramid, are not boat-shaped at all but rectangular, and, although large in themselves, they are too small to contain a fully constructed ship.

It was in one of these pits that a vessel that would come to be known as 'Khufu's boat' was discovered; it is still considered to be one of the world's most incredible archaeological finds. In 1954, one of the huge slabs of limestone – one of forty-one – that formed the ceiling of the eastern-most of the two boat pits was raised and inside was found a disassembled but complete boat. The parts of the boat had been carefully packed into the chamber, arranged in a pattern that corresponded with their positions in the finished boat.

Khufu's buried boat was no replica: this was a fully functioning vessel. It took 14 years of meticulous work to reassemble all 1,224 of the pieces that were found in the pit. A museum dedicated to housing the find was constructed in 1982 next to Khufu's pyramid, and this exhibition allows us to get up close to the boat and examine it in all its glory.

Made of planks of cedar wood, the boat was ingeniously designed to be literally stitched together with rope. When placed on the water, the rope contracts and shrinks, while the wooden planking expands, making a boat constructed in this way totally waterproof.

When fully reassembled, the boat turned out to be 43.3 m in length, twice the length of the *Golden Hind*, the vessel that Sir Francis Drake sailed around the world in the 1570s. The keel of Nelson's flagship, HMS *Victory*, was only marginally longer, at 45.7 m. Six pairs of oars had been buried with the boat – one set would have been used for steering at the stern – as well as a quantity of original rope which was too frail to be used in the reconstruction.

What the ship's purpose was before it was buried is not known. Some speculate that it was always intended to be purely symbolic and was never used, whilst other scholars insist that the boat was fit to take to the water and would have been used, if only on the Nile. Chief amongst those who took this view was the man who spent so long painstakingly reassembling Khufu's boat, Hag Ahmed Youssef Moustafa. It was his belief that the ship was built specifically as a funerary boat to carry Khufu to Giza, and that it had not formed a regular part of Khufu's fleet. As evidence for this theory, he cited the fact that Egyptian boats were traditionally painted green with a yellow bow and stern, with the *wadjet* eye of protection painted on either side of the bow. There is no trace at all of any paint on Khufu's boat. There is some evidence that the boat had been in the water: some of the planks are faintly marked by the ropes that would have shrunk and tightened when placed in the water, and the remains of the rope that were found also show signs of having been immersed in water. So perhaps this boat did carry Khufu's embalmed body from Memphis to his funerary complex at Giza.

While it very likely served this practical purpose before its interment, Khufu's boat is similar in design to the solar barque of Ra – the legendary 'boat of millions of years' – as it was depicted in Egyptian art. It probably also functioned as a symbolic vessel, one which would transport the king in the next world as he accompanied the sun-god Ra on his daily journey across the heavens and through the netherworld. Thus it would seem that the boat was designed to serve Khufu in the afterlife as well as in this world.

The boat that we see today inside the Great Pyramid's Solar Boat Museum is not a one-off. In 1985, the second boat pit, to the south of Khufu's monument, was examined using fibre-optic cameras, and found to contain a second, identical boat. This second boat had also been dismantled before its constituent parts were buried in the chamber. It is hoped that in the future this boat can be removed and reconstructed, just like its twin.

Strangely, the two boats found so far at Giza lie outside the perimeter wall that once surrounded the Great Pyramid. This is thought to be evidence that the two boats were used in the funerary procession of Khufu. Items used in these processions were thought to possess a very powerful force, and in order to contain this they were buried, usually outside the funerary complex. This might explain why the ships were buried outside the pyramid's enclosure wall.

The practice of burying boats seems to have died out sometime during the Middle Kingdom. Either it proved too expensive to continue constructing these huge vessels only to bury them in the sand, or a subtle shift in the religion of the Egyptians allowed them instead to bury their dead kings with mere models of the boats that would enable them to sail into the afterlife.

SEE ALSO: Abydos, Giza, Khufu

CANNIBALISM AND HUMAN SACRIFICE

The elements of Ancient Egyptian culture that we admire include the monumental buildings, exquisite wall paintings and delicate statues of the gods and rulers of this mysterious land. It has been suggested, however, that darker undercurrents lay beneath this civilisation and that practices that we now find abhorrent, such as cannibalism and human sacrifice, were occurring in the Nile Valley. Can this be true?

In his *Library of History* (c.30 BC), Diodorus Siculus notes that the Egyptian god Osiris forbade the Egyptians to eat each other, which suggests that cannibalism was practised at some point. It was only the introduction of agriculture that led Osiris to state that cannibalism was no longer necessary. Hence, rather than being a ritualistic practice, cannibalism appears to have been more of a necessity at certain times in Egypt's history. Despite the bounty produced from the Nile floods, times of high or low flood could lead to years of famine and hardship. Such documented famines occurred in the 3rd Dynasty (c.2687–2649 BC), which experienced seven years of famine, in the 5th Dynasty (c.2513–2374 BC), in 2100 BC, and in the 20th Dynasty (c.1200–1081 BC), in which one year was known as 'the year of the hyenas'.

In a letter written around 1949 BC by a funerary priest and landowner called Hekanakhte to his family, he states that: 'Being half alive is better than death altogether. Look, one should say "hunger" only about real hunger. Look, they are starting to eat people here.' Whether this is an exaggeration on the part of Hekanakhte, who, from his letters, is clearly despairing of his family, who continually moan about the inadequate amount of food he has allotted them, or whether it is a true reflection of actual events, cannot be certified. Even so, it is worth noting the events that occurred in Egypt many years later, during the seven-year famine in the eleventh century AD. With food so scarce, the people of Egypt resorted to eating human flesh, which was openly sold in the streets and sometimes obtained by very underhand means. It was reported that one such method involved dangling a large hook out of a window in order to snare people going about their business in the street below, winching them up, killing and then cooking the unfortunate individuals. Accordingly, whilst not a common practice, in times of severe famine, cannibalism in Ancient Egypt cannot be ruled out.

In the late nineteenth century, the British archaeologist Sir Flinders Petrie excavated a large Predynastic tomb at Naqada (T5), which dates to 3500–3100 BC. The tomb was sealed and intact, and contained the scattered bones of approximately six people. Intriguingly, the human upper-leg bones showed signs of teeth marks – although whether human or animal is uncertain – as well as indications that the bone marrow had been scooped out with a spoon-like implement. Petrie concluded that these individuals had been the victims of cannibalism. Indeed, the taking of bone marrow suggested opportunistic rather than ritualistic cannibalism. When people are starving, the bone marrow and internal organs are the last parts of the body to lose their goodness. However, there are no signs of cut marks on the bones, which in all likelihood there would have been if the flesh had been eaten. In addition, the lack of burn marks on the bones has led to the current view that cannibalism was not the reason behind all of this.

So why had the bone marrow been extracted? Clearly, these practices were part of a ritualistic disarticulated burial, whereby the flesh is allowed to rot off the bones for later interment. The bone marrow was removed not for eating but as part of the cleaning process. Teeth marks on the bones might be due to animal activity whilst the flesh was rotting. Accordingly, it is doubtful that this burial was cannibalistic in origin. So is there any other evidence to suggest that cannibalism was practised in Ancient Egypt?

The Pyramid Texts are spells, or utterances, carved on the walls of a number of 5th- and 6th-Dynasty pyramids (c.2513–2191 BC) intended to aid and protect the King as he ascends to heaven to become a god. In the pyramid of Unas is carved the so-called 'Cannibal Hymn' (Utterances 273–4), which details how the King eats the gods so that he may 'flourish' with 'their magic in his belly'. It states that:

> Unas is the Bull of heaven who conquers at will, who lives
> on the being of every god, who eats their entrails when
> they come, their bodies full of magic . . . Unas is one who
> eats men and lives on gods . . . Unas eats their magic and
> gulps down their spirits . . . Lo, their power is in Unas's
> belly, their spirits are before Unas as broth of the gods,
> cooked for Unas from their bones.

The mention of Unas eating the magic of men and gods is very telling. The Ancient Egyptians believed that a person's magic dwelt in their stomach and so to eat an individual would allow you to acquire their magical qualities, as well as absorbing that person's power, strength and very essence. However, it has been suggested that the Cannibal Hymn's positioning (on the east wall of the burial chamber) makes it more likely that the allusion to eating gods and men is metaphorical. It may signify the King's dominance and greater power over the beings in order to ensure that he ascends unchallenged and undisturbed to heaven and the rewards that await him there.

Whilst Egyptologists deny the practice of cannibalism, it is accepted that human sacrifice did occur. This took two forms: sacrificial killing/burial of servants in order to accompany and serve the deceased king in the afterlife; and the ritualistic slaughter of Egypt's enemies.

The funerary sacrifice of servants is attested to at two royal burial sites, Abydos and Saqqara, from the time of the ruler Aha (c.3100 BC) until the end of the Early Dynastic Period (c.2686 BC). It is also known to have occurred in the Second Intermediate Period (c.1786–1569 BC) at Kerma in Nubia. The evidence for the funerary sacrifices can be found in the large number of subsidiary burials that surrounded the King. Neatly arranged in rows within the royal enclosure, the King's servants were killed at the time of the royal burial. Whilst there is no direct written or pictorial evidence to corroborate this, the architecture of the tombs suggests that it must have been the case. The funerary enclosure comprised a royal double chamber surrounded by brick-lined storerooms and subsidiary burial pits sunk directly into the desert floor. With no entrance except from above, the tombs and superstructure were completely roofed over only after all the incumbents had been buried. The servants were buried with tools and vessels, with one of King Djer's retainers being buried with a writing palette signifying that he was a scribe. It is interesting to note that even Djer's queen was sacrificed and buried alongside her husband, being sealed within the royal tomb's superstructure. George Reisner, who studied the Abydos burials, noted that of 317 subsidiary burials surrounding Djer, at least 162 were sacrificial, based on the shared-roof theory, although another Egyptologist has suggested a figure of 580. Other kings who entered the afterlife with a considerable entourage include: Djet, for whom there were 113 sacrificial burials; Den, with 123; and Semerkhet, with 68.

Although few skeletal remains have survived, those that could be studied show no signs of contortion, suggesting burial whilst still alive. Accordingly, it would appear that these retainers were killed before placement within the tomb. This is in stark contrast to the Kerma sacrificial victims, who entered their graves alive and were then covered over by the mound of earth. In 1923, Reisner stated that it was impossible 'to escape the conviction that these extra bodies are the remains of persons who died in the places where we found their bones, and who had been in fact buried alive'.

Whereas there is no textual evidence for the sacrificial killing of retainers in Ancient Egypt, there is certainly proof that enemies were ritually killed. The depiction of a king (indeed even a queen, for that matter, notably Nefertiti) smiting Egypt's enemies with a mace whilst grabbing their hair was a common one on temple walls, palettes and other votive objects throughout Egyptian history. Although this may have been purely symbolic, Amenhotep II (1454–1419 BC) stated that he personally executed seven Syrian princes within the Karnak temple, signifying that the smiting depictions were not merely for show. Not only did this act serve as a performance of the King's power to defeat Egypt's enemies, it was also recorded on stelae and carved into temple walls in order to perpetuate this power and guarantee the King's eternal victory over them. In the 1960s, the remains of a human sacrifice were unearthed at the 12th-Dynasty Egyptian fortress of Mirgissa. A damaged pottery cup held an upturned skull, near to which was found a flint knife traditionally used in ritual sacrifice. Near by lay the headless disarticulated skeleton. Examination of the skull revealed the victim to be Nubian. The reason the sacrificial slaughter was carried out at Mirgissa is apparent given the role of this fort and the others in the vicinity. The fort, situated at the outer reaches of the Egyptian area of influence, was protected by the killing of the victim in the same way that Egypt was protected by the depictions of smiting enemies on temple walls. At Mirgissa, 197 inscribed red pots, 437 uninscribed red vases, 346 figurines and 3 limestone prisoner figures were also found – all attesting to Egypt's need to negate the power of its enemies through the ritual breaking of the named or depicted foe.

The smiting of the enemy is a complex imagery used to ward off evil spirits and to protect Egypt. The action underlined and underpinned the strength and protective aspect of the King, and there is no doubt that, in this context, ritual human sacrifice by the King or his designated deputy was practised in Ancient Egypt.

SEE ALSO: Abydos, Nefertiti

CARNARVON, LORD

George Edward Stanhope Molyneux Herbert, 5th Earl of Carnarvon, would perhaps have passed almost unnoticed into history but for his involvement in what proved to be one of the great sensations of the twentieth century, with sudden death and mystery at its heart. Born in 1866 and educated at Eton, he was fortunate enough to inherit Highclere Castle, near Newbury in Berkshire, the estate where he had been born. He was also bequeathed a considerable fortune, a financial situation not harmed by marriage to a Rothschild, or, of course, his title.

In 1903, he visited Egypt with his wife, the Countess, for the sake of his health, having been involved in a serious car crash in Germany in 1901. In England, his hobbies had included horse racing, photography, shooting and motoring. He found Cairo rather boring and began to take an interest in the ancient civilisation of Egypt to keep himself active. This was at a time when the authorities were beginning to regulate excavation, but wealthy men could still, if they persuaded the right people, gain permission to sponsor private archaeological work. As a young boy, he had dabbled in excavation in the land surrounding his home.

After moving down to the Winter Palace Hotel at Luxor, he was, perhaps to get him away from those he had been pestering, allowed to supervise a dig at Sheikh Abd el-Qurna. After six weeks of sitting in the shade behind a fly screen giving occasional instructions to the *reis*, or foreman, who was organising the workmen, he came across a mummified cat, complete with coffin; but this limited success does not seem to have dampened his enthusiasm at all.

While he was there, he was fortunate enough to meet Howard Carter, an artist who had become an archaeologist and who was anxious to be employed in that work. Despite Carter's blunt and direct manner, Carnarvon seems to have been impressed by the young man, who had once worked for the American millionaire businessman Theodore Davis, who was at that time desperately searching for an intact royal tomb in the Valley of the Kings. Working for the Earl in areas outside the valley, Carter made some interesting and worthwhile discoveries. By 1914, Davis had grown discouraged and had given up the concession to dig there, leaving the way open for Lord Carnarvon to take it up. He hired Howard Carter to supervise the work. Their discovery of embalming equipment and other funerary items in the valley encouraged them to believe that a mysterious pharaoh virtually ignored by history might have been buried there.

Then war in Europe broke out and, to Carter and his employer's dismay, digging had to be postponed. It did not recommence until 1917. Carter's work was slow and painstaking, clearing the valley floor sector by sector of the debris from previous digs. The Earl of Carnarvon began to feel that he was pouring money into a hopeless enterprise. His capital was being swallowed up to no effect, much as buckets of water poured onto the parched sand of the desert would be. He told Carter he was pulling out. Carter begged for one more season, even offering to fund the final work himself if the Earl would allow him to continue rather than simply relinquishing the concession. Carter had only a relatively small area of the valley left to examine. He was persuasive enough to gain one last season – still at Carnarvon's expense. Then, on 4 November 1922, the Tutankhamun legend began.

Workmen unearthed what appeared to be a step leading downwards. As they feverishly excavated and carried away the spoil in baskets, further steps were revealed, until a flight of twelve was exposed. At the end was a door, carrying the seal of the necropolis priests from 3,000 years ago. The seal bore the imprint of the jackal god, Anubis, who presided over the embalming ceremonies, above nine captive enemies.

The Earl was back in England, but, on receiving a telegram informing him that a 'magnificent tomb' had been discovered with the seal intact, he rushed to Egypt with his daughter, Lady Evelyn Herbert. Meanwhile, Carter had filled in his excavation and was awaiting the arrival of his employer. Towards the end of the month, the wall of the antechamber was breached and everywhere 'the glint of gold' was seen. On 17 February 1923, the burial chamber itself was revealed, at least officially. We cannot tell whether Carnarvon and Carter had permitted themselves a quick peep before that date. It is a widely held suspicion. Neither can we tell whether a few items were illicitly appropriated into private hands before the official audit. There is some evidence that this was the case.

There were major problems involved in the retrieval of the pharaoh's treasures. Originally, it had been agreed that if a disturbed tomb was discovered, the spoils would be divided equally between the Egyptian authorities and the holder of the concession, the latter of course being the one who had borne all the expenses. A dispute ensued in which, perhaps because two apparently quite minor robberies had occurred soon after Tutankhamun's burial, it was argued by Carter that under the terms of the agreement he was entitled to half of the treasures.

A long stand-off followed, during which the tomb was once again resealed for a while until Carter was allowed to complete his work. But by this time, the unfortunate Lord Carnarvon was dead. With the benefit of this death to lend credence, a journalist reported that within the tomb was the inscription: 'Death shall come on swift wings to him that toucheth the tomb of the Pharaoh'. There is, however, no sign of such an inscription, although there are still those today who believe in its existence. Perhaps the nearest thing to a warning inscription is on a shrine of Anubis, the jackal, claiming that he was for the protection of the deceased. Unable to resist temptation, a reporter added to this, 'and I will kill all those who cross this threshold into the sacred precincts of the Royal King, who lives for ever'.

To be fair, suspicion that there was a conspiracy to keep important facts from the public and particularly the popular press was lent force by the fact that the Earl had made a contract with *The Times* newspaper giving them exclusive access to information regarding the discoveries being made, information which only came to the rest of the world's news desks at second hand. The benefit of this deal, of course, was that Carter, when he was allowed to do so, could get on with his task without constant interruption from correspondents.

The intriguing death of Lord Carnarvon was officially from fever and pneumonia following blood poisoning contracted as a result of a small shaving cut. It must be remembered that he had originally gone to Egypt because he was in poor health. The press, who need such stories to sell their papers, made much of the sudden death, which was, they claimed, a consequence of the curse on those who disturbed the tomb. To shore up the sensation there was the story that Howard Carter had a golden yellow canary which the Egyptians who had seen it believed was a good-luck mascot which would lead Carter to discover more gold. Yet, on the very day that the tomb was opened, a snake entered the room where the poor bird was kept and killed and ate it. It was recalled that the snake goddess, Wadjet, was the protector and symbol of Egyptian royalty, her image worn on the brow of the King. Was this deity appearing in her animal form to warn or to take revenge? Proof of the power of the curse, perhaps?

More evidence still may lie in the story that, at the very moment Carnarvon breathed his last, the electric lights suddenly failed all over Cairo. However, those who have visited Egypt, even in modern times, will be aware that power cuts are not at all uncommon there. At Highclere Castle, England, at the very same time, the Earl's dog, Suzie, died howling, the intriguing story continues.

The fact of the matter, in the cold light of reason, is that only six people directly involved in the opening of the tomb died during the decade which followed. Carter himself died, in his 65th year, 17 years later.

SEE ALSO: Carter, Howard; Curses; Tutankhamun; Valley of the Kings

CARTER, HOWARD

Howard Carter was an ailing child, born on 9 May 1874 in Kensington, London, to a family of modest means. He was fortunate enough, however, to visit Norfolk a great deal, and in particular Didlington Hall, where the famous Amherst family had a collection of antiquities. Perhaps it was the artistic education provided by his father that gave him an especial eye for the beauty of Egyptian artefacts.

When he was 17 years old, he met Percy Edward Newberry, Egyptologist and botanist, who invited the young Carter to accompany him to Egypt to copy the ancient art on tomb walls. The expedition, led by Flinders Petrie, set off in October 1891. Though he was extremely meticulous and conscientious in his work, he clearly found what amounted to tracing inscriptions insufficiently fulfilling. Within a few months, he was studying field archaeology and excavation techniques.

Recognition of his talents followed rapidly, and after working for a short time as a draughtsman and overseer at the Deir el-Bahri Temple, he took up the important post of inspector-general of monuments for Upper Egypt, at the age of only 25. He worked on many excavations in Thebes, including some funded by Theodore Davis in the Valley of the Kings. An argument with French tourists, for which he refused to apologise, led to the French director of the Egyptian Antiquities Service, Gaston Maspero, packing him off to the Delta, where there was little for him to do.

Not a man to accept demotion lightly, he decided to resign and scratched a living selling his Egyptian paintings until, probably in 1908, he met the 5th Earl of Carnarvon, who was in Egypt for health reasons. Lord Carnarvon had developed a taste for archaeology early in life and, rather than be bored in Cairo, he had decided to persuade the authorities to allow him a digging concession, which he asked Howard Carter to undertake on his behalf.

Several years passed, during which Carter made some very interesting discoveries; but he and his employer had a goal which others thought unattainable. Evidence existed that there had been a pharaoh, one Tutankhamun, who had almost certainly been buried in the Valley of the Kings. An American businessman, the immensely rich Theodore Davis, held the concession in the valley and had made some spectacular discoveries, greatest of which was the tomb of Yuya and Thuya, parents of Queen Tiye. Perhaps, for the ambitious Davis, the spectacular artefacts he found were insufficient to satisfy him, for they were only parents-in-law to a pharaoh and not actually royal themselves. He searched in vain for an undiscovered royal burial until, in 1914, he gave up and Lord Carnarvon took up the concession. Carter had hardly had time to formulate his plans for a sector-by-sector clearance of the valley floor when the Great War broke out and work was suspended.

In 1917, to his great joy, he was able to begin again. But during four years of painstaking searching, little of huge interest was found. The Earl grew despondent and decided that he was throwing good money after bad. Carter was told that it was all over. Theodore Davis had been correct: the valley was worked out. Howard Carter, though, was not a man to give up without an argument. He was sure that in the small area he had not yet explored the mysterious lost pharaoh's tomb might be found. Would Carnarvon agree to letting him have just one more season, at Carter's own expense if necessary, to finish the work? The Earl, somewhat against his better judgement, he no doubt felt, agreed, although he insisted that he himself would finance this last dig. Carter was in a position to make a final clearance. Would he find his Holy Grail?

On 1 November 1922, the workmen returned to their backbreaking labour, sweating in the heat of what passes for late autumn in Egypt. Just three days later, an excited labourer (no doubt expecting, and, one hopes, receiving, baksheesh) reported that he had found what appeared to be a step near the foot of the hillside. Further, frantic digging revealed a whole flight of steps. At the bottom, Carter discovered an entrance, closed with the seal of the necropolis priests. This tomb, if that was what it was, had been hidden under rubble, spoil from a tomb built immediately above it into the hillside. It must have been with very mixed emotions that Carter ordered his men to fill in the hole while he sent a message to his employer in England to tell him that he believed he had found a tomb, perhaps intact.

The matter of whether the tomb was intact or not was of great importance, not only from the point of view of wanting to find as much as possible but also because the agreement with the authorities specified that if a disturbed burial was discovered, the spoils would be shared between the concessionaire and the state. This would not apply, however, if none of its contents had been robbed, under which circumstances everything would go to the Egyptian authorities.

We can only imagine the excitement felt at Highclere Castle when the message was received from Egypt. The Earl and his daughter, Lady Evelyn Herbert, dropped all their social engagements and packed for the journey at once. Before the end of the month, they were in the Valley of the Kings watching the last of the infill being removed, revealing once again the seal of the necropolis priests, with its nine captives under the domination of the jackal god, Anubis, who presided over the embalming of the dead. The date was 26 November.

An opening was made and the splendid treasures stacked in the antechamber were slowly revealed. Such wonderful things, 'the glint of gold everywhere'. It was to be another ten years before Howard Carter finished his meticulous cataloguing and removal of the belongings of the young king Tutankhamun.

He had, during this time, to endure the arrival of hordes of visitors anxious to see inside the tomb before it was emptied of its wonders. Princes and potentates from the four corners of the world were given permission by the Antiquities Service to interrupt the often irascible Carter's work, while the world's press nosed around the edges like hyenas in the desert, despite the fact that *The Times* had been granted exclusive news access, a deliberate attempt to avoid the attentions of the whole pack. As a consequence, the newshounds were often forced to invent their own stories so that their editors' thirst for copy might be slaked.

So the stories grew over the ensuing months. Carter's yellow pet canary, believed to presage his finding real gold, was regarded by his house staff as a symbol of luck. On the day the tomb was opened, he was greeted on his arrival home with the news that the unfortunate bird had been devoured by a snake, no doubt the animal form of the cobra goddess Wadjet, protector of the pharaohs and their tombs. This provided a wonderful tale for the journalists.

Then the Earl, whose health had not been entirely robust since early in the century, cut himself while shaving, became infected and was unable to shake off the illness, dying shortly afterwards. All the lights in Cairo failed at the moment of his death. Another press coup! Sensational headlines highlighted the 'curse of the pharaoh'. Carnarvon died on 5 April, and it was pointed out that this was only seven weeks after the opening of Tutankhamun's actual burial chamber. This must have been more than mere coincidence.

There was a shrine of the jackal god, Anubis, in the tomb, which was inscribed, 'I prevent the sand from choking up the secret chamber. I protect the dead one.' A reporter chose to add his own, 'and I will kill all who cross this threshold into the sacred precincts of the Royal King, who lives for ever'. It was also claimed that written at the tomb entrance were the words, 'Death shall come on swift wings to him that toucheth the tomb of the Pharaoh.' Powerful words indeed, but unfortunately they were nowhere to be seen on the shrine or at the tomb.

In late March 1923, Marie Corelli, real name Mary Mackay, a novelist, had issued a warning that those who entered the tomb would suffer the consequences. Her words had obviously been truly prophetic. A feeding frenzy of press speculation and misinformation followed, alleging that many deaths among those involved in the tomb opening had occurred. It was claimed by some that 21 people, and by others that 26 unfortunates, were struck down by the curse. In fact, six fatalities over the next ten years was the accurate figure.

The idea of the 'mummy's curse' actually pre-dates the Tutankhamun tomb violation by more than a century, but sensation sells newspapers. Poor Howard Carter, who surely should have been one of the first struck down by such a curse, survived, instead constantly plagued by intrusive interest in the misinformation and rumour. It did not help him in his desire to complete a comprehensive and scholarly assessment of the tomb and its contents. Fanning the flames, the creator of the Sherlock Holmes stories, the respected Sir Arthur Conan Doyle, a believer in the occult, gave it as his opinion that the pharaoh's curse might have been behind the death of Carter's patron. Worse was to follow when, just five weeks after Lord Carnarvon's death, he was unexpectedly followed into the grave by his younger brother. Conclusive proof, if it was wanted by those very willing to believe in the supernatural, that the young pharaoh was avenging the disturbance of his house of eternity. And yet Carter himself lived for a further 17 years and Lady Evelyn, the Earl's daughter, who had been first to set foot in the tomb with the two men, died in 1980 at the ripe old age of 79. Dr Derry, who carried out an autopsy on the body of the king, lived until 1969 and Harry Burton, photographer of the contents *in situ*, survived until 1940.

One young Coptic Egyptian from a privileged family who was allowed to enter the tomb shortly after it was opened later became a much-loved general practitioner in north Birmingham, England, and lived until the age of 90. His name was Dr Awad Sudki, and he was still in medical practice long after what is now accepted as a normal retirement age. He would chuckle merrily when it was suggested that the curse might visit itself on him. He had clearly escaped unscathed. There were many others who entered the tomb and might have been visited by a curse, if one existed, who were mercifully spared.

Yet, for Howard Carter, disputes with the authorities probably caused him the most pain. He was even prevented at one time from entering the tomb, which was again sealed for a while. There was a dispute over ownership of the contents since it seemed clear that soon after the young king had died the tomb had been violated by robbers, although it appeared that few items had actually been removed. However, the Egyptian Antiquities Service claimed that the agreement over the division of grave goods meant that it all belonged to the Egyptian state. It may be that a few items, easily portable, were removed illicitly, as has been claimed, and it is a matter of opinion whether this could ever be justified, given all the circumstances. It can hardly be doubted, though, that Carter made a splendid job of organising, cataloguing and recording what he had found in a meticulous manner, proving to be a model for modern archaeologists in many ways.

After the triumph of making what might be described as arguably the archaeological discovery of the century, what was he to do now? To retire at the peak of his fame seemed a sensible option. This he did, but instead of living with a quiet pride and sense of a job well done, he became reclusive and gloomy.

Returning to England, he failed to receive the recognition his achievement deserved. He was a lonely, sad figure, lacking in social skills, overbearing and obstinate but nevertheless possessing the qualities of industriousness and meticulous thoroughness. He lived until 1939, when he died of heart failure. Was it then that the curse of Tutankhamun's tomb caught up with him? He lies buried in Putney Vale Cemetery, London.

It has been suggested that there may be scientific reasons why people have died 'mysteriously' after entering Ancient Egyptian tombs. Today, we examine mummies wearing face masks and with hands covered in protective gloves. There may be pathogens on the bodies or their wrappings which could cause infections, illness and even death. At the other end of the range of speculation, it has even been proposed that uranium might have been spread on the floors of the tombs, causing the intruder to be affected by radiation sickness and ultimately to die from this. The reader is free to choose whether or not to believe in the power of the curse, whatever its agent.

SEE ALSO: Carnarvon, Lord; Curses; Tutankhamun; Valley of the Kings

CURSES

The 'curse of the pharaohs' has grabbed the imagination of the world thanks to Howard Carter's discovery of the tomb of Tutankhamun in November 1922 and the subsequent exploitation of the curse motif in Hollywood from the 1920s onwards. In fact, the belief in such curses began in the seventh century and the Arab occupation of Egypt. Although they knew little about the Ancient Egyptian culture and were unable to read hieroglyphs, the Arabs greatly respected the Ancient Egyptians, in particular their magic, which they considered to be extremely powerful. So potent, in fact, did they view Ancient Egyptian magic to be that they believed that magical words uttered in tombs could materialise previously invisible objects, that highly effective curses protected the tombs and that to this effect mummies could be brought back to life. A mummy was a terrifying foe – it could not be killed as it was already dead.

Some months after the opening of Tutankhamun's tomb, a certain Marie Corelli, writer of Gothic novels, wrote to *The Times* to inform the reader that those working on the tomb would die as stated by the Arabs' texts, one of which declared, 'Death shall come on swift wings to him that toucheth the tomb of the Pharaoh.' When Howard Carter's sponsor, Lord Carnarvon, died a few weeks later, Corelli's prediction was seized upon by the media, firing everybody's imagination and making the 'curse' front-page news. Carnarvon, who was there at the opening of the tomb, died of complications after he aggravated a mosquito bite on his left cheek while shaving. The bite was in the same position where a wound was discovered on Tutankhamun's mummy when it was unwrapped in 1925. To add potency to the 'curse', it was claimed that on the night of the tomb's discovery Carter's pet canary was eaten by a cobra, an Ancient Egyptian symbol of kingship, that at the time of Carnarvon's death the lights went out across Cairo and that back in England Carnarvon's dog suddenly died. The 'curse' began to take on a reality of its own and even the words quoted from an Arabic text by Corelli were now affirmed as having actually come from the exterior of Tutankhamun's tomb. It was even hinted that at the tomb's opening Carter had found an inscribed curse but had hidden it so that his workers would not be unduly worried.

Even the eminent Egyptologist and Antiquities Service inspector Arthur Weigall added to the curse mania by relating how he, together with an American friend and their respective wives, decided to enact a play in the Valley of the Queens. However, at a rehearsal the wives were inexplicably struck down by acute pains, the American lady experiencing searing pain in her eyes and Mrs Weigall suffering severe abdominal pains which turned out to be a miscarriage. The rehearsal was abandoned and the proposed play was never performed.

By 1935, the press had attributed 21 victims to Tutankhamun's curse, although other calculations were as low as 6 deaths by 1934 among the 22 people present at the opening of the tomb. However, it is now thought that mould spores present in the stagnant air of a long-ago-closed tomb can be toxic, leading to organ failure and, in some cases, death. Even so, the curse of Tutankhamun has gained a foothold in our imagination and, as recently as 1972, it was thought to be responsible for the misfortunes of four of the RAF flight crew who transported the pieces for the Tutankhamun exhibition to London – one who blamed his divorce on the curse, two who suffered heart attacks and another who broke his leg, albeit two years later, which he thought was due to his kicking the case that held Tutankhamun's golden mask.

Ancient Egyptian tomb curses did exist, however, and have been likened to missiles because of the Ancient Egyptians' firm belief in their effectiveness. These curses were seen as a protection against all who dishonoured the tomb. The dead threaten violators of their tombs with crocodiles and snakes or with strangulation: 'as for any man who enters this tomb unclean, I shall seize him by the neck like a bird'. Some state that because the tomb-owner is a powerful *akh*-spirit, or deceased, he has the power to kill a violator and to ruin their entire family as well: 'and assuredly their descendants will be destroyed'. The tomb-owner thus protects himself and his tomb from desecration, threatening the intruder with all the force and fear that a deceased spirit can call upon.

Private curses, which were written down in the Graeco-Roman period but were probably in use well before that, also call upon akh-spirits to enforce them, often being placed within the tomb of a person who had died in a particularly violent or unexpected manner.

Official state curses are found in the Ancient Egyptian Execration Texts, which listed the real or perceived enemies of Egypt. Written on pots, plaques and statuettes, they were ritually smashed and the pieces placed within jars and buried in order to concentrate the energy. These curse inscriptions were applied from the late Old Kingdom onwards. What is interesting to note is that at the entrance of Tutankhamun's tomb was a seal, placed there when the tomb was closed. The seal shows Tutankhamun's name within a cartouche, beneath which is a jackal in repose. Under that are nine bound captives, known as the Nine Bows, who were the enemies of both the state of Egypt and the pharaoh upon whose seal they are depicted. This seal acted as a protection against violation; could it therefore be that the very act of entering the tomb effectively smashed the seal and the Nine Bows shown upon it? In so doing, would the magical potency of the seal be implemented, leading to the destruction of the king's enemies/violators? Perhaps Tutankhamun's tomb was cursed after all.

SEE ALSO: Tutankhamun; Carter, Howard; Carnarvon, Lord

DJOSER

The pharaoh popularly called Zoser or Djoser (as we shall call him) has his 'Horus name', Netjerikhet, inscribed on his monuments, including his Step Pyramid complex at Saqqara. The Horus name was one of the earliest types of royal title used, and it consisted of a square enclosure, or *serekh*, containing the name and surmounted by a falcon, believed to be Horus. Djoser is believed to have expanded his kingdom as far south as the First Cataract of the Nile at Aswan and reigned around 2687–2668 BC.

Until his time, powerful Egyptians had been buried in low mastaba tombs, designed to preserve their earthly remains and the necessities for a comfortable eternal life, often on the plateau overlooking the fertile plain towards the capital city, Memphis. Djoser and his architect, Imhotep, had grander ideas and determined to build, about a mile further away, an edifice much taller than previous tombs and made entirely of stone, surrounded by associated structures. While some stone features had already appeared in earlier tombs, which were basically a core of sand overlaid with mud bricks, it should be emphasised that this concept of building on such a scale with stone was unprecedented. Whereas in earlier times Egyptians had employed wooden posts and matting, in this revolutionary complex stone was carved to look like the original materials. The building known as the House of the North has stone columns imitating papyrus reeds, on which the triangular papyrus stem shapes may be clearly seen. Cult buildings, chapels and processional courts were erected. The more temporary, primitive building materials were being superseded by the new, 'everlasting' stonework, perhaps seen as symbolic of the eternal survival of the Pharaoh. Solid chapels to east and west, entirely filled with rubble but wonderfully carved externally, were designed to allow the deceased king to watch, in the company of the gods, the Heb-Sed, or jubilee, ceremonies which would take place in the afterlife.

By a corner of the pyramid, near the entrance to the mortuary, or memorial, temple, stands a chapel that has two small openings at eye level. Inside the chapel, known as a *serdab*, a seated statue of the king (the original now replaced by a modern replica) stares out for eternity at those who come to pay their respects. It is a most eerie feeling to peer from the outside and catch the mighty ruler impassively gazing back at his visitors. The original limestone figure is now in the Egyptian Museum, Cairo.

The Step Pyramid started out as a mastaba tomb and was progressively enlarged until, when completed, it had six irregular steps reaching more than 62 m into the sky, dominating the plateau surrounding it. Its base measures 109 m by 121 m. There are many shafts inside but it is very difficult to determine which the builders created and which were excavations made by people intent on theft during the next four and a half millennia.

The king's viscera are thought to have been interred, after their removal during the mummification process, in the building known as the South Tomb. It is also believed by some that the *ka* statue, which represented the king's spirit, would have been placed there. The fictive architecture – that is, the non-functional structures – was for the use of the pharaoh's ka in the afterlife. The functional structures were for use in the funerary rituals.

The figure of Djoser may be seen carved on panels in the false doors of the South Tomb running the prescribed circuit during the Heb-Sed ceremony. The Heb-Sed was a royal jubilee festival during which the Pharaoh had to perform a ritual race in a special open courtyard. A large uncovered enclosure in the Step Pyramid complex has been identified as a Heb-Sed court. In theory, the first Heb-Sed ceremony of a king's reign was held to mark 30 years of his rule. During it, his fitness to continue in office was recognised and he was crowned for a second time. While Djoser's reign is generally accepted to have been around 19 years long, in which case his Heb-Sed must certainly have been premature, there are those who argue that the Step Pyramid and its attendant structures could hardly have been erected in such a comparatively short time. It was not the usual practice for a successor to complete a predecessor's tomb, since he would have his own eternity to cater for. The images of the pharaoh running in his Heb-Sed ceremony thus imply that Djoser's reign was longer than is conventionally thought, that he celebrated his Heb-Sed early or that he had prepared depictions of the ceremony in anticipation of celebrations that were still to come either on earth or in the afterlife.

The unusual method of working was one of the factors that must have affected the numbers of stone carvers employed at the site and the time it would have taken to do their work. Today, it would make sense to us to carve the recesses in the stones forming the masonry at a workshop and then assemble the pieces on site. It appears that, after laying the stonework in place, they then carved each block *in situ*. This is clearly not the most efficient way of proceeding, but it should be remembered that there was no precedent for construction in stone on this scale. The craftsmen had not yet worked out the easiest and most effective method. The magnitude of the task was considerable – the enclosure wall alone measured 277 m by 544 m.

Many features at Saqqara emphasise that Djoser was king of two united lands, Upper and Lower Egypt. These signs include: houses for gods from both lands; a double throne raised on a platform; and two pairs of stone structures symbolising the boundaries of the two kingdoms. Towering above all this was the gigantic staircase, the Pyramid, leading to the heavens. This would be the route by which Djoser's spirit would join his fellow immortals after his death.

It is certain that the reign of Djoser was seen as a new era by the Egyptians themselves, and the man credited with being the inspiration for this seminal work, Imhotep the architect, was, likewise, never forgotten and indeed gained status with the passage of time.

SEE ALSO: Imhotep, Heb-Sed, Pyramids

DUAT

The Duat – sometimes also known as the Dwat or Tuat – is the Ancient Egyptian term for what we would describe as the underworld. Many cultures around the world have a belief in the underworld, and that the dead have to make a journey to locate it, but the oldest recorded version occurs in Egypt, in the Pyramid Texts. The hieroglyph representing the Duat is a five-pointed star inside a circle. The word is thought to translate literally as 'zone of twilight', 'other world' or 'heaven by night'.

The Duat was ruled by the god of the underworld, Osiris, and it was his domain. However, there is some debate as to where exactly the Egyptians believed the Duat to exist, whether it was underground or in the sky. Another possibility explored by some Egyptologists, including E.A. Wallis Budge, was that the Duat was actually considered to be a real location on earth. In the introduction to his translation of the Book of the Dead, he says:

> The early Egyptians thought that Egypt was the world, and that it was surrounded by a chain of lofty mountains, like the Gele Kaf of the Arabs, which was pierced in two places, one in the east and the other in the west. In the evening the sun passed through the western hole, and travelling, not under the earth, but on the same plane and outside the chain of mountains it came round to the eastern hole in the mountains, through which it entered to begin the new day above the earth. Outside the chain

of mountains, but quite close to them, was situated the Tuat, and it ran parallel with them. It was to all intents and purposes circular in form. Now as the Tuat lay on the other side of the chain of mountains which surrounded Egypt, and was therefore deprived of the light of the sun and moon which illumined its skies, it was shrouded in the gloom and darkness of night.

Reaching the Duat and the realm of Osiris was the aim of all souls setting out on their journey to the afterlife, but it was not an easy task, according to the Egyptian texts. All sorts of trials and tribulations awaited the travelling soul, and obstacles were thrown up at every turn. There were 12 gates to pass through, each one associated with an hour of the night. As well as being covered with a darkness that was impenetrable, there were said to be countless roads through the Duat – 'many were its ways' – so that only with the help of some friendly being could the disembodied soul hope to locate the heart of the kingdom of Osiris and find the lord of the underworld himself.

Furthermore, fearsome creatures that were hostile to any who passed through inhabited the region and were even said to feast on travelling souls. Only by means of words of power, spells and gifts could these beings be placated. This was one of the many purposes of the lengthy rituals carried out over dead kings, as described in the Pyramid Texts and the Book of the Dead. All the spells that the Pharaoh's soul would need to keep itself from harm were spoken over the embalmed body before it was entombed. In the case of the 5th-Dynasty pyramids at Saqqara, where we find the Pyramid Texts, these spells were also engraved on the very walls that surrounded the tomb. Some examples of the terrible things that could happen to the deceased if they didn't go armed with the correct spells were: being destined to walk upside down in the Duat; having to eat excrement; being devoured by deadly crocodiles; and being attacked by snakes that spat poison.

As further protection, amulets and other powerful items were buried with the mummified pharaoh. These acted both as gifts to be given to the inhabitants of the Duat to placate them and procure their aid and as protective emblems to ward off evil. Quantities of food and drink were also buried with the dead king to sustain the soul during its journey.

As the soul progressed, it was forced to cross streams and

rivers, all of which were tributaries of the great river that flowed through the Duat. This signified that the disembodied soul was approaching the region of the Duat known as Sekhet-Hetepet, the place on which the Greeks would later base their concept of the Elysian Fields. It was here that a place known as the Field of Reeds could be found, and this was where Osiris ruled with his court.

Rather than going through this arduous journey, it was possible for the deceased to reach the Duat by water instead, yet this too had its perils. Budge commented:

> The Egyptians thought that the Nile which flowed through Egypt was connected with the river in the Tuat, but to reach the latter the deceased would have to pass through the two holes in the First Cataract from which the Nile rose, and then he would have to sail over streams of fire and boiling water before he arrived. The banks of these streams were filled with hostile beings which sought to bar his progress, and lucky indeed was that soul which triumphed over all obstacles, and reached the City of God.

There was one way to reach the Duat directly, and that was if the mortal body of the deceased soul had drowned. This was because the god Osiris was said to have been drowned by his brother Seth – anyone dying in this Osirian fashion proceeded straight to the Field of Reeds.

So strenuous and fraught with danger was the journey through the Duat that some scholars have suggested that the Pharaoh spent a considerable amount of time during his life preparing for the treacherous journey that he would encounter once he died.

When finally the deceased's soul reached the Field of Reeds inside the Duat, it had to face the greatest challenge of all. The heart was weighed in the Hall of Two Truths in front of Osiris, Anubis and Thoth. All of the deceased's deeds were considered and appraised as the heart was weighed against the 'feather of truth'. If this test was passed, the soul could progress to its final resting place amongst the stars. Failure resulted in a terrible fate: a hideous monster devoured the heart of the deceased and the soul was forsaken, never to reach its desired destination.

As we have said, some scholars believe that there is evidence in Ancient Egyptian texts such as the Book of Caverns, the Book of Am-Duat and the Book of Gates that the Duat was in fact understood to be a region of the sky, a place that is said to contain the 'imperishable stars'. It is in the oldest of the Egyptian funerary texts, the Pyramid Texts, that most light is shed on this location of the Duat. There are countless mentions of stars and regions of the sky through which the soul must travel. This is from Utterance 481:

> The reed-floats of the sky are set in place for me, that I may cross by means of them to Ra at the horizon. I ferry across in order that I may stand on the east side of the sky in its northern region among the Imperishable Stars. I will stand among them, for the Moon is my brother, the Morning Star is my offspring.

Furthermore, the Pyramid Texts are emphatic on one point: the dead king's soul becomes a star after death. Utterance 466 is in fact titled 'The king becomes a star':

> O King, you are this great star, the companion of Osiris, who traverses the sky with Orion, who navigates the netherworld with Osiris; you ascend from the east of the sky, being renewed at your due season and rejuvenated at your due time. The sky has borne you with Orion.

If this was indeed where the Duat was located, it would also explain the presence of the river that flows through it, for if the Duat was situated in the sky then the river would clearly be the Milky Way, that celestial watercourse that flows amongst the stars.

So it would seem that all of the events that occurred in the underworld, as described by the Egyptian texts, were considered to take place in the sky rather than in an underground location. Dr E.C. Krupp in his book, *In Search of Ancient Astronomies*, elaborates on this:

> The Pyramid Texts describe the ascent of the departed king to the sky. He joins Orion (Osiris), and Sirius is his guide. They continue together as participants in the cosmic cycle. A similar wish is expressed in other texts. The spirits of the dead hope to join the never-setting, never-dying, circumpolar stars.

The Duat, then, seems to have been a stellar world rather than a netherworld. Once the dead king had successfully negotiated all the trials and obstacles, he would become as one with Osiris and live for ever as an imperishable star.

SEE ALSO: Astronomy, Osiris, Sokar, Thoth

ENNEAD

An ennead in Egyptian mythology is a collection of nine gods. The word 'ennead' itself comes from the Greek for 'nine'. The Egyptian equivalent term was *'pesdjet'*, which seems to have applied to any collection of deities, not to a group made up of a specific number.

Several enneads are mentioned in Egyptian literature, and these include the Great Ennead, the Lesser Ennead and the Dual Ennead, amongst others. Of primary importance was the Ennead of Heliopolis (the Great Ennead), which comprised the nine chief gods of Egyptian mythology. They were Atum, Shu, Tefnut, Geb, Nut, Osiris, Isis, Seth and Nephthys.

Atum was the god who first arose from the primeval waters of Nun and is associated with the Benben, the mound of creation. He either masturbated on the mound to create his offspring, Shu and Tefnut, or he produced them from his spittle. It has been suggested that Atum was a hermaphrodite and so able to reproduce alone.

Shu was the god of the air and Tefnut the god of water. Together, they gave birth to Geb and Nut, the gods of the earth and the sky respectively. It was said that when Geb and Nut copulated, their father, Shu, interposed himself between them, thus creating a space between the earth and the sky. Many depictions of this immortal couple show Nut, the sky, arched over her husband. Despite this paternal interference, Geb and Nut had four children: Osiris, Isis, Seth and Nephthys, the four gods who play a crucial role in the Osirian myth that was central to Egyptian religion for a long period of time.

It is very likely that Osiris was not always considered part of the original Great Ennead, but, as his popularity rose throughout Egypt, his inclusion became necessary. His addition to the group was a clever manoeuvre by the priests of Heliopolis, because with Osiris sitting in the Great Ennead, there was a clear succession from Atum, the founder of all creation, through to the Pharaoh himself, who was seen as the physical incarnation of the son of Osiris, Horus.

The Lesser Ennead, sometimes called the Little Ennead, consisted of a succession of gods, including Thoth, Maat and Anubis, under the leadership of Horus.

SEE ALSO: Atum, Benben, Heliopolis, Osiris

EXODUS

One of the most dramatic biblical stories involving Egypt is the account of the Exodus, when the Israelites escaped from their bondage. They were led by the prophet Moses, who had been brought up as an Egyptian, and his legend is a fascinating one. According to the Bible, the ruling pharaoh, who was concerned that the Hebrews did not become too large a population group in his country, decreed that all male Hebrew babies were to be killed. Moses' parents kept him hidden for three months after his birth, but further concealment would have been impossible. His mother made a basket out of bulrushes and then, putting the baby into it, floated the basket down the river.

A daughter of Pharaoh had come down to the river to bathe, when she saw the baby and took pity on it. She hired a nurse and raised the child in her household. The Bible explains that she gave the baby the name Moses as a play on the Hebrew word '*masha*', 'to draw out' because she 'drew him out of the water', implying that the Egyptian princess spoke Hebrew. It is perhaps more likely that Moses is an Egyptian name: it has the stem *mesi*, which means 'to be born' and forms part of composite names such as Ahmose ('the moon is born').

There are parallels between the story of Moses' infanthood and other legends. In one version of the story of the goddess Isis, she hides her son Horus in the marshes of the Nile to prevent him being harmed by his uncle Seth. Sargon of Akkad, in the Mesopotamian myth, was said to have been placed in a bitumen-covered basket on a river as a baby.

Moses was brought up as a high-ranking Egyptian, and it was only after he reached adulthood that he understood that God wanted him to lead his original Hebrew people out of Egypt. The figure of Moses has been compared to the monotheist pharaoh Akhenaten, who ascended the Egyptian throne in around 1372 BC. There are certainly similarities between the two charismatic leaders, who both tried to establish new religious observances among their people, Akhenaten with his worship of the Aten and Moses with the Ten Commandments. Ahmed Osman, in his 2002 book *Moses and Akhenaten: The Secret History of Egypt at the Time of the Exodus*, postulates that they are in fact the same person. In 1939, Sigmund Freud suggested in *Moses and Monotheism* that Moses had been at the court of Akhenaten and adopted monotheism there, leaving Egypt after Akhenaten's death and the collapse of the new religion. Several parallels between Akhenaten's 'Hymn to the Aten' and Psalm 104 are often quoted, suggesting either a direct link between the two traditions or at least a common heritage. Whether Moses and Akhenaten were the same figure or whether one was an archetype of the other must continue to be a matter for speculation, as there is no proof one way or the other.

Unfortunately the Book of Exodus does not provide us with the name of the pharaoh involved, so dating the Exodus is problematical. In the First Book of Kings, it is described as taking place 480 years before the reign of Solomon (generally accepted to have begun around 960 BC), which would suggest a date of around 1440 BC. However, Exodus 1:11 contradicts this, stating that the Hebrews had built the cities of Pithom and Raamses. The latter is generally accepted to refer to the city of Piramesse in the Delta region of Egypt, which was established during the reign of Ramesses II (1304–1237 BC). This would mean that the Exodus could not have occurred before the thirteenth century BC. There are a number of possible explanations for these anomalies. For example, the 480-year figure may have been based on a number of generations calculated at 40 years each, a symbolic but inaccurately high figure.

A piece of archaeological evidence sometimes used to date the Exodus is held in the Egyptian Museum in Cairo. The so-called Israel Stela attracts much attention from visiting groups, as it contains the only mention of the word 'Israel' in the surviving Ancient Egyptian written records – which are copious. Originally from the mortuary temple of Amenhotep III, the stone was usurped and recarved by Merenptah. It contains the line: 'Israel is devastated, her seed is no more, Palestine has become a widow for Egypt.' This is the expression that has caused some scholars to think that Merenptah (who reigned from 1237 to 1226 BC) was the Pharaoh at the time of the Exodus. Even if you can't read hieroglyphs, the shiny part of the huge granite slab near the bottom is easily identified, worn clean by hundreds of fingers rubbing the stone at the name 'Israel'.

The Victory Stela, as it is more correctly called, was found – as most things in Egypt seem to have been – by Flinders Petrie, in 1896 at Merenptah's mortuary temple in Luxor. If the inscription was evidence that a state of Israel existed and was attacked by Merenptah, it would in fact imply that the nation was established by this time and therefore that the Exodus occurred much earlier. This interpretation of the stela, removing Merenptah from the running as the Pharaoh of the Exodus, also confounds related speculation about his body. When the mummy of Merenptah was examined, salt crystals were found on the body, leading some to speculate that the Pharaoh had drowned in the Red Sea when God brought its waters crashing down on the army of Egypt. Dramatic though this explanation is, the more prosaic, and more likely, explanation for the presence of these crystals is that excessive amounts of embalming salts were used during the mummification process.

The biblical version of the story of the Exodus, in which the Red Sea is parted to let the Israelites across and then engulfs the pursuing Egyptians, also raises questions about the geography of the Exodus. In order to reach the Red Sea, the departing Hebrews would have travelled south-east from Goshen (an area in the Delta around Piramesse), covering a great distance within Egypt. A more logical route would have been east towards the Reed Sea, a series of salt lakes on the way to Canaan. If we read the account of the Exodus in the Torah, the body of water is actually translated there as the Reed Sea, suggesting that the Bible version many of us are familiar with has become confused during one of the many translations it has undergone.

Ultimately, in looking for evidence of a large number of people leaving Egypt – a civilisation with extensive records – in an exodus as described in the Bible, we find a remarkable lack of hard facts. Unable to pinpoint a ruling pharaoh or a date on which scholars can agree, we are left with various speculations. The author Ralph Ellis, for example, suggests that the Tempest Stela of Ahmose I, recording severe storms in Egypt at the beginning of the 18th Dynasty, may bear witness to some of the calamities visited on Egypt by God to persuade Pharaoh to let his people go. Ellis also suggests a link between the Hebrews and the Hyksos, a group from outside Egypt who for a period ruled the country and who were expelled by Ahmose I.

SEE ALSO: Akhenaten, Hyksos, Joseph, Old Testament Egypt

FUNERARY BOOKS

Egyptologists have located a wealth of funerary books amongst the tombs, temples and pyramids of Ancient Egypt. Perhaps the most well-known is the Book of the Dead. This is the name Egyptologists have given to a group of texts known in Ancient Egypt by the collective name 'the Book of Coming Forth by Day'. The purpose of this text was for the many spells and verses that it contained to accompany the deaceased on the voyage to the afterlife. Originally, these texts were not books as we know them; instead the text was inscribed onto the walls of the deceased's tomb or onto his sarcophagus.

E.A. Wallis Budge does a good job of describing this very complex 'book' in the introduction to his *The Egyptian Book of the Dead*:

> 'Book of the Dead' is the title now commonly given to the great collection of funerary texts which the Ancient Egyptian scribes composed for the benefit of the dead. These consist of spells and incantations, hymns and litanies, magical formulae and names, words of power and prayers, and they are found cut or painted on walls of pyramids and tombs, and painted on coffins and sarcophagi and rolls of papyri. The title 'Book of the Dead' is somewhat unsatisfactory and misleading, for the texts neither form a connected work nor belong to one period; they are miscellaneous in character, and tell us nothing about the

lives and works of the dead with whom they were buried. Moreover, the Egyptians possessed many funerary works that might rightly be called 'Books of the Dead', but none of them bore a name that could be translated by the title 'Book of the Dead'. This title was given to the great collection of funerary texts in the first quarter of the nineteenth century by the pioneer Egyptologists, who possessed no exact knowledge of their contents.

The Pyramid Texts found inside the 5th-Dynasty pyramids at Saqqara are the earliest such texts to survive, and elements from the Pyramid Texts, along with the Coffin Texts – passages inscribed in ink on the wooden coffins of wealthy Egyptians during the Middle Kingdom – are found in the funerary texts that eventually superseded these earlier ones.

The later Book of the Dead was no longer carved onto the walls of the tomb, instead its spells and incantations were elaborately written on papyrus. Probably the most famous and fullest existing version of what we call the Book of the Dead is the Papyrus of Ani. When it was discovered in Thebes inside the tomb of the scribe Ani, it was a continuous scroll of papyrus some 78 ft long. Budge purchased the papyrus in 1888 on behalf of the British Museum, but before he shipped it back to London he had it cut into 37 pieces of roughly equal length, with little regard for the integrity of the text. Each of these pieces was then glued to a wooden board before being sent back to London for translation – just one of many acts of vandalism carried out in the name of Egyptology over the years.

Along with all the spells, charms, hymns and words of power that the soul of the deceased would require to navigate safely the 'many ways' of the underworld, there were also detailed images of what it would encounter on its journey. The aim of all this complex detail was to ensure that the soul made it safely to the Hall of Two Truths, where Osiris resided and where the final ceremony – the weighing-of-the-heart ritual – would take place. It seems that individual papyri were created specifically for the rich and powerful. A total of up to 200 chapters could be included, and these were tailored to meet the needs of the particular king or noble concerned. No single version of the book found so far contains all of the possible 200 chapters.

As for the age of the ideas contained in these books, I.E.S.

Edwards, in his book *The Pyramids of Egypt*, discussed the origins of the Pyramid Texts, which formed the basis of the Book of the Dead:

> For the most part, the Pyramid Texts were certainly not inventions of the Vth or VIth Dynasties, but had originated in earlier times; it is hardly surprising, therefore, that they sometimes contain allusions to conditions which no longer prevailed at the time of Unas and his successors. As an example, Spell 662 includes the words 'Cast the sand from thy face', which could only refer to the burial practices of pre-dynastic times, when the king was interred in a grave dug in the sand.

This assertion that certain portions of these funerary texts were being used in Predynastic times is astounding: these writings could not have appeared fully formed overnight – it has to be assumed that they took many years, possibly centuries, to develop as a body of religious thought – so if they were in use at such an early stage in Egyptian history, they must have originated in much earlier times.

Another sacred funerary text is the Book of Gates. This dates from the New Kingdom and covers similar material to the Book of the Dead, detailing the hours of the Duat. The Duat was in some ways viewed as the night itself, and was divided into hours, each with its own attributes and character. It also stresses the importance of the gates that are to be found in the underworld, each of which is guarded by a god who will not let the dead king go through without the required password. Once he has given the correct passwords and safely navigated the gates, the deceased can proceed through the netherworld, accompanied by Ra, until he meets Osiris in the judgement hall.

The Book of Caverns is another text, this one dating from the 20th Dynasty. The earliest surviving version is found at Abydos, carved onto the walls of the Osireion. It contains some of Egypt's most graphic accounts of the perils of the underworld and describes it as the 'place of annihilation', where Ra condemns the enemies of Osiris to eternal damnation.

Other Egyptian funerary books, all dwelling on similar themes, include the Book of Amduat, the Book of the Earth, the Litany of Ra and the Books of the Heavens.

The funerary books of Egypt are complex, profound and hard to comprehend. Much study and a detailed knowledge of Egyptian religious thought are required to even begin to pierce their veils. Some scholars have argued that, at such a distance in time, we can never begin to understand them fully. There are, however, passages that anyone who has ever feared mortality or believed in an afterlife can identify with. Furthermore, many followers of modern religions in today's world will recognise the themes present in these texts:

> O dweller in the Land of Holiness, thy face is beautiful . . . The gods come before thee bowing low. They hold thee in fear. They withdraw and retreat when they see the awfulness of Ra upon thee; the [thought] of the conquests of thy Majesty is in their hearts. Life is with thee. Let me follow thy Majesty as when I was on earth, let my soul be summoned, and let it be found near the Lords of Truth. I have come to the City of God, the region that is eternally old, with my soul (ba), double (ka) and spirit-soul (aakhu), to be a dweller in this land. Its God is the Lord of Truth . . . he giveth old age to him that worketh Truth, and honour to his followers, and at the last abundant equipment for the tomb, and burial in the Land of Holiness. I have come unto thee, my hands hold Truth, and there is no falsehood in my heart . . . Thou hast set Truth before thee: I know on what thou livest. I have committed no sin in this land, and I have defrauded no man of his possessions.
>
> E.A. Wallis Budge, *The Egyptian Book of the Dead*,
> Chapter CLXXXIII

SEE ALSO: Abydos, Duat

GIZA

Standing some 12 km to the west of modern Cairo is a limestone escarpment which marks the edge of what we know today as the Giza Plateau. This in turn stands at the far eastern tip of a great western desert that stretches to Libya and beyond. It was here at Giza that four of the most remarkable structures ever conceived by the mind of man were executed in stone. Guarding the plateau behind is the immutable Great Sphinx; to the west of this enormous statue are three stone pyramids of gargantuan size.

At 30° north, 31°20′ east, the Giza Plateau rises some 30 m from the Nile Valley. Interestingly, some of the early archaeologists and authors who studied Giza pointed out that this remarkable high, sandy formation stands at what has been referred to as the centre of the earth's land mass. In other words, if one were to draw a line through Giza stretching from east–west around the earth and a second line through Giza passing from north to south, one would find that these lines crossed more land than sea, and indeed more land than any other two such axes.

There is evidence that the Giza Plateau has been used as a necropolis since early in Egyptian Dynastic history. What we see today confuses the eye with an amazing jumble of Old Kingdom and later structures. However, Predynastic pottery has been found close to the Great Pyramid and, in an area just to the south of the three pyramids, tombs from the first three dynasties have been found. These include Covington's tomb (so-called because it was excavated in the early 1900s by the American philanthropist

L. Dow Covington), which may well be a royal burial of 2nd- or 3rd-Dynasty origin.

Orthodox Egyptology is of the opinion that the first major structure to be built at Giza was the 4th-Dynasty Great Pyramid of Khufu (also known as Cheops). Khufu, who reigned from approximately 2609 to 2584 BC, is credited with planning one of the most ambitious building projects ever undertaken by man, a pyramid so large that until the Eiffel Tower was completed in 1889, it was the tallest structure on the planet. The Great Pyramid of Khufu at the north-eastern edge of the plateau is laid out with such amazing accuracy that most authors, both orthodox and alternative, agree that astronomical alignment must have been used in its initial setting out. Several boat pits lie to the east and south of the Great Pyramid. The wooden boat found buried in one of these pits has been painstakingly reconstructed and is now housed in its own permanent museum next to the pyramid.

Due to its positioning, alternative theorists have questioned whether the Great Pyramid of Khufu was indeed the first to be built on the plateau, pointing out that the pyramid ascribed to Khafre, one of Khufu's sons, is placed on a higher and more dominant part of the plateau and so looks taller than the Great Pyramid itself. They argue that the most obvious location for the first great structure would have been the higher, and therefore more impressive, spot.

Conventional history would have us believe that these immense monuments on the plateau were conceived and designed individually and not as a unified whole. In other words, there was no overall plan for the entire Giza Plateau necropolis. We are led to believe that Khufu, Khafre and the assumed builder of the third pyramid, Menkaure (Khafre's son), each in their turn, chose their location and then instructed their architects and stonemasons to begin construction of their pyramid. As many alternative authors have pointed out, this interpretation seems to defy the evidence on the ground that indicates that these 4th-Dynasty monuments and their accompanying precincts were designed and laid out to a master plan.

In 1994, authors Robert Bauval and Adrian Gilbert published the bestselling book *The Orion Mystery*, in which they postulated that the three great pyramids of the Giza Plateau were laid out in a pattern mirroring the alignment of the three stars of Orion's Belt. The book received plaudits and criticism from both sides of the orthodox/alternative divide and still stands as a seminal work in the alternative-history genre. This correlation theory proposed that the three 'belt' stars of the constellation Orion in the southern sky had been mimicked on the ground in the formation, construction and placement of the three pyramids at Giza, particularly in the offset of the third pyramid from the diagonal line. Although this theory has been discredited on various levels since the book's publication, it remains a serious attempt to explain the layout and design of the Giza Plateau monuments.

SEE ALSO: Astronomy, Boat Burials, Giza, Khufu, Pyramids, Sphinx

HALL OF RECORDS

Over the past 20 years or so, many alternative writers and researchers have descended upon Giza to search for something that has become known as the Hall of Records, believed to preserve ancient wisdom and arcane knowledge. The term 'Hall of Records' stems from the prophetic writings of American medium Edgar Cayce (1877–1945). Cayce was a remarkable man who seemed to have genuine abilities when it came to treating and diagnosing diseases and conditions in people who had previously been misdiagnosed by their doctors. He also issued prophecies while in a trance-like state, many of which related to Atlantis, earlier races of advanced people and, not least, the Great Pyramid and the Hall of Records.

So where did the idea of a Hall of Records come from? Did Cayce make it up, did he genuinely receive information about it from a higher source or is there evidence that this mysterious place has been sought for millennia?

By his own account, Edgar Cayce was an avid reader, and as a teenage boy and young man, he worked in a bookshop. He had become familiar with the writings of such people as Madame Blavatsky, a Russian medium who set up the Theosophical Society, and Rudolf Steiner, the Austrian philosopher and spiritualist, and he seems to have been much influenced by the works and theories of such figures. Incidentally, the distinguished Egyptologist Mark Lehner, who is currently excavating on the Giza Plateau, was originally a Cayce devotee, having written a book in 1974, *Egyptian Heritage*, about Cayce's Egyptian prophecies.

The quest for a hidden repository of lost knowledge, for that is what the Hall of Records supposedly is, is one that we can trace back to Khufu himself. In the Westcar Papyrus, a 15th-Dynasty collection of stories, we find the remarkable tale of Khufu and the magician Djedi. In this story, which seems to be intended to legitimise the origins of the late-5th-Dynasty kings, we find Khufu requesting the presence of the famous magician Djedi at his court. It was said that Djedi was such a talented sorcerer that he could reattach a severed head to a corpse and restore the body to life. After the sage proved that he could perform this feat, demonstrating on a goose, Khufu asked him a strange question: did he know the secret of Thoth (the symbol used for 'secret' here may also refer to a book or document) so that the King could complete his pyramid? Djedi answers that he does not but that the answer Khufu seeks is to be found in a room called 'Inventory', about which no explanation is given.

What we have here could well be the first kernel of the idea that a secret set of documents or a book containing arcane knowledge exists in the vicinity of Giza. Add to this the recollection of the Greek historian Herodotus, who claimed that Khufu was buried on an island surrounded by water in a mysterious subterranean chamber, and the historical context behind the Hall of Records story starts to become clearer.

Modern researchers such as John Anthony West, Robert Bauval and Graham Hancock have searched for the Hall of Records underneath the Great Sphinx. Their work was prompted by that of the Stanford Research Institute, which in the 1970s used ground-penetrating radar to detect cavities beneath the Great Sphinx. Adding to this mystery was an archaeological discovery. Granite, which in Egypt occurs naturally only at Aswan in the south, was found deep below the limestone bedrock just in front of the Sphinx temple. The discovery means one of two things: either a piece of granite brought to the plateau for use in the monuments has fallen down a once-visible fissure; or there remains to be discovered a subterranean structure or chamber constructed with granite blocks. Could this be the Hall of Records?

We believe there could be an alternative solution to the mystery. Our research has led us to conclude that a hidden and possibly subterranean shrine or temple to the god Sokar exists at Giza. It is this domain of the god that is represented by the fifth hour of the Duat, a place known as Rosetau. That place is Giza. So it is our theory that this undiscovered tomb, temple or shrine fits the theoretical picture of a Hall of Records at Giza. We hope to have the opportunity of expanding upon this theory in the future.

SEE ALSO: Duat, Giza, Khufu, Pyramids, Sokar, Sphinx

HATHOR

Hathor is one of the most important goddesses worshipped by the Ancient Egyptians, and she is also associated with many other goddesses whose characteristics she shares. The name Hathor (Hwt Hor) means 'the house of Horus', and she was closely linked to the god Horus, both as his nurse and his wife. This connection is apparent in the hieroglyphic representation of the name of Hathor, which shows a square house enclosing a falcon, symbol of Horus.

There were several different ways in which Hathor herself was shown: as a woman with cow's horns on her head framing a sun disc, as a woman with a cow's head, or entirely as a cow. The head of Hathor is often shown in full face, as opposed to the profile view much more common in Egyptian art. Many temples have supporting columns with the head of Hathor in this aspect carved into the capital.

The origins of the figure later worshipped as Hathor can be seen in the so-called 'cow-dancing woman' figure painted onto Predynastic vases. A woman with her arms curved up over her head, seeming to imitate a cow's horns, is often shown standing in a boat. By approximately 3000 BC, the familiar image of a cow-horned, full-face depiction of Hathor is found on the Narmer Palette, an important artefact showing an early ruler of Egypt. It has also been suggested that the shape represented by the face and two upward-curving horns resembles the female reproductive organs, the uterus and fallopian tubes. The fact that Hathor was associated with fertility is used to support this hypothesis.

In common with most aspects of Egyptian culture, Hathor is an example of the duality that the Egyptians were clearly comfortable with and fundamentally understood. In one myth, Hathor is sent in the form of a lioness by her father, the god Ra, to punish mankind, with whom he was displeased. She set about devouring man with great enthusiasm and developed a taste for blood, threatening to completely destroy rather than simply punish the erring humans. Hathor acquired the name Sekhmet ('she who prevails') and showed no inclination to halt her killing spree. Finally, the other gods devised a plan that involved mixing beer with red ochre to dye it red, thus making it resemble blood, and spreading it on the land. Hathor drank deeply, relishing what she believed to be blood, and eventually became so intoxicated that she forgot her vendetta against mankind.

The vengeful aspect of Hathor described previously is in complete contrast to many of her other roles. Women who looked for protection during pregnancy and childbirth particularly worshipped Hathor as a gentle and benign deity. For pharaohs, the goddess also performed the role of wet nurse, and she is sometimes depicted as a cow suckling the King from her udder. The Seven Hathors, all different forms of Hathor, were able to predict the futures of babies and are similar to the Greek Fates. Her other titles included 'Lady of the Sycamore', 'Lady of the West' and 'Lady of Turquoise'. In this last guise, she was worshipped at a temple built in the Sinai near the turquoise mines.

In the myth describing the conflict between the gods Horus and Seth, Hathor plays a healing role in restoring Horus's sight after his eye has been gouged out by Seth. Hathor and Horus were also married, and with their son Ihy form one of the triads prevalent throughout Egyptian mythology. The Sacred Marriage between Hathor and Horus was celebrated as a festival at the temple of Edfu each year. The statue of the goddess Hathor left her temple at Denderah to be placed on a boat and transported up the river Nile towards Edfu. During the journey, the goddess would pay her respects to other deities in their sanctuaries along the route. On her arrival at Edfu, the statue of Horus greeted Hathor and various rituals, culminating in their marriage, were celebrated. For the next 14 days, there would have been a holiday atmosphere surrounding the temple as visitors came to celebrate the festival, known as the 'Feast of the Beautiful Meeting', and join in the celebrations. At the end of the festival, the statue of Hathor was once more embarked onto her boat to journey back to her own temple.

Denderah was not the only site at which Hathor was worshipped but it was the most significant one, and the surviving temple on the site is one of the most impressive monuments in Egypt today. Worship of the goddess at Denderah goes back to Predynastic times, with a succession of buildings occupying the site, one of which was attributed to the pharaoh Khufu. The temple of Hathor that the modern visitor can enjoy was constructed in the Ptolemaic and Roman eras, roughly 120 BC to AD 30. Surrounding the temple is the remarkably well-preserved mud-brick wall that defined the temple precincts.

On the roof of the temple there are a number of chapels or shrines, one of which used to contain the Denderah Zodiac; the original is now in the Louvre Museum, Paris, and has been replaced with a copy. This remarkable map of the sky, showing the 36 decans which the Egyptians used to tell the time at night, is regarded as one of the great treasures of Egypt. The constellations are depicted in a style that illustrates the fusion between Greek and Egyptian cultures at the time of construction. Another famous feature of this temple is a depiction of many gods, led by Hathor, receiving offerings from the Pharaoh. The pharaoh in question is Cleopatra VII, with her son by Julius Caesar, Caesarion, and this is one of relatively few illustrations of a woman who has inspired such speculation over the centuries.

Hathor is closely associated with a musical instrument known as the sistrum, a type of rattle comprising metal discs which were shaken rhythmically. Many surviving examples of the instrument are decorated with the head of Hathor, and her son Ihy is normally shown carrying a sistrum. As a goddess rejoicing in love and beauty, Hathor was equated with Aphrodite by the Greeks. Her worship was also often linked to the consumption of wine and beer, in an echo of the myth in which the drunkenness of Hathor saved mankind.

SEE ALSO: Astronomy, Horus, Khufu, Queens Reigning as Pharaoh

HEB-SED

Traditionally, the first Heb-Sed festival of a pharaoh's reign was a celebration of the 30th anniversary of his rule. Thereafter, the Heb-Sed was performed every three or four years until his death. During the festival, the King's right to rule Egypt was ritually tested, although there is no record of a pharaoh being found unfit, and he seems always to have been re-crowned. It is thought that the festival first took place after the unification of Upper and Lower Egypt and that the legendary pharaoh Menes was the first to celebrate it. The Heb-Sed is said to have taken place after the New Year, in June, at the same time as the annual inundation of the Nile – a time of renewal and rebirth.

Heb-Sed festivals were elaborate and lavish affairs. They included temple rituals and processions as well as proofs of the King's fitness to rule. The most crucial stage of the Heb-Sed was designed to demonstrate his physical prowess. In an open court between two sets of shrines (one for each of the kingdoms, Upper and Lower Egypt), the King was required to run a ritual race. The course was known as 'the field' and the Pharaoh completed eight circuits of this course, four for each of the two kingdoms.

The most detailed representations of the Heb-Sed are preserved in the Sun Temple of the pharaoh Niuserre at Abu Ghurab and contribute greatly to our understanding of what happened during the festival. They show the king sitting on a double throne in one of the two pavilions wearing the traditional attire for the Heb-Sed, a short cloak that reached just to the knees and which left the shoulders almost entirely free. In his hands, he holds the three-pronged flail that indicates his position as King.

The scenes at Abu Ghurab suggest that the festivities proceeded in the following fashion. They began with foundation rituals, ceremonies that were carried out when the construction of a sacred building was commenced, then the King visited building works he had commissioned. Next, there was a procession in which he appeared in the Heb-Sed cloak for the first time. After this, the Pharaoh took part in rituals that were concerned with the rebirth and regeneration of the King and his supernatural powers. This was followed by audiences in which the King appeared before people from all over Egypt, and then there was a procession in honour of the god Min, a deity known for his male vitality. The King visited the chapel of Wepwawet, the 'Opener of the Ways', and anointed the standard of this jackal god. Wepwawet was closely associated with the god Sed, whose name is incorporated into the festival. This was followed by the famous Heb-Sed race, which appears to have been the most significant of all the festivities and the focus of the celebrations. At last, a census of cattle was presented to the gods. Finally, a carrying chair was brought before the Pharaoh and, taking his place in it, he paraded in front of the people.

It would seem that the Heb-Sed, as well as being a time of celebration for the renewal of the King, could also have been seen as a test of his ability to rule, and perhaps in even earlier times, where surely the ritual had its roots, it was seen as a way of ridding the country of a ruler whose power and grip on the throne was waning. The fact that the Heb-Sed was repeated every third or fourth year after the first festival celebrating thirty years on the throne gives a strong indication that this was the case.

Some pharaohs bent the rules more than a little, and it is documented, for example, that Hatshepsut celebrated her Heb-Sed on the 16th anniversary of her ascension to the throne. The fact that some pharaohs moved the Heb-Sed forward implies that, whatever had been the case in the past, the balance had now shifted towards the pharaohs, and that rather than representing a challenge or test, the Heb-Sed had become a powerful means of confirming their position.

So deeply rooted was this festival in Ancient Egyptian culture that even the so-called heretic king, Akhenaten, is shown performing the Heb-Sed, in the colonnaded Temple of Aten at Karnak. However, it would appear that Akhenaten also celebrated his Heb-Sed prematurely, possibly even as early as Year 3 of his reign. What is remarkable about the scenes in the Temple of Aten is that the Aten is also pictured taking part in the festival, the only depiction of a god performing the rituals associated with the Heb-Sed.

In Djoser's Step Pyramid complex at Saqqara, the remains of the king's Heb-Sed court still exist today. It is thought by some that this was never intended to be used in the king's lifetime but was constructed for his eternal spirit to use after his death. This is therefore seen as strong evidence that the Ancient Egyptians believed that the dead king would continue to carry out the Heb-Sed festival in the afterlife. What is interesting is that many scholars believe that the structures we see in stone in Djoser's Heb-Sed court are precise replicas of the actual, more temporary structures where the pharaoh would have carried out the rituals associated with the festival while alive.

There is evidence that the Heb-Sed was practised right up until the dying stages of the pharaonic era. At Kom Ombo, we see depictions of one of the last pharaohs, Ptolemy VIII, being handed Heb-Sed symbols by Horus.

SEE ALSO: Akhenaten, Djoser

HELIOPOLIS

Heliopolis was one of the oldest and the most sacred of Ancient Egypt's many cities. It was the chief location of the cult of Ra and the centre of sun worship in Egypt, as well as the Egyptian capital for a time. The city was named by the Greeks, and Heliopolis means, appropriately, 'city of the sun'. Heliopolis's Ancient Egyptian name can be transcribed as Iunu, which, when translated, seems to mean 'place of pillars'; it may have been so called due to the large number of obelisks we know once stood there. The Hebrew version of Iunu was On and appears to have meant 'light'.

Today, hardly anything remains of this sacred city. Its temples, its sanctuaries, all have disappeared, thought to have been destroyed during the construction of medieval Cairo. Many ancient buildings were diminished or destroyed during the raising of Cairo's holy places, fortresses and minarets – including much of the Old Kingdom pyramids' outer casings – but surely one of the sorest losses is the disappearance of Heliopolis.

Believed to have been occupied since Predynastic times, Heliopolis was at the heart of Egyptian religion for centuries. The Heliopolitan cosmogony taught that Heliopolis was the precise spot where the primeval mound rose from the waters of chaos and where Atum first set foot, the place from which all creation sprang. Even when Thebes became the state capital around the year 2100 BC, Heliopolis continued to thrive, becoming a centre for learning and sciences, especially astronomy.

The Greek historian Herodotus visited Heliopolis sometime around the year 450 BC, and although he was reluctant to speak of the secrets he had learned while he was there, he did say that the scholars of Heliopolis were the most knowledgeable in all the land. Plato, Solon and Pythagoras are all said to have visited the city in their lifetime, and it was home to a school of philosophy of great repute. Plutarch, in his work *Moralia*, wrote of the influence that Egypt and the great academic centres at Heliopolis had on the Greeks:

> This is also confirmed by the most learned of Greeks such as Solon, Thales, Plato, Euxodus, Pythagoras, and as some say, even Lycurgus going to Egypt and conversing with the priests; of whom they say Euxodus was a hearer of Chonuphis of Memphis, Solon of Sonchis of Sais, and Pythagoras of Oenuphis of Heliopolis. Wherefore the last named, being, as is probable, more than ordinarily admired by the men, and they also by him imitated their symbolic and mysterious way of talking; obscuring his sentiments with dark riddles. For the greatest part of Pythagoric precepts fall nothing short of those sacred writings they call hieroglyphical.

However, by the time of the historian Strabo, in the first century BC, the city seems to have been largely abandoned. During his visit with the Egyptian prefect Aelius Gallius, he wrote, 'Today the town is completely deserted.' Its scholars and priests had left, presumably for other centres of learning – the newer city of Alexandria, perhaps.

After that, it appears that Heliopolis was gradually lost to the sands, and in Roman times the city was plundered when the many obelisks that guarded the entrances to its once-sacred temples were uprooted and taken to Alexandria and even as far as Rome itself.

When Napoleon Bonaparte arrived in Egypt during his Egyptian expedition of 1798, he found the remains of walls marking a huge enclosure or temple, some 1,200 m by 1,000 m. These ruins were reported to have been still 10 m high by the year 1898, but today absolutely nothing remains.

As the sources above show, almost everything we know about Heliopolis comes from literary sources. However, there is some archaeological evidence. For example, a funerary stela found near the site and attributed to someone called Djedatumiufankh describes the construction of walls 15.6 m thick at one of the temples of Heliopolis. Walls of such monstrous proportions, together with the size of the site – going by Napoleon's finds and the amount of obelisks raised in the city, it must have been enormous – indicate that in all likelihood the temples and shrines of Heliopolis would have far exceeded even those at Karnak, near modern Luxor, in size and scale.

Today, the suburbs of Cairo have encroached upon what was once Heliopolis, and the remains of the Temple of Ra and the famous Mansion of the Benben, along with many other buildings, now lie beneath a district called Ain Shams. The name means 'eye of the sun', in deference to the sacred ground upon which it sits. Heliopolis continues to give up its secrets slowly, despite being buried below a thriving metropolis. In 2006, a solar temple thought to date from the time of Ramesses II was located beneath a market in Ain Shams. Perhaps one day someone will even stumble upon the fabled Mansion of the Benben.

There is a lone reminder of Heliopolis's lost grandeur. A single obelisk stands near the spot it must once have occupied. It was one of a pair dedicated by Senusret I, a pharaoh of the 12th Dynasty, and is now the oldest of the obelisks still standing in Egypt. Even this was raised long after Heliopolis was founded, but today it is almost all that remains of the once-great capital of Ra.

SEE ALSO: Atum, Benben, Obelisks, Ra

HIEROGLYPHS

The Ancient Egyptian writing system known as hieroglyphs (from the Greek for 'sacred writing') was fully formed by 3000 BC. It consists of phonetic symbols and pictorial signs such as body parts, natural objects, plants, buildings, equipment, tools, insects and birds. Indeed, over 80 bird signs are used and Islamic writers referred to hieroglyphs as 'bird writing'. Hieroglyphs could be read from left to right, right to left or top to bottom, the directional clue taken from the faces of the various signs so that the reader, for example, reads towards the mouth of birds or the front of a leg.

To spell a particular word, certain types of signs were used: ideograms, which visually represented particular concepts; phonograms, which represented one, two or three consonants; and determinatives, which represented the type or sense of the word and helped determine its reading, particularly important in a writing system that did not indicate vowels. Accordingly, an abstract word such as 'death' was determined by a black hole, 'wind' by a sail, and words of motion by walking legs. Colour played an important role, too, with every sign given a particular colour: plants were always painted green; body parts red; and earth or water black. Often, colour helped distinguish between two similar signs, thus serving as an aid to the reader.

Because of their pictorial, stylised writing system, the script of the Ancient Egyptians was able to transcend its purely literal meanings, allowing for a more subtle and symbolic interpretation and conveying the myths, allusions and powerful statements of the time and place. Thus, in its most basic form, the *wadjet* eye conveyed the meaning 'observe', but it also suggested the myth of the wounding and healing of the eye of the god Horus or created magical protection.

The hieroglyphic script was more than just a means of communication. Indeed, the Ancient Egyptians considered their script to be the gift of Thoth, the ibis-headed god of wisdom and learning. The Egyptians themselves called their writing system *medu netjer* – the words of god. Coming as it did from the mouths of gods, the script was impregnated with all the power and magic of a divine utterance, giving it multidimensional and metaphysical facets. Added to this was the Ancient Egyptian belief that an image of a situation or object could create its own reality and bring that which was depicted into existence. As the hieroglyphic script was based upon pictorial signs, the 'letters' were affected by that supernatural force and were living beings in their own right. Added to this, throughout the Early Dynastic Period (3050–2687 BC), when the script developed considerably from its administrative function, writing obtained a political importance, underpinning and expressing the superiority, prestige and position of the elite. This political role, allied with its link to kingship, gave writing a position of prominence and power, and further enhanced the magic of the written word.

Symbolism was integral to the script, which contained its own magic and power that could be mobilised and released under particular circumstances. It is apparent that context and ceremony played an essential part, with writing's potency intensified in especially sensitive areas where symbolism was particularly relevant. Thus hieroglyphs written on labels for administrative purposes would not have had the same power as those written in tombs, or which were intended to serve a magical function, such as those carved into amulets. Accordingly, the writing of the funerary formulae, such as the offering of food, drink and goods to Osiris, was sufficient to provide the deceased with the necessary benefits in perpetuity. An added advantage was that, once written, the words endured for ever and would continue to assist the deceased, who would not have to rely on a living person to recite the formula. The potency of hieroglyphs could protect the deceased from a permanent death and could be used to benefit the departed by stating how beneficent the tomb-owner had been:

'Never did I deprive any person of anything . . . Never did I do anything by means of violence against anybody' (Hetepherakhti, 5th Dynasty). By these written guarantees of guiltlessness, any sins in life would be counteracted. Sins were not absolved through repentance and forgiveness; rather, by denying in writing the existence of any transgressions, they simply ceased to be. In view of the efficacy and creative power of the written word, such a negation became a reality.

Whilst the written word's influence could prove a benefit for the deceased, the very power, vigour and living quality of the signs also posed a potential threat, either directly, by attacking the deceased, or indirectly, by interfering with the offerings and hence sustenance of the deceased or leaving the tomb and taking their power with them. Probably the most obvious expression of the implicit power of hieroglyphs was the modification or suppression of certain signs, as found in the Pyramid Texts, the spells and utterances written on the walls and funerary equipment of nine Old Kingdom and First Intermediate Period pyramids and some private tombs of that time. Some signs were altered or not included at all in order to diminish the potency of those images and their possible bad effect upon the deceased. Dangerous creatures could be shown cut in half, or the word spelled phonetically, omitting the animal sign. Cattle and fowl might be shown cut in half, with just their head, with just their front half or not shown at all. Fish were always omitted, as, according to Egyptian myth, a fish had eaten the cut-off phallus of Osiris. In general, birds were untouched, as were serpents. Whilst there are no set patterns as to which hieroglyphs were altered or erased, the human form was always suppressed or modified, appearing without body or legs, or sometimes with arms only, indicating the great threat humans were thought to pose to the deceased. In the few cases where Old Kingdom private tombs modified the hieroglyphs within the burial chamber, actual depictions of the tomb-owner and other tomb scenes were not affected, because such scenes appeared inside the entrance or in the antechamber of the tomb, rather than within the burial chamber, where words were potentially dangerous.

The writing of a name held great power, especially as it was an essential prerequisite for incarnating into the afterlife, because without a name you did not exist and would therefore be condemned to a second, permanent death. By changing the form of a name, an object or creature would be made less effective. Thus, in the Old Kingdom tomb of Ti, a crocodile – *meseh* – is spelled out as *mehes*, effectively removing the crocodile's personality and minimising the potency of its name. Within a ritual context, the writing of an enemy's name was used to call upon the power of the hieroglyphs, and the magic contained within them, to bring the inscribed curse into reality.

Because of the force of the written name, it had to be guarded carefully as it could be open to abuse and erasure. As a protection, the royal name was enclosed within a cartouche (*shenu* – circuit). Magically encircling the name, it trapped within its oval shape any negative energy or hostile force sent by an enemy, thereby preventing it from reaching the person concerned. Despite the threat to a written name, however, the benefits far outweighed the drawbacks.

As the mysterious quality of the written word was able to bring objects to life, individual hieroglyphic signs were considered entities in their own right and imbued with divine power. Hieroglyphs such as *ankh* (life), *sa* (protection) and *djed* (endurance) were used for magical amulets because of the intrinsic power of the sign. By wearing the symbol, the appropriate sympathetic magic was conjured up, with the beneficial attributes of the hieroglyphs bringing the relevant energy to the wearer, and incorporating the properties and strength of that sign to inspire, promote and encourage protection and virtue.

SEE ALSO: Symbolism, Thoth, Wadjet Eye

HORUS

Portrayed as a falcon or a hawk-headed man, Horus was the god synonymous with the power of kingship in Ancient Egypt. Each pharaoh was known by five names, one the name given to him at birth and the other four conferred at the time of his accession to the throne. Two of these names are connected with Horus, indicating the god's importance to the concept of kingship in Ancient Egypt. The 'Horus name', preceded by a falcon symbol, signified that the King was the earthly reincarnation of Horus. The meaning of the 'Golden Horus name' is disputed. It may represent the victory of Horus over his uncle Seth or, as gold is an imperishable metal, it may indicate the eternal link between the Pharaoh and Horus. These elements date back to the earliest recorded rulers, and a fragment of ivory from the tomb of the 1st-Dynasty ruler Den shows his Horus name as a hieroglyph in a *serekh* (a rectangular enclosure thought to represent a palace façade) surmounted by a falcon. (It should be mentioned here that, as with many other facets of Ancient Egypt, there is some controversy surrounding the god, as to whether all early depictions of falcon gods are actually Horus or whether they show other deities, for example Sokar, whose characteristics Horus may have acquired.)

The Egyptians believed that the gods had once ruled the earth, and on one example of a king list (the Turin Canon) the intermediate stage between the gods and the mortal rulers is the reign of the *shemsu hor* – 'Followers of Horus' – who are credited with a total of 13,400 years on the throne, demonstrating the importance of this deity.

Horus was a sky or solar god. One meaning of his name is 'distant', reminiscent of a falcon flying high above the earth to observe possible prey. As we have seen, the ruling king was associated with Horus, and on his death this connection passed to his successor. One aspect of Horus (Harsiese) performed the opening-of-the-mouth ceremony on the deceased king, an important part of the funerary ritual that mystically transferred power from one ruler to the next. The deceased king was then identified with Osiris.

Horus was the son of Isis and Osiris, conceived after his father's death by means of magical intervention. The trinity of Osiris – the resurrected god – Isis and Horus is probably the best-known in the Egyptian pantheon. Statues or images of Isis cradling or suckling her infant son Horus are identical in their iconography to those of the Virgin Mary with Jesus in the Christian tradition. The story of Osiris and his murder by his brother Seth is dealt with elsewhere in this book; however, there is also a complicated myth surrounding the subsequent feud between Horus and his uncle.

One colourful version of these 'contendings', as they are called, is contained in the Chester Beatty Papyrus that describes various stages in the conflict between Horus and Seth to succeed to the throne of Egypt. When the other assembled gods are unable to decide between Horus and Seth, it is suggested that they change into hippopotamuses and jump into the sea in a trial of strength. Isis, the mother of Horus, decides to help her son and makes a harpoon that she throws into the water. Unfortunately, the hippopotamus that she hits is Horus, who shouts at his mother to remove the harpoon, which she does. Her second strike successfully hits Seth, who in turn cries out to Isis, his sister, for mercy, and again the harpoon is withdrawn. Horus is by now furious, and he comes out of the water to attack Isis, cutting off her head and then fleeing into the mountains.

The god Ra restores Isis's head and then commands that Horus be punished for what he has done. Seth is the first god to find Horus, who is sleeping, and he gouges out his nephew's eyes. Hathor comes across the injured Horus and restores his eyesight using magic and the milk of a gazelle.

Seth next tricks Horus into meeting him at his house, and at night they lie down together. To dominate Horus and discredit him in the eyes of the other gods, Seth ejaculates between Horus's legs, and when Horus wakes up, he discovers semen on his hand. Seeking help from Isis, who has forgiven him, Horus has this hand cut off, thrown into the water and replaced. In turn, Horus now masturbates, and his semen is placed onto a lettuce, which Seth eats. When the two opponents appear before the judging gods, Seth is dismayed to find that he has been the victim of this trick, and he calls for another challenge.

Horus and Seth are to race in stone boats, but while Seth builds his boat out of a mountain-top, Horus cheats and constructs a boat that is actually of wood but disguised to look like stone. Naturally, the stone boat sinks, and after intervention by Osiris, judgement is finally awarded to Horus. The story is notable for the human attributes displayed by the gods; they are not above jealousy, cheating or revenge.

At the temple of Edfu dedicated to Horus, a celebration called the 'Festival of Victory' was held each year to commemorate the triumph of Horus over Seth, and inscriptions describing the contest are carved into the walls. Also to be found at Edfu are the Building Texts, which not only describe in great detail the construction and function of the temple itself but also unusual and mysterious creation myths involving strange gods who are unique to Edfu.

First mentioned in the Pyramid Texts of the Old Kingdom, four gods referred to as the Sons of Horus – all mummiform and often represented with animal heads – came to have an important role in funerary practice, as protectors of the body's internal organs. By the time of the 19th Dynasty, the Canopic jars which contained the preserved organs had stoppers in the shapes of the heads of these four deities:

- Imsety has a human head and protects the liver;
- Hapy has an ape head and protects the lungs;
- Duamutef has a jackal head and protects the stomach;
- Qebehsenuef has a falcon head and protects the intestines.

Each of these male gods also has a female counterpart, in true Egyptian dualistic fashion. For example, the goddess Nephthys assists Hapy.

SEE ALSO: Hathor, Isis, Mummies, Osiris, Sokar

HUMAN BODY

When the human body was depicted in two dimensions, Ancient Egyptian craftsmen followed an unusual convention. The head and legs of the individual were shown in profile, while the shoulders and torso were depicted facing forwards. Although this sounds an awkward style in which to portray the body, the results look surprisingly natural, and this method was used for the duration of Ancient Egyptian civilisation. Working in three dimensions, artists created statues that depicted details of the body such as the muscles, despite sculpting in very hard materials like granite.

Various medical papyri show that the Egyptian understanding of the working of the human body was quite sophisticated. The Ebers Papyrus describes a circulatory system centred on the heart and extending to the extremities. Presumably, the process of mummification had provided Egyptian doctors with sufficient opportunity to study anatomy to enable them to reach conclusions such as this.

Egyptian society seems to have accepted physical deformity among the 'working classes', with many examples shown on wall paintings. It is common to see blind harpists in scenes of musicians. A very famous statue in the Egyptian Museum in Cairo shows Seneb, who has dwarfism, in a statue with his wife and children, who are of normal size. It appears that dwarfs were often employed as jewellers and metalworkers, as portrayed in the tomb of the nobleman Mereruka at Saqqara. Excavations of the cemeteries at Giza have discovered the body of Perankh, a dwarf who, on a statue found in his tomb, is described as 'He who pleases and amuses the king'. This acceptance included the god Bes, who protected women in childbirth and the family, and was depicted in his statues as a dwarf, with shortened limbs.

This tolerance, however, seems not to have been extended to the ruling class. With the notable exception of Akhenaten, who chose to have himself portrayed with an elongated face and exaggerated wide hips, the royal family and nobility were depicted as being youthful and healthy. This clearly was not always the case, as was attested to when the mummy of the 19th-Dynasty pharaoh Siptah was examined and it was discovered that he had a deformed left foot, possibly caused by polio. In contrast, however, the walls of his tomb in the Valley of the Kings show Siptah as an able-bodied and handsome young man, which is how he must have wanted to appear in eternity.

The title *swnw* (physician) is recorded from very early in Egyptian history, and the profession was divided into different categories. The historian Herodotus made the following observation in his *Histories*, after his visit to Egypt in the fifth century BC:

> The art of medicine among them is distributed thus: each physician is a physician of one disease and of no more; and the whole country is full of physicians, for some profess themselves to be physicians of the eyes, others of the head, others of the teeth, others of the affections of the stomach, and others of the more obscure ailments.

An Egyptian doctor would make an examination of the patient and take the pulse before coming to his diagnosis. The cure would be accompanied by magic spells designed to help the patient by invoking the assistance of the gods and increasing the power of the medicine. Remedies were based on plants and on more exotic substances such as 'the milk of a mother who has borne a son', which was believed to be beneficial in the treatment of colds. Honey (now known to contain natural antibiotics) was used to treat wounds; dill for stomach problems, including excessive wind; poppy seeds to ease headaches and insomnia; and parsley was used as a diuretic.

Physicians were under the direction of Thoth as well as other divinities, including Isis, Amun and Imhotep. The goddess Selqet was associated with scorpions and snakes, and her priests treated snakebites and scorpion stings. The deadly threat from snakes is countered from the time of the Old Kingdom with magic spells against snakebite, included in the Pyramid Texts.

Evidence from a variety of sources – medical papyri, human remains and pictorial representations of the body – provides us with information about the diseases suffered by the Egyptians in pharaonic times. It seems that eye diseases were widespread, and several are described in the Ebers Papyrus, including one that is probably a cataract. Trachoma, an eye disease caused by a parasite that is still prevalent today, was also a scourge thousands of years ago. Other parasitic infections such as malaria, tuberculosis and schistosomiasis were endemic and in addition to causing specific symptoms would also have weakened patients and made them more susceptible to other illnesses.

Fractures were successfully treated, and examination of bodies found at Giza and identified as those of the pyramid builders shows several examples of bones that have healed neatly. Male circumcision appears to have been a common but not universal practice and may have been associated with hygiene and ritual cleanliness, since it was particularly associated with priests.

The study of the mummies in various collections has enabled elements of healthcare such as dental hygiene to be researched. Probably due to a diet without refined sugars, most Egyptians did not suffer significantly from tooth decay as we often do now. Their affliction was a wearing away of the teeth caused by tiny, hard particles, such as sandstone from millstones, found in their staple foods, like bread. Over a lifetime of chewing foods made from flour containing particles of stone, the enamel and dentine of the teeth were eroded. X-rays of the mummy of the pharaoh Ramesses II, who died a very old man of about 90, show that extreme wear of his teeth had led to abscesses forming. It is difficult to see what assistance dentists or doctors could have provided for this gradual erosion of the teeth, but for other problems, it seems that there were solutions available. An example of a dental bridge from the 4th Dynasty, with two teeth fixed with gold wire to the existing ones, suggests that the patient had received skilled treatment.

The Egyptian diet contained two staple foods, both based on grain: namely, bread and beer. Those who could afford it supplemented these, depending on availability, with meat, fish, vegetables and legumes, such as lentils and peas. Food was sweetened with honey and carob. From records of offerings made and tomb paintings of agricultural life, the animals domesticated by the Egyptians can be identified. Cattle, sheep and goats were used for their milk and meat, and ducks and geese appear to have been consumed, as well as quails and partridges. Pigeons, still much prized by contemporary Egyptians for their alleged aphrodisiac qualities, were also part of the ancient diet. The vegetable that most often accompanied bread was the onion, with radishes and garlic also widely consumed.

In the tomb of the pharaoh Tutankhamun was found the food that had been left to nourish him for eternity. He was buried with a bulb of garlic, chickpeas and lentils, as well as grain and a model granary to provide an everlasting supply of bread. There were boxes containing meats including the shoulder blade of an ox, duck breasts, geese and ribs from either a goat or a sheep. Also discovered were coriander, juniper berries and sesame for flavouring and two jars of honey for sweetening. To accompany the food were almost 40 jars of wine, each labelled with their vineyard, year of production and the name of the chief vintner.

SEE ALSO: Akhenaten, Imhotep, Magic, Mummies, Spells, Thoth, Tutankhamun

HYKSOS

The Hyksos ruled Egypt for over 100 years between approximately 1664 BC and 1555 BC. They were a group of invaders who, according to the Egyptian scribe Manetho, took the country almost without a fight. The name seems to have derived from the Egyptian phrase '*heka khasewet*', which means 'rulers of foreign lands'. This term is used in Egyptian literature to denote kings of lands outside Egypt, so it is easy to see how the phrase could evolve to denote these kings who originated from foreign lands to rule Egypt.

Where precisely the Hyksos came from and who they were is one of the enduring mysteries of Ancient Egyptian history. The common belief is that they were Semitic in origin, a theory which is borne out by their royal names. Some have posited the idea that these rulers were Hurrians from northern Mesopotamia or even Indo-Aryans. Many other cultures have also been put forward as candidates in the past.

The Hyksos entered Egypt and took control during an era known now as the Second Intermediate Period. When the female pharaoh Sobeknefru died, the 12th Dynasty came to a close and a second period of unrest in Egypt's history was ushered in. The Second Intermediate Period began with a succession of weak Egyptian kings before the Hyksos arrived to take control of the country. A vulnerable Egypt is therefore seen as the reason why the Hyksos were able to invade and wrest control of the country from its rulers.

The first-century Jewish historian, Josephus, wrote a two-volume work called *Against Apion*, which contained quotations said to be taken directly from the writings of the Egyptian priest and scribe Manetho. One of these excerpts described the Hyksos' arrival in Egypt:

> Tutimaios. In his reign, for what cause I know not, a blast of God smote us; and unexpectedly from the regions of the East invaders of obscure race marched in confidence of victory against our land. By main force they easily seized it without striking a blow. Having overpowered the rulers of the land, they then burned our cities ruthlessly, razed to the ground the temples of the gods, and treated all the natives with cruel hostility, massacring some and leading into slavery the wives and children of others. Finally, they appointed as king one of their number whose name was Salitis. He had his seat at Memphis, levying tribute from Upper and Lower Egypt, and always leaving garrisons behind in the most advantageous places.

If Manetho was accurate, it would seem that, although the myth of the Hyksos marching in unopposed was correct, their invasion was not without some degree of bloodletting and the occupation, at least in the early stages, seems to have been cruel and heavy-handed.

The Hyksos chose a city called Avaris as their capital, and later they also used Memphis as an administrative centre. It is thought today that Avaris was at Tell el-Dab'a. Archaeological evidence dating from the exact period in time when the Hyksos would have occupied the city shows that it was indeed laid out differently to other Egyptian towns, indicating that it probably was inhabited by foreign rulers.

Despite having the whole of northern, or Lower, Egypt under their control (northern Egypt was called Lower Egypt because the names of the two lands were based on the course of the Nile, so Upper Egypt was the south of the country, while Lower Egypt was the north and the Nile Delta), the Hyksos do not seem ever to have occupied the whole of Egypt. During this period, Upper Egypt was in the hands of noble Theban families, although their power was very limited.

The Hyksos were finally driven out of Egypt by Ahmose I. The

Theban princes had continued to rule Upper Egypt from Thebes, and they began a war of independence which culminated in the overthrow of the Hyksos capital Avaris by Ahmose I, probably around the year 1569 BC. The Hyksos were chased out of Egypt and pursued deep into southern Canaan. This event marked the beginning of the New Kingdom and the end of unrest in Egypt.

One popular misconception is that the name Hyksos translates as 'shepherd kings'. Josephus himself propagates this idea, explaining that '*hyk*' meant 'king' and '*sos*' 'shepherd' in the Egyptian language. Another alternative he puts forward is that the word meant 'captive shepherds', with 'hyk' also being an Egyptian word for 'captive'. While it is possible to argue this case, it is much more likely that the word has its origins in the phrase 'heka khasewet', which, as we have said, means 'rulers of foreign lands'.

This mistranslation has led to a whole series of false trails, and, even today, many Egyptologists believe that the biblical story of the Exodus and the Israelites in Egypt has its roots in the Hyksos, that the Hebrews were in fact none other than the Hyksos, or 'captive shepherds' as they choose to call them. They suggest that it is possible that there was no invasion, that those who were captives became kings during a period of weakness in Egypt. In other words, the Hebrews rose to be rulers of the country until finally they were forced out. In this interpretation, the flight of the Hyksos is equated with the story of the Exodus. This dubious connection with shepherds has also led to the belief that Joseph was linked with the Hyksos.

One thing that is puzzling is that, although we see some differences in certain aspects of Hyksos rule, there was a tremendous degree of similarity between them and the Egyptians they had conquered. They even worshipped Egyptian deities, including, for example, Seth. This is attributed to the extensive trade and communication between Egypt and her neighbouring states over the preceding centuries. However, it does raise the interesting possibility that the Hyksos were not actually outsiders at all but exiles from Egypt. To what period their banishment might date is not clear, but it is an intriguing line of enquiry. If the Hyksos were in fact exiled Egyptians, it might explain why they took the country almost without a fight: large sections of the population might have welcomed their return. It would also explain why they acted as they did when they finally took power, subduing certain elements of the population and sending many into slavery. By no means a solid theory, it is an entirely possible and highly intriguing proposition.

Looking back, it would now appear that the rule of the Hyksos wasn't as disastrous a period of Egyptian history as many believed at the beginning of the New Kingdom. Several technological improvements were introduced during this era, including the chariot and the composite bow, advances in pottery and weaving, and the introduction of new food crops.

Probably the most lasting benefit of the Hyksos rule was that, during the reign of the Hyksos king Apophis, many old Egyptian texts such as the Westcar Papyrus were copied, with the result that they were preserved for posterity. So today we have a large body of literature that otherwise might have vanished for ever had this line of foreign rulers not invaded Egypt.

SEE ALSO: Exodus, Joseph, Queens Reigning as Pharaoh

IMHOTEP

Inscribed on a pedestal base which once supported a statue of the pharaoh Djoser are the words: 'Chancellor of the King of Lower Egypt, First after the King of Upper Egypt, Controller of the Great Palace, Hereditary Lord, High Priest of Heliopolis (Iunu), Imhotep the Builder, the Sculptor, the Maker of Stone Vases'. In truth, it sounds a little unlikely that his hands would actually have had much time to hollow out a vase or carve a stone block, but it was Imhotep's mind which created the design for the Step Pyramid complex. It was Imhotep who conceived of constructing in stone a funerary and ritual site which would previously have been made of perishable materials such as wood and matting. Rather than a rectangular, quite low table tomb, or mastaba, fashioned of sand and mud brick, he devised a series of six such buildings, decreasing in size as they were piled one on the other, to create a series of huge steps reaching to the sky. This structure, too, was to be in stone. We call it the Step Pyramid, and it is generally recognised as the first building in the whole world made totally of stone. In its day, it was an entirely novel concept.

It has been estimated that around a million tons of limestone – high-grade stone called Tura for use in prominent positions and poorer limestone for infill – were used in the Step Pyramid complex. The logistics involved are quite staggering, and Imhotep must have had a great deal of self-confidence to conceive such a revolutionary design on such a huge scale. One wonders if there may have been times when even he was at least a little uncertain whether some of the demands he made of the stone blocks were reasonable. Would they support such a weight? What would be the overall practical and aesthetic impact? Other questions spring to mind. Would his royal master be happy? Where would sufficient skilled masons be found? Would the necessary food rations and other essential supplies be sufficient and would they arrive on site in good condition and at the right times? Even storage must have been a problem. He would have had to be very confident that his lieutenants were reliable, capable men.

The royal mastabas of the Early Dynastic Period (3050–2687 BC), at Abydos in the south of the country, were burial chambers covered with sand mounds. These may have been intended to represent the Benben, the first land which appeared, according to Egyptian mythology, from the primordial ocean when the world was first created. The structures may therefore have embodied ideas of creation and renewal, symbolising the rebirth in the afterlife of the tomb-owner. Perhaps the reasoning behind Imhotep's new design was to make the mound more permanent by constructing it of stone, more conspicuous by taking it to a great height and more practical by providing steps by which the soul of the dead king could mount to the heavens. The site chosen for this architectural innovation was at Saqqara, an already important necropolis near the capital city, Memphis. Visitors to the Step Pyramid complex today will see many structures that have been rebuilt and columns that have been restored by the French architect Jean-Philippe Lauer, who worked at and was associated with Saqqara from 1932 until his death in 2001.

There are few who would deny that Imhotep was the greatest creative mastermind known to the preclassical world. It is thought that his family originated in Upper Egypt and that his father was Kanefer, the Royal Superintendent of Works. It is quite possible that Imhotep began his education under his father's direction and began to develop his innovative ideas as an assistant to his father.

Many years after his death, his genius was transformed in legend so that he began to be associated with medical knowledge, which, in the ancient world, was connected with magic. After all, what could be more magical than the mysteries of life and death, the effects of healing potions and drugs upon the body, and the power of the physician to cure, sometimes when all hope appears to be gone? Imhotep is credited with having written medical treatises.

If this is true, he was a remarkable polymath and his diverse achievements rival those of Renaissance artists and architects. By the time of the Greek Ptolemaic dynasty, more than 2,000 years after Imhotep's life had ended, he was regarded as a god. Imhotep was assimilated with both the Greek god of healing, Asclepius, and the Egyptian Thoth, god of wisdom, who is pictured in Ancient Egyptian art recording the verdict of Amun when the heart of a dead person is weighed in the scales to decide whether the deceased should be eaten by a terrible composite beast or join the justified ones in eternal life. Offerings of mummified ibis birds were made to Imhotep/Thoth by those seeking favours and wishing to leave offerings to ensure their prayers were heard by the gods. Egyptologists believed that Imhotep had been buried, having reputedly died at a great age, near his master at Saqqara, and it was during searches for his tomb that the huge, sacred animal cemetery there was found. The mummies of baboons, falcons and ibises were excavated by Walter Emery from 1964.

The main cult centre for Imhotep in Graeco-Roman times was the Asclepion at Memphis. Believers might bring models of afflicted parts of their bodies or those of their loved ones to emphasise what particular healing process was required. In many Roman Catholic countries today, similar appeals are made by desperate devotees of the saints, the main difference, apart from the particular divine power invoked, being that wax body parts are usual today, whereas in Ancient Egypt the models were generally made of clay. The healing sanctuary housed in the great mortuary temple of Hatshepsut at Deir el-Bahri was another centre for the cult of Imhotep the Wise. A common belief was that by sleeping in the sanatorium and being blessed by the god with a dream, a sufferer might be cured. The process was known as 'incubation'.

Imhotep the god became thought of as the son of Ptah, chief god of the city of Memphis, who had visited his mortal mother Khereduankh. The logic behind this is that the High Priest of Ptah had as one of his titles 'Master Builder', and during construction of religious buildings he directed the craftsmen in their work. Another link is that Ptah himself was known by the title 'Ptah of the Primeval Mound', which may be thought of as a reference to raised tombs being analogous to the first land which appeared above the primordial flood at the creation of the earth. Images of Imhotep usually show him as a kilted figure with a papyrus scroll in his lap and a skullcap on his head.

In contemporary culture, Imhotep's name has been used for characters in films, notably 1999's *The Mummy*, starring Brendan Fraser and Rachel Weisz. Ironically enough, given that Imhotep is the vengeful, cursed villain of the film, the name can be translated as 'He who comes in peace'.

SEE ALSO: Abydos, Djoser, Magic, Thoth

ISIS

There is no Egyptian goddess whose name resonates more with people than that of Isis. In fact, she is perhaps the world's best-known goddess, and long after Egypt's power had waned, her cult was still spreading.

Isis was unusual in that for a large part of Egyptian history she was not worshipped in her own right but as part of a holy trinity along with Osiris and Horus. It is thought that not until sometime around the 30th Dynasty were temples dedicated solely to Isis constructed. However, from this point onwards, her importance grew until, according to Barbara Watterson in her book *Gods of Ancient Egypt*:

> The cult of Isis was widespread in the Egypt of the dynastic period. From Egypt it spread northwards to Phoenicia, Syria and Palestine; to Asia Minor; to Cyprus, Rhodes, Crete, Samos and other islands in the Aegean; to many parts of mainland Greece – Corinth, Argos and Thessaly amongst them; to Malta and Sicily; and, finally, to Rome. In the first century BC, Isis was perhaps the most popular goddess in the Eternal City, from which her cult spread to the furthest limits of the Roman Empire, including Britain: her only rival was Mithras.

The goddess's name translates literally as 'queen of the throne'. Another possibility that has been suggested is 'stone seat'. Isis was always depicted as a woman in a long dress, with a headdress shaped like a throne. Manly P. Hall commented on the meaning of this symbolism in his book *The Secret Teachings of All Ages*: 'Among the Egyptians, Isis is often represented with a headdress consisting of the empty throne chair of her murdered husband, and this peculiar structure was accepted during certain dynasties as her hieroglyphic.'

She also had many titles. Amongst numerous other names, she was known as 'the Brilliant One in the Sky', 'Lady of the Countries of the South', 'the Great Lady', 'the Divine One', 'the God-mother', 'the Queen of all Gods', 'Opener of the Year', 'She Who Knows How to Make Right Use of the Heart', 'the Female Ra', 'Queen of the Earth', 'Great Lady of Magic', 'Lady of Warmth and Fire', 'She Who Is Greatly Feared in the Duat', 'Wife of the Lord of the Abyss' and 'Moon Shining Over the Sea'.

Like Osiris, Isis was originally a minor deity of the Delta region of Egypt who rose to become one of the most prominent gods of the Egyptian pantheon. At first, she was associated with Horus as his wife and not his mother. At this point in the development of Egyptian mythology, Isis was considered, as the wife of Horus, to be the wife of the living pharaoh, and so her role was a very important one, especially once the King had died, because it was Isis's duty to assist the dead king's soul. This is borne out by the sheer number of times her name appears in the Pyramid Texts. As a goddess of protection, she became second to none. Later on in Egypt's history, Isis is found on coffins and sarcophagi, her winged arms outstretched in a gesture of protection. It is not the only context in which she is shown with wings, and in a key moment in the Osirian myth she hovers over the prone form of Osiris as a kite.

Perhaps these funerary duties for which Isis was responsible are the key to the way the story of Osiris – another god with strong connections with the dead, as lord of the underworld – evolved to include the goddess as an integral character. It has also been suggested that it was actually the merging of Isis with Hathor that brought about changes in her role. However exactly it came about, Isis moved from her position as the wife of Horus to become his mother and the wife of his father, Osiris, instead. Thus, in keeping with her new position, she became the mother of the Pharaoh, not his wife, and depictions survive of her breastfeeding the King in her new role as throne-mother.

So it was that Isis began to be viewed as the devoted wife and mother, searching tirelessly for her husband Osiris's mortal remains after he has been murdered by Seth, chopped into numerous pieces and scattered across all Egypt. It is in this strand of the Osirian myth that Isis's great magical powers come to the fore. She manages to create an artificial phallus for the dead king's mummified remains and brings Osiris briefly back into his body with complex words of power, resurrecting him for long enough to conceive their child, Horus.

Isis's magical powers were said to have come from Ra himself. Back in the legendary times before history began, Isis desired to wield more power so she cunningly tricked Ra into telling her the secret name that was the source of his potency: she created an invisible snake and Ra was bitten; he was unable to heal himself, but Isis promised she would cure him as long as he revealed his secret name to her. Ra, fearing death, complied, and so it was that all of his knowledge and power passed to Isis.

It was not only in magic that Isis was skilled; she was also an expert healer. Richard Patrick, in *Egyptian Mythology*, reveals some of her other talents:

> [Isis's] magic was allied to the wisdom of Thoth and given to mankind as a skill in Healing; she was also responsible, as the counterpart of Osiris, for teaching the household arts to women. She taught them weaving and spinning, and how to grind the corn. Her strongest appeal was to the sorrowing wife and devoted mother − every woman could identify with her and she has been seen by some commentators as the archetype of a cult that continues in the Christian churches to the present day.

This brings us to another important aspect of Isis: her identification with the Virgin Mary. Many have pointed out that the myth of Isis, Osiris and Horus bears a striking similarity to the story of Jesus, and it would be easy to mistake some images of Isis and the young Horus for depictions of the Virgin Mary and Jesus. This is no coincidence, and some scholars have gone so far as to point out that during the early stages of Christianity the worship of Isis was simply merged with the worship of the Virgin Mary, that the two became one. Furthermore, the tale of the Virgin Mary fleeing with the baby Jesus to protect him from the purge of Herod echoes the story of Isis going into hiding with the infant Horus to avoid the wrath of Seth. When we consider the myth of the resurrection of Osiris, we start to see a group of central themes of Egyptian theology embedded in Christianity.

Isis was symbolised in the heavens by the star known today as Sirius, the brightest object in the night sky after the planets and the moon. The appearance of this star on the horizon towards the end of June heralded the Egyptian New Year and also coincided with the annual inundation of the Nile. It was through Isis's power and magic that the flooding of the Nile was believed to occur, and it was as a result of this deluge that fertility returned to the Nile Valley.

So we can see that the symbolism of the myths related directly to the environment in which the Ancient Egyptians lived: the drama of the gods was repeatedly played out on earth. Just as Isis was the medium through which Osiris was resurrected, so too did her appearance in the sky bring about the flooding of the Nile and the rebirth of Egypt. It was Isis who brought the land back to life, just as she had revived Osiris. Up and down Egypt, all the thousands of moulds in the form of Osiris that were built to celebrate this time of new life sprouted, honouring the moment when Isis brought Osiris back to the living, however briefly, and Horus was conceived. In all of Egypt there was no greater magic than this.

SEE ALSO: Hathor, Horus, Osiris, Ra

The Step Pyramid of Djoser and its associated complex at Saqqara.

Scenes from the Giza Plateau, showing the incredible Great Pyramid of Khufu (below) and that of his son Khafre (above right; inset).

Above: The Great Pyramid dominates the landscape.

Inset: The boat found alongside Khufu's Great Pyramid has been painstakingly reconstructed.

Below: The Great Pyramid is the last surviving wonder of the ancient world.

Above: The so-called Bent Pyramid of Sneferu at Dahshur.

Below: The Great Sphinx of Giza. Is this the image of King Khafre?

An obelisk from the Temple of Amun at Karnak.

Above: The enigmatic face
of the lioness goddess Sekhmet.

Inset: A statue of Horus from his temple at Edfu.

Below: A Hathor-headed column.

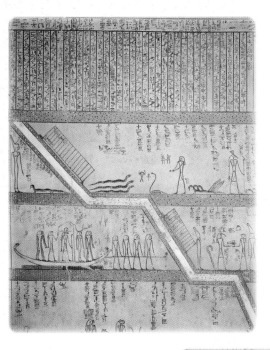

In the tomb of Tuthmosis III in the Valley of the Kings are found these depictions of the fourth (above) and fifth (right) hours of the Duat.

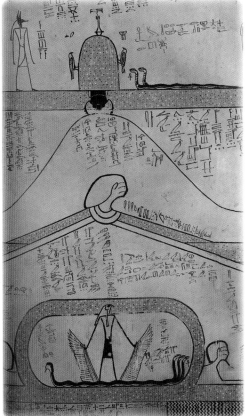

The golden death mask of the boy king Tutankhamun.

JOSEPH

The story of Joseph, the biblical prophet who could interpret dreams and who saved Egypt from famine, is familiar to us from portrayals in many media – even including a stage musical, *Joseph and the Amazing Technicolour Dreamcoat*. The key events in Joseph's story take place after he is sold as a slave by his jealous brothers and enters the house of an Egyptian official who is called Potiphar. According to the biblical account, Joseph was a conscientious servant who performed his duties well. However, he resisted the advances of Potiphar's wife, following which she denounced him for seducing her.

Joseph was put into prison as a result of this false allegation, and while incarcerated he interpreted dreams for some of his fellow inmates. For a cupbearer, he had good news, that the man would be released and restored to Pharaoh's favour. A baker was less fortunate: Joseph correctly foresaw that he would be executed. Word reached the Pharaoh about the prisoner who could unravel the meanings of dreams, and he demanded to see Joseph. Given this great opportunity to improve his position, Joseph was able to interpret the meaning of Pharaoh's dream. The seven fat cows of which he had dreamed represented seven years of good harvests to come, and the seven lean cows were a warning of seven years of famine. In Egypt, where agricultural success was dependent on the inundation of the Nile, the prospect of repeated poor harvests was taken very seriously.

The Pharaoh – who, frustratingly, is not named – placed Joseph in charge of the operation to prepare the country for the difficult time ahead. Stores of food were gathered during the good harvests and this meant that when the crops failed in the famine years, there were reserves that could be used to feed the population. Joseph, by his managing of this crisis, became a favoured servant of Pharaoh and was given the Egyptian name Zaphnath-Paaneah. He married Asenath, the daughter of Potiperah, a priest of Heliopolis. Attempts have been made to interpret these as Egyptian names. For example, Asenath could be a derivation of '*as neith*', 'favourite of the goddess Neith'. However, there are those who argue that these names are Semitic in origin, which would challenge conventional wisdom regarding the dating of Joseph's story. Names of this type were not in use in Egypt until much later than Joseph is generally thought to have lived.

Famine across the region eventually led Joseph's father Jacob to send his other sons into Egypt to buy food. The brothers did not recognise the successful and powerful man at the court as their brother, but when he revealed his identity, they were afraid of his revenge. Joseph in fact welcomed his errant brothers and agreed that they would bring Jacob and the rest of the family into Egypt to live. After his death, Jacob was mummified according to Egyptian methods so that his body could be taken for burial at his chosen location in Canaan. Joseph was also embalmed following his death, having left instructions that his body should be taken out of Egypt when the Israelites left.

If we look at this story from an Egyptian perspective, there is little in the surviving records that can help to verify the story. Very accurate information regarding the Nile inundation was kept, and there is some evidence of famine in Egypt, but there is no mention of a seven-year famine of the magnitude of Joseph's. There is a so-called Famine Stela dating from Ptolemaic times that is believed to be a copy of a 3rd-Dynasty record, but nothing suggestive of a sustained famine during the Middle Kingdom, where most scholars place Joseph.

On the walls of the tomb of Khnumhotep at Beni Hasan, there is evidence, dating from around 1900 BC, that the Ancient Egyptians traded with Asiatic people. Some bearded men in striped clothing are leading animals in a trading caravan, and their leader has the Semitic name Abishai. This shows that the Egyptians were trading with people from the Near East, although the guides who tell visitors that these are the Midianite merchants who sold Joseph to Potiphar are surely engaging in wild speculation.

The element of Joseph's story in which Potiphar's wife tries to seduce him is very similar to an Ancient Egyptian narrative called 'The Tale of the Two Brothers'. In this story, the wife of the older brother is spurned by the younger when she tries to start an affair with him. Conflict erupts between the brothers and it is only after many adventures that they are reconciled, in the same way that Joseph and his brothers are finally reunited in Egypt.

In his book *A Test of Time*, the historian David Rohl dates Joseph's life to the time of Amenemhat III and argues that his great labyrinth at Hawara may have been an administrative building linked to the preparations for dealing with the famine. He develops his theory further by locating Joseph's tomb at Tell el-Dab'a, where a statue of a man has been found featuring an unusual style of wig and remnants of paint suggesting a brightly coloured garment. The theory is that Joseph was buried in this tomb until Moses removed his body at the time of the Exodus.

One very interesting point regarding chronology arises if we return to the biblical story of Joseph. The Pharaoh lets Joseph ride in a chariot as a mark of his favour, which brings into the equation the time when chariots were introduced into Egypt. There are no records of chariots before the Second Intermediate Period, and their introduction is usually associated with the Hyksos rulers of Egypt. This means either that Joseph could not have been in the service of a Middle Kingdom pharaoh such as Amenemhat III or that the story was embellished at some stage.

Ahmed Osman, who has made a series of links between biblical characters and Egyptian historical figures, puts forward another possibility for the tomb of Joseph. In *Stranger in the Valley of the Kings*, he shifts the timeframe to the New Kingdom, in the reign of the pharaoh Amenhotep III. The tomb of Yuya and his wife Thuya, which was discovered virtually intact in 1905, was, Osman suggests, that of Joseph himself. He points out that Yuya had the title '*it ntr n nb tawi*', 'Holy Father of the Lord of the Two Lands', in other words, father of the Pharaoh. In the Bible, Joseph tells his brother, 'So now it was not you that sent me hither, but God: and he hath made me a father to Pharaoh.' Conventional Egyptologists argue that this title was bestowed on Yuya because he was the father of Queen Tiye, the chief wife of Amenhotep III, and therefore his father-in-law.

Several observers have noted that Yuya's well-preserved mummy has his arms tucked under his chin, rather than crossed on his chest in the usual way, which mimicked depictions of Osiris. His features, and in particular his nose, are also said to be unusual compared with those of other mummies, and it has been suggested that he looks non-Egyptian. Osman suggests that the name Yuya is an attempt to render in Egyptian the name of this man's god, Yahweh, in the same way that his pharaoh had the name of his god, Amun, as part of his name, Amenhotep or 'Amun is pleased'. Notably, another of Yuya's titles is 'Commander of the King's Chariotry', and he was buried with a very fine chariot.

The name of Joseph is used today for the Bahr Yusef, a branch of the Nile that brings water to a lake, Birket Qarun, near Hawara in the Faiyum region. This connection encourages speculation that the stores Joseph built up in anticipation of the seven-year famine were housed in the Labyrinth of Hawara.

SEE ALSO: Exodus, Heliopolis, Hyksos, Labyrinth of Hawara, Ra

KHUFU

Considering he is one of the most famous Old Kingdom pharaohs, thanks to his association with the Great Pyramid at Giza, surprisingly little is known about Khufu (also commonly known by the Greek name Cheops), the second ruler of the 4th Dynasty. Even the length of his reign is uncertain, although it is generally believed that he ruled for 25 years (2609–2584 BC). However, other sources state that his rule was considerably longer, notably Manetho, who records a 65-year reign. Herodotus, meanwhile, attributes to him a 50-year reign.

What we do know about Khufu is that his name was Khnum Khufu – 'Khnum (the creator god) protects me'. He was the son of the pharaoh Sneferu, a prolific pyramid-builder. His mother, Hetepheres, was buried or perhaps reburied in a shaft tomb on the Giza Plateau. Two of Khufu's sons became pharaohs: Djedefre, whose pyramid is at Abu Roash, 8 km to the north of Giza; and Khafre, who is credited with building another of the Giza pyramids.

Like those of other pharaohs, Khufu's name has been found carved in a number of quarries, including the granite quarries of Aswan and the Hatnub alabaster quarries. Inscriptions also record that Khufu ordered raids on the Sinai peninsula, Nubia and Libya, probably as part of mining expeditions. In stark contrast to the scale of the Great Pyramid, the only attested artefact of Khufu is a minute statuette of the seated king wearing the red crown of Lower Egypt. Carved in ivory, the statuette stands less than 7 cm tall and was found in 1903 at Abydos. Khufu's 'Horus name' – Her-Mejedu – is inscribed on the side of the throne. Interestingly, recent research put forward in a paper by Dr Zahi Hawass, Secretary General of the Supreme Council of Antiquities, shows that this statuette is in fact from the much later 26th Dynasty, and is therefore very unlikely to be a direct likeness.

There are, however, two other surviving statues that are thought to represent Khufu, and although these are not inscribed with his name, there are sufficient similarities to suggest that they represent the king. One is a colossal red-granite head wearing the white crown of Upper Egypt, now in the Brooklyn Museum; the other is a miniature limestone head, again wearing the Upper Egyptian crown, now in Munich. A few cylinder seals bearing his name can be seen in the Petrie Museum, London, and some vessels from the temple of Horus at Nekhen (modern Hierakonpolis) are also inscribed with his name.

Apart from that, little information about him remains, although, surprisingly, Khufu appears in three 'Tales of Wonder' dating from c.1600 BC, during the Hyksos period. Recorded in what is known today as the Westcar Papyrus, one of these tales depicts Khufu as a man who cares little for the value of human life, so that when the great magician Djedi, who can rejoin severed heads, is brought before him, Khufu orders a prisoner killed so that he can see Djedi bring him back to life. When Djedi objects, the magician's powers are successfully tested on a goose. The tale also relates how the pharaoh sought to obtain knowledge regarding the number of the secret chambers of Thoth. This desire on his part has led some to suggest that Khufu had an impious attitude towards the gods of Egypt, but this is questionable, as the tales do not indicate that Khufu adopted a particularly irreverent stance. Indeed, in the tales, Khufu is portrayed as very human: his discourses with Djedi are not condescending in any way, and, at the end of the tale, the king shows concern for the well-being of the magician, providing him with a home within the household of his son, Prince Hardedef. However, it has to be remembered that the Westcar Papyrus was written 1,000 years after Khufu lived, so it is uncertain how accurately he has been portrayed in these tales.

It is interesting to note that Herodotus considered Khufu to be a less-than-savoury character, suggesting in Book Two of his *Histories* that he was a tyrant who was hated by his people even centuries later:

> Till the death of Rhampsinitus [Sneferu], the priests said
> Egypt was excellently governed, and flourished greatly;
> but after him Cheops succeeded to the throne, and plunged
> into all manner of wickedness. He closed the temples and
> forbade the Egyptians to offer sacrifice, compelling them
> instead to labour, one and all, in his service.

Herodotus relates that such a despot and an immoral man was Khufu that when he had spent all the resources of the royal treasury on pyramid-building, he sent his own daughter into prostitution in order for her to replenish the royal coffers: 'The wickedness of Cheops reached to such a pitch that, when he had spent all his treasures and wanted more, he sent his daughter to the stews [a brothel], with orders to procure him a certain sum.'

Dr Hawass has suggested that hatred of Khufu was in some way similar to the loathing felt for Akhenaten, who was seen as a heretic by his successors. Hawass suggests that Khufu sought to exclude all gods except Ra, identifying himself closely with that god. Such a strategy would explain Herodotus's assertion that Khufu closed down the temples and forbade sacrificial offerings to gods. However, there is no firm evidence in this regard, and the idea that Khufu was a tyrannical ruler occurs only in later tales about him and is probably related to the enormous scale of his pyramid and the strain its building must have been on Egypt's economic and social structure.

But how certain are we that Khufu *was* the builder of the Great Pyramid of Giza? Certainly, his mortuary temple sits beside the pyramid, but, without any official inscriptions within the pyramid itself, its designation as Khufu's is considered by some to be somewhat tenuous. The problem of attributing the Great Pyramid to Khufu was first raised by the author Zecharia Sitchin in his book *The Stairway to Heaven* and then taken up by Robert Bauval and Graham Hancock in *Keeper of Genesis* as part of their theory that the pyramids of the Giza Plateau were built earlier than is generally accepted. Sitchin pointed out that the evidence relating the pyramid to Khufu is sparse and inconclusive, and claimed that vital aspects of it were in fact forged in 1837–8 by Colonel Richard Howard Vyse.

It was Vyse and J.S. Perring, an engineer, who discovered, among other things, the names Khnum Khuf (three instances) and Khufu (one instance) written in red ochre on the ceiling or walls of four out of the five 'relieving chambers' within the Great

Pyramid. (These chambers were originally thought to take the strain off the King's Chamber so that the enormous weight of the completed pyramid above did not cause the King's Chamber to collapse. However, modern research by French structural engineer Jean Kerisel has shown that the so-called relieving chambers are nothing of the sort. In fact, according to Kerisel, it is these very chambers that have contributed to the various cracks in the ceiling of the King's Chamber.)

In 1765, a relieving chamber directly above the King's Chamber had been discovered by Nathaniel Davison, although no markings were found on the walls. It was in 1837 that Vyse and Perring noted that a reed could be pushed through a small crack in the ceiling of Davison's Chamber, indicating that another room existed above. Vyse and J.R. Hill (a mill superintendent) blasted their way through and, according to Vyse's diary, made a thorough examination of the chamber. He makes no mention of discovering any red markings. Not until the next day, when Perring and a Mr Marsh (a civil engineer) were shown the chamber, were the marks noticed. Subsequently, similar red marks were found in another three relieving chambers which were discovered above the first.

However, Sitchin believes that the circumstances in which all these markings were found are suspect: Hill was there most nights and therefore able to make the marks prior to their 'discovery'. Sitchin also notes that the red marks were only found in the chambers discovered by Vyse and that there are a number of orthographic problems with them. They appear to be a mixture of writing and styles used in a number of different periods, some Middle Kingdom, some 26th Dynasty, some letters unique or so slovenly and inexpertly written that they are indecipherable. At the time, copies of the red markings were examined by Samuel Birch of the British Museum, who, although he stated that the king mentioned within the cartouches was Khufu, nevertheless had reservations about the writings and their inconsistency with what was known of Old Kingdom hieroglyphs.

However, most Egyptologists today have no problem ascribing the Great Pyramid to Khufu on the grounds of dating and the instances of his name within four of the five relieving chambers. Indeed, modern research has shown major flaws in Sitchin's theory, not least of which is that at least one of the marks has been made around a corner of one of the stones which has then been integrated into the masonry, meaning that it must have been written on the stone before or during construction. The marks are so-called 'quarry marks' believed to be graffiti from the work gangs who constructed the pyramid and to relate to the names of the various gangs, with each taking a form of the king's name, either Khnum Khuf or Khufu. Mark Lehner, the distinguished Egyptologist of the Giza Plateau, states in *The Complete Pyramids* (1997): 'Since nobody had entered this from the time Khufu's workmen sealed it until Vyse blasted his way in, the gang names clinch the attribution of this pyramid to the 4th-dynasty pharaoh, Khufu.'

Ultimately, the question of whether Khufu was responsible for the building of the Great Pyramid is related to the uncertainty about what happened to his body. His final resting place has as yet remained undiscovered. Herodotus related that Khufu was buried on an island beneath the Great Pyramid – he says that water was 'introduced from the Nile by a canal' – but nothing to this effect has been found. There is no evidence that the sarcophagus found in the King's Chamber was Khufu's or indeed that anyone was ever buried within the pyramid. Khufu's funerary cult (whereby his statue was venerated and daily tended) lasted until the 26th Dynasty, almost 2,000 years after his death.

SEE ALSO: Giza, Pyramids, Sneferu

LABYRINTH OF HAWARA

Despite the many impressive buildings left to us today by the Ancient Egyptians, the effects of time and human interference have diminished the legacy of this great civilisation. One of the greatest losses is that of the labyrinth at Hawara, which was described by classical scholars as a greater and more impressive achievement than the pyramids.

The labyrinth was surveyed in the 1820s by John Gardner Wilkinson, who published his findings, and excavated in 1843 by Karl Richard Lepsius. It was Lepsius who made the first detailed drawings of the remains. The labyrinth was identified as the mortuary temple of the 12th-Dynasty pharaoh Amenemhat III. It is located in the Faiyum region near a mud-brick pyramid of the same ruler. The Faiyum is an area 60 km south-west of Cairo, a fertile district around a lake now known as the Birket Qarun, called Lake Moeris in the classical period. During the Middle Kingdom, the capital of Egypt moved to the area and several pyramids were built in the Faiyum, for example at El-Lahun.

Herodotus described the labyrinth as a huge building; in the second book of his *Histories* he writes:

> Furthermore, they resolved to leave a memorial of themselves in common, and in pursuance of this resolve they made a labyrinth, a little above Lake Moeris, and situated near what is called the City of the Crocodiles [in the Faiyum, known to the Greeks as Crocodilopolis]. I saw it myself and it is indeed

a wonder past words; for if one were to collect together all of the buildings of the Greeks and their most striking works of architecture, they would all clearly be shown to have cost less labour and money than this labyrinth.

The pyramids, too, were greater than words can tell, and each of them is the equivalent of many of the great works of the Greeks; but the labyrinth surpasses the pyramids also. It has twelve roofed courts, with doors facing one another, six to the north and six to the south and in a continuous line. There are double sets of chambers in it, some underground and some above, and their number is 3,000; there are 1,500 of each.

When Herodotus visited in the middle of the fifth century BC, he was told that the lower rooms contained the tombs of the kings who had built the labyrinth and also those of crocodiles, which were sacred in the Faiyum, worshipped as the crocodile god Sobek. The historian recorded that the building had a total area of about six acres.

Pliny the Elder (AD 23–79) also described the crocodile vaults and he stated that the building was the template for the labyrinth in which the Minotaur was kept at Knossos in Crete. He was repeating the claim made by Diodorus Siculus in his *Library of History*, in which he asserted that Daedalus was inspired by the architecture of the labyrinth in Egypt in building his for King Minos. After discussing the conjecture over who built the structure, he too pays tribute to its enormous size:

> Whatever the truth may be, there is no doubt that Daedalus adopted it as the model for the labyrinth built by him in Crete, but that he reproduced only a hundredth part of it, containing passages that wind, advance and retreat in a bewilderingly intricate manner.

Strabo (*c*.64 BC–*c*.AD 23) wrote about the labyrinth in his *Geography*, Book XVII. Strabo said that the labyrinth had 42 halls, corresponding to the number of *nomes*, or administrative districts, in Egypt:

> It is said that this number of courts was built because it was the custom for all the nomes to assemble there in accordance with their rank, together with their own priests and priestesses, for the sake of sacrifice and of

offering gifts to the gods and of administering justice in matters of the greatest importance. And each of the nomes was conducted to the court appointed to it.

Flinders Petrie, during his excavations in 1888, found limestone remains of a building suggesting a size of 300 m by 250 m wide. He also found crocodile burials, as described by Herodotus and Pliny the Elder. At the time of Petrie's dig, there were mounds of limestone chippings covering the area. Much of this material was removed during the building of the railways, however, and the site is now much depleted.

It is believed by some biblical scholars that the labyrinth housed the storerooms and granaries of Pharaoh, used by Joseph to store food up against the seven lean years he foresaw. It has also been postulated that the pyramids at Giza were the storerooms, which – given their limited internal space – seems unlikely.

The correlation between biblical chronology and Egyptian historical dating is fraught with difficulties. If, however, the date of Joseph's time in Egypt is taken to be around 1900 BC, as is usual, then he would have been there during the Middle Kingdom. At this time, the pharaohs of the 12th and 13th dynasties were ruling from their Faiyum capital Itjtawy, and the labyrinth, if it was indeed built for Amenemhat III, would have been contemporary with this. Interestingly, the waterway that links the Nile with the Birket Qarun lake is known as the Bahr Yusef, so Joseph's name is linked with the area to this day.

Amenemhat III built two pyramids, one at Dahshur and the other as part of the labyrinth complex at Hawara. The internal structure and passageways of the pyramid at Dahshur are particularly complex, including two sets of burial chambers for queens. This pyramid was abandoned, possibly used for only a queen's burial, and the second complex at Hawara was begun around Year 15 of the pharaoh's reign. The route to the pyramid's burial chamber employs techniques such as a passageway hidden in the ceiling to try to foil attempts at robbery, and yet it was nonetheless empty when excavated. Unfortunately, the use of mud bricks as the principal building material has meant that, in comparison with the Giza pyramid field, against which it was once so favourably measured, the site at Hawara is now rarely visited, and the pyramid and labyrinth are shadows of their former glory.

SEE ALSO: Exodus, Joseph, Old Testament Egypt

LETTERS TO THE DEAD

Despite their apparent preoccupation with death and the afterlife, the Ancient Egyptians' actual outlook was one of loving life and hating death. Whilst death as a human experience is inescapable, and whilst the Ancient Egyptians knew that magic could not prevent it, they did believe that magic could be used in order to persuade the dead to aid the living, utilising their potency to cure illnesses, promote good health or fertility, prevent bad dreams or end the malicious effect of a deceased person, or *akh*-spirit.

By writing a letter to the dead, an unresolved or unjust matter could be sorted out by appealing directly to the akh-spirit. It was hoped that such entreaties, written on a bowl, jar stand, linen or papyrus, and placed inside the tomb of the deceased whose help was sought, would compel the akh-spirit to act on the behalf of the living. The surviving examples, of which there are fewer than 20, date from the Old right through to the New Kingdom, and in all cases it would appear that an akh-spirit was thought to be the cause of the problem suffered by the living. The author of the letter, usually a wife, husband, son or daughter, stresses that they are an innocent victim and should not be made to suffer the hardships with which they are afflicted. By beseeching the help of an akh-spirit, it was believed, the antagonist could be prevented from continuing its malicious influence, the complainant often calling upon the Underworld Tribunal to prosecute their case.

It was believed that akhu-spirits were interested in and able to influence the world of the living. In fact, the dead continued to dwell with their family and were often thought to be jealous of the living, being a force for good or a cause of trouble and illness. They could possess the living, making individuals irritable and petulant, and their magical potency, obtained through death, meant that the akhu-spirits were a force to be feared.

The letters to the dead begin by stating who is sending the letter and to whom, followed by the complaint or problem that the deceased is required to rectify, such as a son who is being dispossessed of his inheritance, another son complaining of the loss of his land, a wife asking her husband to end the illness of a loved serving-maid, a daughter seeking a son for herself and for her sister, as well as many unspecified complaints. The author's blamelessness and friendship with the deceased when still alive is stressed, often highlighting that the proper burial rituals had been observed, sometimes at great expense, and/or that the author continues to provide sustenance for the deceased. The complaint is therefore, 'I've done all this for you, so why are you not protecting me and allowing me to suffer so?'

Even if a living person was the obvious cause of an individual's misfortune, it was thought that a malevolent akh-spirit was the reason why the person was acting that way. Only another akh-spirit could counter the malicious influence of the dead and the only way, therefore, to cure the problem was to appeal directly to the akh-spirit that was thought to be the cause of the difficulty or ask, even order, a dead relative to intercede on your behalf. This was especially pertinent if a request was made to a deceased parent, as it was believed that even in death parents would protect their children as they would in life. In fact, the letters to the dead make it clear that a dead parent was expected to stay with their children as a guardian or protective ghost in order to ward off evil.

That the Ancient Egyptians wrote letters to the dead is important, as it reflects their belief in the permanency of the written word; it ensured that the appeal's potency was eternal and meant that the presence of the aggrieved individual to personally say the words or enact a ritual was not required in order for the deceased to hear their plea. The care with which the letters to the dead and the utensil they are written upon were made and designed indicates that they must have been pre-planned and carefully formatted. Not only are the bowls, for example, well made, they also feel nice to hold. Sensation is important to magic and it must have been important that the letter and the medium used should attract the attention of the deceased, calling upon the senses of sight, touch, and perhaps even taste and smell, if the bowls were filled with food offerings as has been suggested.

The letters indicate that the malicious person is usually dead and it appears that only a fellow akh-spirit can judge or bring to justice a harmful ghost. There is no indication that a living person could carry out an exorcism but the evidence of these letters suggests that they were being used to conjure up the deceased. As the akhu-spirits were thought to be responsible for disease and torment, they were to be feared and treated with respect so that they did not become annoyed and cause harm. Accordingly, the malicious influence of an akh-spirit was not solely due to neglect by the living but also to the jealous nature of the dead, their unstable emotions and their power to interfere with the living.

It is unknown what level or form of responsibility was involved when attempting to communicate with the dead. The intention of the letters was to invoke the dead in order to persuade them to affect the living in a positive way. This was done by degrees of persuasion, including the remembrance of past friendships, reminders that the correct burial rituals had been observed or the threatening of the dead with the cessation of funerary libations. The failure to perform the necessary rituals would affect the very sustenance and life of the akh-spirit, causing the tomb-owner to shrivel and desiccate due to the lack of revitalising water. Threats to the dead must have been a tremendously serious matter, bearing in mind that the power and possible pernicious effect of the akh-spirit was considered real and tangible.

Letters to the dead were considered so important that a person would chance violating the purity of the tomb in order to place the letter there. Was the act seen as a desecration and if so how was this overcome? What rituals or observances were needed in order to place the letter within the tomb without disturbing its purity and without activating the tomb-owner's curse? The letter to the dead known as the Leyden Papyrus was written by a general to his wife who had died three years previously, suggesting that her tomb was specifically reopened in order to deposit the letter.

The letters to the dead invariably produce more questions than answers, although as a corpus they help us to understand how the average Ancient Egyptian interacted with the mysteries of the afterlife and its inhabitants. Even though so few survive, it is believed that the practice of writing letters to the dead was widespread, considering the formulaic construction and phrases used, and the distribution of the finds throughout Egypt. It is evident from reading the letters that the concern of Ancient Egyptians was not whether the practice was logical, or even whether it worked, but how a person's plight might be redressed and improved.

SEE ALSO: Magic, Spells

MAGIC

Throughout the history of Ancient Egypt, magic played an essential and integral role. Indeed, for the people of antiquity, Egypt had the reputation of being without rival in magic and the divinatory arts. The Jewish Talmud even states that 'ten measures of sorcery descended upon the earth, nine of which were taken up by Egypt'. By the fourth century AD, the historian Ammianus Marcellinus was writing that 'knowledge of the divine and the origin of divination . . . has spread abroad from Egypt'.

In the Western world today, the term 'magic' conjures up images of something superficial and simplistic that is part of the entertainment industry. However, rather than dismissing the relevance of magic out of hand, it is worth noting that the Ancient Egyptians had absolute faith in magical practices and a belief that magic worked, even if not immediately. If by any chance it did fail, this was put down to errors in carrying out the ritual or spell, to hostile forces or even to the failure of the gods. In fact, the Egyptians saw magic as part of the natural world, indeed it was the essential power that had made creation possible. This magical force – *heka*, often translated as 'awesome power' – was seen as a gift from god, who, according to the 'Instructions of Merikare', dating to approximately 2060 BC, 'made for them magic as weapons to ward off the blow of events'. Magic was therefore seen as a means of defence in life against fate and any evil an individual might meet, and in death as a necessary method of avoiding a second and everlasting demise.

Not only was magic part of the natural order, it was actively endorsed and approved by the gods. Magic was therefore legal, respectable and effective, although it worked outside accepted modern laws of cause and effect. Ancient Egyptian magic was closely linked, indeed intertwined, with religion and with medicine, each being an integral factor within the other. In Egyptian magic, the practitioner was usually what is known as a lector-priest, with many magical practices involving prayers to the gods. Medical prescriptions encompassed prayers to the gods and magical words and actions to be performed over the patient as well as medication. By way of a definition, Egyptian magic was considered a non-judgemental, natural/supernatural force used to influence the course of events by means of words or actions, often seeking the help of a god to obtain the desired result. Such a force was inherent in all animate forms either living or dead, in words, symbols or depictions.

Although Egyptian magic was part of everyday life, those who performed it or who were associated with it state that they were privy to secret magical knowledge. For example, the 6th-Dynasty noble Aba writes: 'I have learned every secret magical spell of the court, every secret formula through which one becomes a spirit in the necropolis.' Another noble from the same period, Ankhmahor, relates that 'no potent magical spell was ever concealed from me', which suggests that certain people had been initiated into its mysteries and that an elitist attitude towards magic existed amongst the educated echelons of society.

Many stories surround Ancient Egypt's greatest magicians, notably Djadjaemankh, from the 4th Dynasty (2613–2492 BC), who folded a lake in half in order to retrieve a jewel; Djedi, another 4th-Dynasty magician, from the time of the pharaoh Khufu, who was able to join the severed heads of birds back to their bodies and bring them back to life; and Naneferkaptah, whose magical powers were obtained through finding a magical book written by the god Thoth himself. *The Sorcerer's Apprentice*, as made famous by Disney's Mickey Mouse, is based upon an Egyptian story of a magician's assistant who overheard a spell pronounced by his master that made inanimate objects perform tasks. Unfortunately, the assistant lacked the experience to control the magical forces, resulting in chaos and confusion.

Even the Bible makes reference to Egyptian magicians, when Moses seeks permission from Pharaoh to leave Egypt with the Israelites:

> When Moses and Aaron came to Pharaoh they did as
> the Lord had told them. Aaron threw down his staff in
> front of Pharaoh and his courtiers, and it turned into a
> serpent. At this, Pharaoh summoned the wise men and
> the sorcerers, and the Egyptian magicians too did the same
> thing by their spells.
>
> (Exodus 7:10–11)

Parallels have even been drawn between Egyptian magical practices and the miracles performed by Jesus. The Talmud notes that Jesus learned magic in his early years spent in Egypt, that he practised Egyptian magic and that this was why he was arrested.

Egyptian magic worked by utilising three elements, namely words, actions and materials. Actions were a very important element, as they served to harness and control the magical energies. Such actions included the tying of knots, encirclement, spitting, swallowing, licking, pointing and certain gestures used as a means of protection. Hand actions were particularly important in magic, as confirmed by studies carried out on the wide variety of hand amulets found, including flat open-palmed amulets, closed hands with thumbs extended, or one or two fingers pointing. Each had their own meaning, with the colour of the amulet and the material used conveying their own connotations. The ingredients used within magic were varied, including milk, water, garlic, blood, semen and urine, with blood and sperm used in a love potion, and blood and sweat used in a spell to increase the magician's power.

Amulets, or charms, were an important element in medical magic and can be traced back to the Archaic period (3050–2687 BC). They were used by both the living and the dead as a means of protection, and took the shapes of human body parts, creatures or individual hieroglyphs. It was believed that the wearing of an amulet would conjure up the appropriate sympathetic magic and bring the relevant energy to the wearer. To enhance an amulet's potency, spells written on strips of linen or papyrus were sometimes placed within it.

Funerary magic, as portrayed in the Pyramid Texts, Coffin Texts, Book of the Dead and tomb scenes, related to the general protection of the deceased, their sustenance and their ascension to the afterlife. Other, everyday spells concerned protection from problems associated with childbirth, love spells and charms, fertility magic, medicinal spells, protection for children and protection against poisonous creatures.

Linked to the concept of protection was the temple ritual of 'breaking the red jars', designed to ward off evil. The red pots, upon which the names of hostile forces and enemies of Egypt were written, were smashed, thus negating their power. The writing of an enemy's name within a ritual context was used to call upon the potency of hieroglyphs and the magic contained within them. Hence, through the breaking of the pots the power of Egypt's enemies was also destroyed. Any ritual that accompanied this played a significant part in the magical efficacy of the Execration Texts. Figurines were also used in this context and could be bound, broken, buried, burnt or decapitated.

Magical practices were also connected with wooden, wax or clay figurines which acted as substitute bodies. Wooden figures could be animated by magic in order to serve the deceased in the afterlife for eternity, whilst wax figures, which could be easily destroyed, were used in magical rites that centred upon the destruction of an enemy. Other wax figurines, dating to the Roman period, have been found studded with nails, although the intention behind this is uncertain, considering these figures were placed in pots along with love charms.

The magical power of figurines was considered so potent and effective that they were used in an attempt on the life of the pharaoh Ramesses III (c.1198–1166 BC). The Harem Conspiracy, as it is known, was an attempt by 28 courtiers and an undisclosed number of women to kill the king and replace him with a lesser queen's son. One of the courtiers, Hui, was charged with stealing a book of magic from the royal library and using certain spells contained within it to inscribe figurines representing the king's guard in an attempt to nullify them. Hui also fashioned wax gods in order to harm the king. The trial notes of the incident survive and state that Hui 'began to make inscribed people of wax . . . for the exorcising of the one crew and the enchanting of the others' (Papyrus Lee, column 1). The plot was discovered before the king was harmed, and all but five of the conspirators were executed or forced to commit suicide, with four of the others being mutilated. What is interesting about this case is that Hui used the three elements of magic in order to create the most effective result: the word (spell), action (making the figurines) and material (wax).

It is the idea that Ancient Egyptian magic was the oldest and therefore the most potent and effective form of magic that is the reason for its abiding attraction. The second- to fourth-century AD

Hermetica, which supposedly contained the wisdom and magical knowledge of the Ancient Egyptian god Thoth, in fact bears little resemblance in reality to the early Egyptian mysteries and more to later, Greek-influenced mysticism. However, its respectability was directly linked to its supposed Egyptian esoteric knowledge.

Even in modern times, Ancient Egypt's renown in the magical arts continues, although it is often distorted by romantic or provocative images of ancient rites, incantations and curses, or by those interested in the occult or black magic. Most notable was the Hermetic Order of the Golden Dawn, founded in 1886, whose most infamous member was Aleister Crowley. His *Book of Thoth*, published in 1944, revealed his interpretation of an Egyptianised tarot, based upon Egyptian symbolism and magic, and was no doubt inspired by the eighteenth-century Court de Gebelin, who wrote a book arguing that the tarot pack had Egyptian origins.

The idea that Ancient Egyptian magic was the purest and most potent form has not only led to its association with some New Age cults that call upon the power and magic of Isis or the reinterpretation of Egyptian funerary books, but also to its representation within the cinematic sphere. Such films as *The Mummy* revolve around the idea of Ancient Egyptian magical books, their power of rejuvenation and rebirth, and their control over nature and the natural order of things.

SEE ALSO: Exodus, Hieroglyphs, Khufu, Spells, Symbolism, Thoth, Ushabtis

MUMMIES

To the Ancient Egyptians, the preservation of a person's image and body was a central tenet in their belief in rebirth in the netherworld after death. Without this preservation, the deceased would suffer everlasting death and be unable to partake in the joys of the afterlife. Mummification was the ritualised preservation of the body so that a person's living force, the *ka*, could recognise the body and return to it in order to receive sustenance for the *ba* and *akh* to survive. The ba was a combination of the reputation and power of an individual, perhaps best described as their soul. The akh was the effectiveness of the individual, the aspect of the deceased that was believed to act for either the benefit or detriment of the living.

Mummified bodies dating from the Predynastic period have been discovered but these were the result of burial in the hot, dry, shallow sand of the Egyptian desert, under which conditions the body desiccates and is naturally preserved. No doubt this effect was noticed by the Ancient Egyptians, who gradually developed the process so that by the 3rd Dynasty an extended, rather than foetal, position was adopted, possibly indicating the removal of the internal organs, and the body wrapped in bandages soaked in resin. From the 5th Dynasty, plaster was moulded onto the body to give a realistic impression, the face being painted to enhance the likeness. Although the outsides of mummies from this period appear intact, the bodies beneath the bandages have decomposed, as no method had been found for the removal of moisture. It was not until the breakthrough with the use of natron that it became possible to completely preserve a body. Natron is a compound of natural salts, mined in the Wadi Natrun in Lower Egypt, which absorbs moisture and could therefore prevent deterioration of a corpse.

From an account by Herodotus, it is apparent that 70 days was set aside for the mummification process, which began with the washing of the body and the removal of the brain through the nostrils using an iron hook. The internal organs were then removed through a cut made in the left side of the abdomen, dried, washed, wrapped and either placed in four containers called Canopic jars or wrapped in parcels. Everything was taken out of the body except the heart (where the ka lived) and kidneys. The body cavity was then rinsed out with a mixture of palm wine and spices and the incision stitched up. The next stage involved drying out the corpse by placing it on a sloping bed and covering it in dry natron for 40 days. The sloping bed allowed any fluid to pour away and once this process was completed the body was washed, wrapped and covered in resin. In order to produce a lifelike body shape, resin-soaked bandages, even sawdust and papyrus, were used as padding placed under the skin. Sometimes, however, over-packing occurred, as in the mummy of Henuttawy from the 21st Dynasty, the face of which is split and bloated. The wrapping of a mummy was a painstaking process that used enormous amounts of linen strips. Each toe and finger, arm and leg, the trunk and, in the case of a man, the genitalia were wrapped separately, covered in resin and then wrapped as a whole with protective amulets and jewellery added between the layers. Depending on the period, the mummy was then covered in a shroud, red-leather straps or faience-bead net. From the time of the Middle Kingdom, a painted cartonnage mask was placed on the mummy, although royal mummies wore golden masks, as the body of Tutankhamun attested.

Each stage of the mummification process was accompanied by specific rituals, carried out by the Overseer of the Mysteries, who acted as the god Anubis. It was Anubis who was believed to have wrapped the body of Osiris, and he therefore became associated with funerary practices. An assistant was called 'the seal-bearer of the god' and also present was a lector-priest, who read out the relevant spells at the appropriate moments. A number of helpers were responsible for the evisceration and bandaging of the body.

Animals were also mummified in Ancient Egypt, notably those connected to cults, such as the sacred Apis bulls, cats, baboons, crocodiles and birds. In fact, so many birds were mummified that it has been estimated that for the ibis alone the figure is approximately four million. It appears that some animals were specially bred in areas within temples, presumably for sacrificial purposes, killed and then mummified.

A great deal of information can be obtained from a mummy, such as lifestyle, diet, and illnesses suffered. From the examination of royal mummies, it can be gleaned that many depictions of royalty do not truly represent the physique of the living person. For example, Siptah from the 19th Dynasty suffered from polio, whilst Amenhotep I, who died young, was diagnosed with curvature of the spine. He also had protruding teeth, a trait common to many of the 18th-Dynasty royal family. At the time of death, Amenhotep III was an obese man with badly decaying teeth and abscesses in his jaw, whilst Ramesses II, who died in his late 80s, was of slender build, over 6 ft tall, and sported a hook nose. This famous king suffered from arthritis of the hip – no doubt connected to his age – heart disease and bad teeth. Many of the mummies of kings examined indicate that they enjoyed a diet comparatively rich in sugar and carbohydrates, as shown by the high incidence of tooth decay and abscesses. In non-royals, badly worn teeth were a common problem, as were arthritis, lung disease and intestinal worms.

The discovery of a number of royal caches has greatly enhanced Egyptology and allowed us to look at the faces of the pharaohs and their queens. In 1881, a shaft was discovered near Deir el-Bahri, in modern Luxor, that led to a tomb filled with coffins containing over 50 mummies and 6,000 objects. Of those mummies, 32 were royal, and they included the remains of Tuthmosis II, Seti I and Ramesses I. So immense was the cache that it took five days to remove all the coffins and equipment, which were then taken up the Nile to Cairo. From the dockets written on the bandages and coffins it is evident that the mummies were moved a number of times, initially to the tomb of Seti I, then to the tomb of Queen Inhapi and finally, during the reign of Shoshenq I (22nd Dynasty), to the tomb of the high priest Pinudjem II. No doubt the caches were originally moved to protect the royal mummies from tomb robberies, but a great deal of the royal funerary equipment relating to the mummies found in the 1881 cache was actually reused by 21st- and 22nd-Dynasty rulers for their tombs in Tanis.

Another cache of royal mummies was found in 1898 within the tomb of Amenhotep II in the Valley of the Kings, consisting of the mummies of eight kings and seven unidentified individuals. Of these, a great deal of debate has surrounded the two unwrapped and plundered mummies known as the Elder Lady and the Young Woman, tenuously identified as Queen Tiye, mother of Akhenaten, and Nefertiti. Because of political power struggles at the time, these bodies were left within the tomb, an unfortunate decision leading to the careless and forceful unwrapping of Amenhotep II's mummy by robbers in search of amulets and jewellery, and to the theft of the king's bow and the mummy of an unidentified prince.

Many mummies have proved enigmatic and problematic – take, for example, the identity of the individual in Tomb 55 in the Valley of Kings – whilst others are intriguing. A curious discovery relates to a 6th-Dynasty (c.2374–2191 BC) mummy found at Saqqara. The inscriptions stated that the owner of the intact tomb was a Princess Khentkawes, eldest daughter of the King. However, examination of the body found that the princess was actually a male who had obviously chosen to live as a woman, and had presumably been accepted as such. However, the inclusion in her tomb of manly hunting equipment suggests that, unlike in life, Khentkawes intended to enjoy the afterlife as a man.

Whilst Khentkawes seems to have been accepted in the royal household, a body of a male found in the 1881 cache told a different story. Discovered inside an uninscribed white coffin was his unwrapped body enveloped in a sheepskin. The awful smell that emanated from the remains suggested that he had not been mummified, a state confirmed upon examination, which revealed that the internal organs were intact and that the man had been bound hand and foot. The unfortunate individual's face was distorted in agony, suggesting that he had been placed within the coffin alive, the sheepskin providing an air-tight environment for natural mummification to occur within the dry tomb. Just what he had done to deserve such a hideous and unique treatment can only be guessed at, but it certainly was not a pleasant death.

Unfortunately, the Egyptian embalmers did not handle all their mummies with the care that anxious relatives of the deceased would have expected. From CAT scans carried out on the remains of the Lady Teshat, for example, it has been discovered that the teenage girl had suffered several broken bones due to rough handling by the embalmers. Rather surprisingly, the CAT scan also revealed the presence of an adult skull between her legs. It is not unusual for mummies dating from the 21st Dynasty onwards to be missing body parts, and although a wrapped mummy might appear to be normal, the bandages might actually contain a jumble of bones. One unfortunate individual had been mummified with their foot in their abdomen and their arms where their thighs should be.

In the modern era, the appalling misuse of mummies has been a common theme since the Middle Ages, when mummies were often used for medicinal purposes. Those that had been buried in the sand and desiccated naturally were ground down to powder and used as a remedy for stomach problems, whilst the bodies that had been purposely mummified were greatly sought after in Europe, where they were considered a cure for a wide variety of ailments. By Victorian times, mummies drew enormous curiosity and were used as tools to amuse visitors to Egypt with the witnessing of the discovery (pre-planned) and unwrapping of a mummy, the body discarded once the entertainment was over. These unwrappings proved so popular that the surgeon Thomas Pettigrew shipped mummies to London in order to lecture on and unwrap a mummy before an inquisitive audience. These lectures were always sold out, although the methods employed by Pettigrew, such as resorting to a hammer and chisel to free the body, left a lot to be desired – a method, incidentally, used in 1923 by Carter and Derry on Tutankhamun's mummy. Mummies were seen as a commodity to be used for medicine, entertainment, even making paper and stoking steam trains, and it is thought that over the years thousands of mummies must have been mistreated in this way. Viewed merely as objects of commercial value rather than deceased people, mummies were treated without respect or dignity. However, with the founding of the Egyptian Antiquities Organisation (now known as the Supreme Council of the Antiquities) in 1858, and the imposition of excavation controls, the wholesale misuse of mummies discontinued.

One interesting twist to this situation is the recent triumphant return to Egypt of the mummy of Ramesses I. In October 2003, Ramesses I finally arrived in Cairo, an Egyptian flag draped over the crate, accompanied by scholars, the media and representatives from the Egyptian government. Privately sold to a Canadian collector in around 1860, the then unidentified mummy had been installed in the Niagara Falls Museum until finally being sold, along with the rest of the museum's Egyptian collection, to the Michael C. Carlos Museum of Emory University, Atlanta, in 1999. Up to that point, it was unknown who the mummy was, but certain clues, notably the position of his arms and the high quality of the mummification, had led the Emory University team to believe it could be royal. CT scans and computer imaging showed a marked facial resemblance to Seti I and Ramesses II, the father and son of Ramesses I. Once the identity was confirmed, the Carlos Museum offered the mummy to Egypt – an offer which was readily accepted. Before leaving Atlanta, however, an exhibition of Ramesses I and the other mummies was held at the Carlos Museum, running from April to September 2003 and drawing in over 115,000 people. After a short spell in the Egyptian Museum in Cairo, Ramesses I was finally returned to Luxor, where he will rest within the museum there.

SEE ALSO: Akhenaten, Apis Bulls, Human Body, Nefertiti, Tutankhamun

NEFERTITI

In 1912, whilst excavating a sculptor's workshop at the Middle Egyptian site of Amarna, the German Egyptologist Ludwig Borchardt uncovered an outstandingly beautiful painted limestone head of Nefertiti. This discovery propelled Nefertiti into a league of her own as the most beautiful woman in antiquity. However, despite her face being one of the most recognisable in history, surprisingly little is known about her origins, early life and death. This state of affairs is even more amazing given that more images of her exist than of any other Egyptian queen.

Nefertiti was the 'Great Royal Wife' of Akhenaten, the so-called heretic king who ruled Egypt in the mid-fourteenth century BC. Concerning her personal qualities, Akhenaten asserts that 'one is happy to hear her voice' and that she is 'sweet of voice' and 'possessed of charm'. These are all very delightful attributes but what of her parentage? Because so little is known of Nefertiti, there is a great deal of speculation surrounding her pedigree.

Throughout the years, Nefertiti has been described as a foreigner, outsider, commoner or sibling of Akhenaten. The name Nefertiti translates as 'A Beautiful Woman Has Come'. Given that this appellation must have been conferred upon her in her youth rather than at birth, it has been hypothesised that the name was given to her only once she had 'come' to Egypt. The most likely candidate for this is the Mitannian princess Tadukhipa, who had been brought to Egypt as a wife for Akhenaten's father, Amenhotep III, very late in his reign. At the time of his death, and with part of Tadukhipa's dowry still unpaid, she could easily have been given over in marriage to Akhenaten. Whether this was the case is impossible to verify, as once on Egyptian soil the princess would have taken an Egyptian name and her old identity would have been lost for ever. However, in 1887, nearly 400 clay tablets were found at Amarna. These turned out to be a part of the diplomatic correspondence for that period between Egypt and her neighbours. The letters from Tushratta, King of Mitanni and father of Tadukhipa, to Akhenaten are enlightening, as Tushratta sends his best wishes to: 'Tiye, your mother, the mistress of Egypt; for Tadukhipa, my daughter, your wife; for the rest of your wives . . .'. Although his mother is mentioned, and sundry other wives, Nefertiti, the Great Royal Wife, is not referred to specifically. Surely, given her standing within Egypt, it would have been unusual not to mention her. Perhaps he does, though – perhaps Nefertiti was Tadukhipa.

The various theories regarding Nefertiti's ancestry are confusing and contradictory. Whilst many assume that she was not of royal birth because her titles and epithets do not state that she was a sister or daughter of a king, others state that one of her titles, 'Heiress', implies that she was. The Egyptologist Percy Newberry thought that Nefertiti was the daughter of Amenhotep III by the Lady Ti, wife of Ay, a later king of Egypt and purported brother of Tiye, Akhenaten's mother. This was based upon one of Ti's titles, 'Nourisher of the Goddess', although this signifies the role of wet nurse rather than mother. Another hypothesis put forward is that Ay was Nefertiti's father, again based on rather doubtful interpretations of one of his titles, 'God's Father'. The argument goes that as he could not be Akhenaten's father (the god mentioned here), he therefore had to be his father-in-law – quite a stretch of the imagination, especially considering that 'father' was open to many usages. Ay himself called Tutankhamun his father, an impossibility given that Ay was by far the older man. Added to this, Ay never mentions that he was the father of Nefertiti. Even the possibility that Akhenaten and Nefertiti were twins has been suggested, based on their similar facial features, the obvious closeness and bond between them, their often parallel portrayals, and their association with the twin deities Shu and Tefnut.

There may be little that we know with certainty about Nefertiti's background but the many depictions of her make it clear that she was a powerful individual who acted as her husband's equal and held a unique role for an Egyptian queen. At Thebes, where

Akhenaten held court for the first five years of his reign, Nefertiti is represented on her own and in specifically kingly roles. She is invariably depicted with all the signifiers of kingship, including the ritual killing of the enemies of Egypt, a role synonymous with Egyptian kingship from its earliest history; driving a chariot; wearing the *atef* crown, usually only worn by kings; and officiating bare-chested and attired in the kingly kilt. From Year 5, however, when the court moved to the new capital Akhetaten (modern Amarna), her role changes to emphasise the loving and equal relationship between her and her husband. They are shown embracing each other, holding hands, with Nefertiti sitting on her husband's lap. She shares the various religious and ceremonial duties with the king, so that Nefertiti is portrayed wearing the same pleated robes as Akhenaten, offering directly to the Aten, on her own or with her husband. The rays of the sun disc give life to her and Akhenaten equally and she is shown in proportion to Akhenaten, unlike the usual minuscule representations of Egyptian queens. Unusually, the 'a' in the '-aten' part of her name (Neferneferuaten – 'Beauty of the Beauties of the Aten') faces her depiction, an extremely unusual and unique style of writing that was never afforded to anyone else. All this points to the fact that Nefertiti was considered a queen regnant and not a mere consort.

But what of a coregency, as has been suggested by some Egyptologists? Although an *ushabti* statue of Nefertiti shows her holding kingly regalia, her titles indicate that she was considered a queen regnant and not a coregent. The very fact that kingly titles were not present on her funerary items is telling.

So do we know what happened to her? As with most of Nefertiti's life, her final years are a mystery. The last positive date for Nefertiti is in Year 12, when she is shown at the great celebrations of that year along with her six daughters. The next, undated depiction is from the royal tomb at Amarna, in which Akhenaten and Nefertiti are shown mourning the death of their second-born daughter, Meketaten. Given that all six daughters were around in Year 12, this would indicate that Nefertiti was still alive sometime after that, although probably no later than Year 14. These years appear to have been particularly hard for the Amarna royal family and by Year 13 Tiye, Kiya (another wife of Akhenaten's) and at least three of Nefertiti's daughters are no longer mentioned. It is known that there was a plague at this time, probably brought to Egypt by the hundreds of foreign dignitaries who went there for the Year 12 celebrations. But whether Nefertiti died at this date, or took on another persona, is open to debate.

From Year 14 until his death in Year 17, Akhenaten shared a coregency with an individual named Neferneferuaten Ankhkheperure, Beloved of Akhenaten, about whom nothing is known. For the next three years, this individual ruled alone, to be followed by Smenkhkare Ankhkheperure, a pharaoh who reigned for only a few months. Nefertiti's full royal name as enclosed within a cartouche was Neferneferuaten Nefertiti, Beloved of Akhenaten. Based on the similarities between these names, it has been suggested that these rulers were in fact Nefertiti. Interestingly, at the gateway to Nefertiti's northern palace there is no mention made of her, although Smenkhkare's name appears, an unusual fact considering to whom the palace belonged, unless Smenkhkare and Nefertiti were one and the same. Alternatively, perhaps it came to Smenkhkare upon Nefertiti's death. Whereas there is little or no evidence as to who the individual Neferneferuaten Ankhkheperure might have been, there are many who believe that Smenkhkare was a royal prince and perhaps brother of Tutankhamun. However, even this is open to debate, as Smenkhkare was never called 'King's Son' as Tutankhamun was, this being the normal designation for a male, living heir.

Yet more theories propose that Nefertiti fell out of favour or was disgraced and hence banished to the northernmost part of Amarna, where her palace can be found. However, evidence suggests that she did actually die at Amarna and was buried in the Royal Tomb there. Although the second burial suite is unfinished and undecorated, it has been noted that a level area would have been suitable for a sarcophagus. In the vicinity, two objects belonging to Nefertiti were found, notably an ushabti figure (which would have been made at the time of embalming) and a gold ring. This alone points to her death at Amarna and indicates that she died before Akhenaten, underlined by the inscription that reads: 'The Heiress, high and mighty in the palace, one trusted of the King of Upper and Lower Egypt Neferkheperure Waenre, the Son of Ra, Akhenaten, great in his lifetime, the Chief Wife of the King, Neferneferuaten Nefertiti, living for ever and ever'. With no indication of Osirian funerary practices (for example, use of the term 'justified'), which came back into usage after Akhenaten's death, it points to the fact that Nefertiti was buried by her husband, who would have insisted on Atenist rites for her.

But even then, we are no wiser as to the whereabouts of Nefertiti's final resting place. In 1898, three unidentified mummies were found in a side chamber of Amenhotep II's tomb. All had been looted in antiquity, with wrappings ripped off in the search for plunder, some bones being broken off in the process. One of the bodies, described as the 'Elder Lady', was thought to be approximately 30 to 35 years old. Her well-preserved face showed that she was a beautiful woman, and her shoulder-length hair was luxuriant and wavy. The Elder Lady had been mummified with care, as there was no unsightly stretching of the lips over the teeth or squashing of the nose, giving her a realistic appearance. Her long neck has a regal air and her left arm, placed across her chest, had been clutching something as in a royal pose.

Initially, the Elder Lady was thought to be the female pharaoh Hatshepsut, although this idea fell out of fashion in favour of an identification of the body as that of Tiye, Amenhotep III's Great Royal Wife. Such a conclusion was based upon some rather dubious hair analysis, notably comparing her hair with a lock of hair found in Tutankhamun's tomb that had been placed within a small chest engraved with Tiye's name. As the hair was more likely to be Tutankhamun's sidelock of youth, the use of such an analysis to prove the Elder Lady was Tiye would be flawed. Blood-group analysis carried out suggested that there was only a remote possibility that the Lady was linked to Thuya, thought to be Tiye's mother.

However, facial similarities, the long neck, her beauty and the age of the mummy have led others to conclude that the Elder Lady is actually Nefertiti herself. The suggested deformation of the mummy's left eye has also heightened speculation that this is Nefertiti through comparison with the limestone bust now in the Egyptian Museum in Berlin, which lacks the left eye inlay, thus leading to the belief that Nefertiti was either blind in that eye or suffered an eye affliction. However, this is not conclusive proof, as it seems that early photos of the Berlin bust show faint traces of pigmentation on the left eye, suggesting that an inlay had originally been present. One other point to mention is that Nefertiti is never shown with hair. It was common practice to shave off the hair or wear it cut short to accommodate wigs and prevent lice, and the crowns worn by Nefertiti are shown resting high up on the back of her neck, well into the hairline without any hair being visible, suggesting that she followed this custom.

A recent theory identifies the 'Young Woman' found in the 1898 cache as Nefertiti. Found naked, the head shaven, the right arm missing and with large holes in the face and chest, the identification is based on the royal pose given to the mummy, her shaven head and double ear-piercing, distinctive of royal women at the time of Nefertiti, the mummy's facial features and the assessment of her age, which fitted Nefertiti's supposed age at death of between 30 and 35. However, it was later reported that X-ray analysis gave an age range of between 15 and 30, that it was in fact a 15-year-old boy or that it was a girl aged between 15 and 20. Accordingly, the mystery surrounding Nefertiti continues.

SEE ALSO: Akhenaten, Tutankhamun

OBELISKS

Obelisks played an important role in Ancient Egypt. They always stood in pairs and were situated at the entrances to temples. Their function was to represent the physical manifestation of the sun-god Ra himself, and the shape of each one was intended to imitate a ray of sunlight. They were often seen as a cosmic gateway between earth and sky, as well as between this world and the afterlife, perhaps in the same way that the pillars on either side of the false doors found in Old Kingdom tombs seem to symbolise the portals of a magical gateway.

Furthermore, the pyramidion (pyramid-shaped capstone) at the top of the obelisk would originally have been gilded so that it reflected the sun's rays, thereby conferring solar energy on the obelisk itself and also on the person whose name was inscribed on the face of the monolith.

The word 'obelisk' comes from the Greek for 'roasting-spit'. The Arab word for obelisk was *misalla*, 'large packing needle'. To the Egyptians, an obelisk was known as a *tekhen*, and although the precise translation is not known, this has been thought to mean 'door-leaf', possibly referring to the obelisk's position at the temple entrance as well as hinting at its role as a representation of a cosmic gateway. Pliny the Elder suggested that *tekhen* might actually mean 'ray of sunlight', which would also make sense given the symbolism of the obelisk. The pyramidion at the top of the obelisk – often gilded, as mentioned – was known as the *benbenet*, attesting to its connection with the mythological Benben, a word the meaning of which included the idea 'shine' or 'radiate'.

How far into antiquity obelisks were created we are not certain. All of the Egyptian obelisks that have survived to the present day date from the Middle Kingdom onwards. However, there is a reference to obelisks in the Pyramid Texts of the 5th Dynasty. The passage is found in Pepi I's pyramid and mentions the two *tekhenui* that belong to Ra. It is therefore probable that obelisks were in use before the Middle Kingdom and that these earlier examples have simply been lost to us.

We can see a precursor to the traditional obelisk at Abu Ghurab, in the ruins of the sun temples that still stand today near the pyramids of Abusir. Here we have E.A. Wallis Budge's description of these sun temples:

> In the temples built at Abusir by some of the kings of the Vth Dynasty in connection with their pyramid tombs, the Ben Stone, or as we may call it, the 'Sun Stone', was the principal symbol of the Sun-god Ra, who was then represented in human form. It preserved the form of the Ben Stone, and was a short, thick obelisk which stood upon a base in the form of a truncated pyramid.

It was said that the original Benben stone in the Mansion of the Benben at Heliopolis stood on an obelisk, although this has been lost in antiquity. It seems likely that the obelisks which survive today developed from this pillar that supported the sacred Benben. That the pillar itself, together with the stone atop it, was supposed to symbolise the primeval mound of creation is without question, so it seems possible that there was a shift from the design used in the sun temples, the much thicker and shorter obelisks, to the later, much narrower obelisks that we see still standing today. Of course, it is entirely possible that, rather than one replacing the other, the two developed side by side.

The Romans had a fascination for obelisks and there are more Egyptian obelisks in modern-day Italy than stand in Egypt itself. In total, there are 13 Egyptian obelisks in Rome today.

The appropriation of these awe-inspiring objects began long ago, in antiquity. The first was relocated to Rome in AD 10 by the emperor Augustus, who brought two obelisks back to Rome. He set one up at the Campus Martius and the other at Circus Maximus, the first and largest public arena in all of Rome. At its height, it could accommodate 150,000 seated spectators and was famed for its chariot racing.

The removal, transportation and raising of these obelisks in Rome must have been a massive feat of engineering. We do have records that show how it was done, and they describe the incredible amount of effort that was expended to import these ancient artefacts. The emperor Constantine had an obelisk of Tuthmosis III (later usurped by his grandson Tuthmosis IV) removed from where it stood at Karnak and transported to Alexandria, ready to be shipped to the 'New Rome' – Constantinople. Constantine died before he saw it raised in the city, and it was left to his successor, Constantius, to ship it instead to Rome, in the year AD 357. Accounts from the period state that a huge lighter (a shallow barge) was constructed to carry the obelisk across the seas and that this was towed by a trireme manned by 300 oarsmen. It is not surprising that such a powerful vessel was required, given that the obelisk weighs some 460 tonnes and is 32 m in length.

The Roman writer Ammianus Marcellinus captured in prose the dramatic erection of this obelisk in the Circus Maximus:

> Vast beams having been raised on end in a most dangerous manner, so that they looked like a grove of machines, long ropes of huge size were fastened to them, darkening the very sky with their density, as they formed a web of innumerable thread; and into them the great stone itself, covered over as it was with elements of writing, was bound, and gradually raised into the empty air, and for a long time suspended, many thousands of men turning it round and round like a millstone, till it was at last placed in the middle of the square; and on it was placed a brazen sphere, made brighter with plates of gold; and as that was immediately struck by lightning and destroyed, a brazen figure like a torch was placed on it, also plated with gold – to look as if the torch were fully alight.

Many obelisks have been through turbulent times, and this one is no exception. It fell to earth long ago, possibly when Rome was sacked. It was repaired and re-erected by Pope Sixtus V in the sixteenth century. Today, it stands proudly at the centre of the Piazza San Giovanni, outside the Lateran Palace – home for a long time to the popes of Rome – and is hence known as the Lateran Obelisk.

The seizure and transportation of these rare Egyptian objects continued throughout the centuries, right up until the late 1800s, and today it is possible to view Egyptian obelisks in Rome, New York, Paris, London and several other cities of the world.

One of the most famous obelisks outside of Egypt is the one that was brought to London. This obelisk is one of a pair known as Cleopatra's Needles, the other now standing in Central Park, New York. Neither of these, however, has anything to do with Cleopatra. They were carved long before her time, sometime around the year 1450 BC, during the reign of Tuthmosis III. They were originally erected outside the great pylon, or gateway, of the temple of Ra at Heliopolis. It was only later, in the year 12 BC, that the Romans moved them to Alexandria.

It was in 1877–8 that one of these so-called needles was brought to London, by Sir William James Erasmus Wilson, who paid for the operation, with the engineer John Dixon overseeing the procedure. It was fraught with difficulties, and the airtight iron ship, the *Cleopatra*, that was built specifically to carry the obelisk was waylaid in heavy weather on the way home and broke free of the ship towing her, with the loss of six lives. The obelisk was recovered and was finally erected in London, on the Thames Embankment, where it remains today.

The tallest of all the remaining obelisks around the world is the Lateran Obelisk of Tuthmosis III, which is reckoned to be around 32 m in height. Not much shorter is the obelisk of Hatshepsut, which still stands in its original location at the Temple of Karnak in Egypt: the top of its pyramidion is some 29 m from the ground.

However, these figures only take into account standing obelisks. There is an unfinished obelisk in a quarry at Aswan that is over 41 m long and estimated to weigh over 1,100 tons. It seems to have been abandoned because of a fault in the rock that developed into a crack. Had it been successfully completed and erected, it would have been the largest obelisk ever raised, the single largest monolith in the world. The feat of engineering required to move such a huge obelisk is immense, yet the Egyptians must have been confident that they could achieve the task, or they would not have started to carve out this monstrous standing stone.

Finally, before we leave this fascinating subject, we must return to the top of the obelisk, the pyramidion. This was considered the most important part of the sacred object, and there is one major difference between the obelisks we see today and the way they would have once appeared, one that we have mentioned briefly. Originally, the pyramidion would have been gilded or covered with electrum – an alloy of gold and silver – causing it to gleam in the sun. Wallis Budge thought, based on inscriptions he had found, that a large amount of this precious alloy was used to cover the pyramidion:

> Of the style and thickness of such a casing we know nothing, but a great deal of metal must have been needed for its construction, for Queen Hatshepsut says about her obelisks, 'I allotted for them the refined *tcham* [which] I weighed out by the *heket* measure, like sack[ful]s of grain.' In other words, she used the precious *tcham* not by the pound but by the hundredweight. These words suggest that the casings of the pyramidions of her obelisks were made of thick plates of *tcham*.

For obvious reasons, none of today's surviving obelisks possess their original pyramidion casings of precious metals, and so we are not generally able to appreciate fully how they would once have appeared.

However, in a ceremony in Paris in 1997, in the presence of the Egyptian president Hosni Mubarak, the obelisk of Ramesses II that now stands in the Place de la Concorde had its pyramidion fitted with a bronze plate gilded with 23.5 carat gold. Now, for the first time in thousands of years, we can see exactly the dramatic effect these obelisks would have had when they guarded the great pylons of the temples of Egypt, bathed in sunlight and reflecting its rays brilliantly.

SEE ALSO: Benben, Heliopolis

OLD TESTAMENT EGYPT

Many of the early Egyptologists were specifically interested in verifying elements of the Bible story by investigating their historical and geographical background. The Egypt Exploration Fund, when it was founded in 1882, stated in its Articles of Association that its exploration work would be in part 'for the purpose of elucidating or illustrating the Old Testament narrative'.

Ahmed M. Abo el Ela, in his 2003 book *Prophets and Pharaohs: Egypt and the Old Testament*, discusses the major connections between the Old Testament narrative and Egyptian history. In his study, he weighs the Egyptological evidence for many of the references to Egypt in the Old Testament and explores the links between the two traditions.

There are parallels between some of the biblical stories and Egyptian literary texts, for example between the story of Joseph and Potiphar's wife and 'The Tale of the Two Brothers'. Similarities between the 'Hymn to the Aten', a text which appeared during the religious upheaval of the reign of Akhenaten, and Psalm 104 have been identified. Also, the moral system advocated in a Late Period text called 'Instruction of Amenemope' may have influenced the writers of the Book of Proverbs.

One of the first of around 500 biblical references to Egypt comes in Genesis 12:10: 'And there was famine in the land: and Abram went down into Egypt to sojourn there.' Unfortunately, the Pharaoh took Abraham's wife Sarah into his household, believing that she was Abraham's sister, although he returned her to Abraham once his mistake became clear and he had suffered plagues from the Lord. The story of Joseph and his family in Egypt is discussed separately, as is the Exodus, and these two episodes together with Abraham's story demonstrate the movement of people and populations across the ancient Near East.

After the Exodus and the establishment of the kingdom of the Hebrews, the relationship between Israel and Egypt is described in the First Book of Kings 11:1, where we discover that 'Solomon loved many strange women, together with the daughter of Pharaoh'. For the ruler of a powerful country such as Egypt to make a marriage alliance with Solomon reflects the prestige of the land of Israel. Solomon was tolerant of the faiths of his foreign wives and allowed them to worship their own gods, which made the Lord angry with him. Whether religious tolerance weakened the nation or not, it was certainly the case that the successors of Solomon could not maintain the unity of the country, and the southern territories became the separate state of Judah. The Judean city of Jerusalem was attacked during the reign of King Rehoboam by a pharaoh who is called Shishak in the Bible. Shishak is usually equated with the historical pharaoh Shoshenq, which would mean that this attack on Jerusalem occurred around 920 BC.

In the Second Book of Kings 23:29, we read that: 'In his days Pharaoh-nechoh king of Egypt went up against the king of Assyria to the river Euphrates: and king Josiah went against him; and he slew him at Megiddo.' After the Pharaoh killed Josiah, he made one of Josiah's sons the next King of Judah and took another brother back to Egypt with him, presumably as a hostage.

Later in the Old Testament, the prophets Isaiah, Jeremiah and Ezekiel describe the ascendance of the Assyrian nation and the subjugation of Egypt to foreign rule. This corresponds to the period in the eighth century BC when the rulers of Egypt were unable to prevent the Assyrian empire dominating the region.

One of the Gospels of the New Testament, that of Matthew, mentions that, after the birth of Jesus, the Holy Family travelled to Egypt to escape Herod's edict that the infant children of Bethlehem were to be killed. One of the churches in Cairo, Abu Serga, claims that it was in the crypt beneath the church that the family took shelter. Once the danger had passed, an angel appeared to Joseph to let him know that it was safe to return to Israel. Some researchers claim that Jesus's time in the country fits into a common historical narrative in which wisdom or knowledge is gained by spending time in Egypt, a nation with millennia of mystical history. Other examples include Alexander the Great's journey to the oracle at Siwa and Napoleon Bonaparte's Egyptian expedition of 1798, when he took a great number of scientists and historians with him to the Land of the Pharaohs.

SEE ALSO: Akhenaten, Joseph, Exodus

OSIRIS

Perhaps the most well-known of the Ancient Egyptian gods is Osiris. The earliest recorded mention of his name dates from the 5th Dynasty, although it is highly likely that he was venerated before this date. By the 18th Dynasty, he had become arguably the most widely revered of the whole Egyptian pantheon.

Osiris is a god of the dead and of the underworld, as well as of the earth and vegetation. This might seem a paradox at first – that he is a god of death and of all growing things at the same time – but the tale of Osiris is one not only of death but also of rebirth and resurrection, so this duality is apt. In fact, in Ancient Egypt, Osiris came to represent both the year-long drought and the miraculous flooding and flowering of the Nile Valley.

'Osiris' is actually the Greek version of the god's name. It has been proposed that to the Ancient Egyptians he was known as Asar, Wesir, Ausare, Usire and a whole host of other variations. The problem is that we still do not know the precise origins of the god's name, so the exact pronunciation of the hieroglyphic form is unclear. The individual glyphs that form his name are those of a throne and an eye. Some attempts to translate it suggest 'He who is strong', 'To create a throne' and 'Seat of the eye'. Perhaps the most likely explanation is that it is a derivation of the word *woser*, in which case it would translate as 'mighty one'.

It is in the funerary inscriptions of the 5th Dynasty that we first come across Osiris. He is referred to as one of the gods of the Great Ennead, the first child of Geb and Nut. Osiris married his sister,

Isis, and they had a son, Horus. It would appear that Osiris was first worshipped as a local deity in the vicinity of Busiris in the Nile Delta, and there are many legends and tales linking him with this place.

The earliest religious texts to mention Osiris refer to him as the god of the dead. They are very clear on one point: they state that Osiris once possessed human form and lived on earth. Because he was the first born of Geb, he assumed his father's throne when Geb stepped down. It is said that, at the time, before history began, the people of Egypt were uncivilised, even resorting to cannibalism. It was Osiris who taught them agriculture and gave them laws.

It was during these very earliest of times that the events of the Osirian myth are supposed to have taken place. This ancient story is the tale most widely known concerning Osiris. While it has its roots in Egyptian texts, the Greek historian Plutarch retold it in his work *On the Worship of Isis and Osiris*, and it was also referred to by Diodorus Siculus in his *Library of History* Book I. It is a dramatic tale, a story ripe with tragedy and themes of death, revenge and resurrection. There are many versons of the myth but perhaps the fullest retelling is Plutarch's.

Osiris and Isis were not the only offspring of Geb and Nut; they had another sister, Nephthys, and a brother, Seth. Apparently, Seth was jealous of the kingship of Osiris and wanted the throne for himself. While Osiris was civilising the peoples of Egypt and teaching them all that he knew, Seth plotted to acquire the throne. When Osiris returned, in the 18th year of his reign, Seth, with the help of 72 conspirators, murdered his brother. Seth had developed a crafty plan. He had obtained his brother's measurements and had an elaborate coffer built. At a banquet, Seth announced that whoever might fit the chest exactly could take possession of it. Of course, it fitted Osiris perfectly.

As soon as Osiris lay inside, the 72 accomplices of Seth nailed the lid shut and it was then thrown into the Nile, whereupon Osiris drowned. It was said that those who died by drowning in Ancient Egypt reached the kingdom of Osiris directly and did not have to take the convoluted route that other dead spirits were forced to navigate. The coffer containing the dead body of Osiris floated all the way downstream until it reached Byblos. Here, it became encased inside the trunk of a tamarisk tree. A local king had the tree felled and it was taken off to his palace, where it became a pillar in the royal palace.

After many adventures, Osiris's wife, Isis, discovered the

location of her husband's body and she managed to remove it from the pillar, after which she returned with it to the Nile Delta. Seth, however, did not let the dead body of his brother rest, and he recovered the corpse while Isis was absent. In an effort to prevent Osiris from having a sacred burial, he chopped the body into numerous pieces (the most common number mentioned is 14). Seth then distributed the pieces across Egypt so that the body of Osiris should never be whole again.

Once again, Isis's loyalty to her husband was unfailing and she embarked on a long quest to find all the pieces of his body. She buried each part, but not before manufacturing a replica of each. The only part that she failed to find was the phallus, so she created a replica and, with the help of her sister Nephthys and Anubis, she rebuilt the body of her husband. With the form of Osiris complete, Isis herself transformed into a kite and breathed life into the dead king using her beating wings. Osiris was brought back to life just long enough for Isis to become impregnated by the reconstituted phallus, and so Horus was conceived.

After this event, Osiris returned to the realm of the gods and it is left to the young Horus to conclude the events of the story. The tale ends with Horus growing up to avenge his father's death. Seth and Horus have their legendary battle, in which Seth loses a testicle and Horus an eye. Horus reclaims his father's throne and Seth is banished to the desert.

The origins of a number of Ancient Egyptian beliefs are present in the Osirian myth. The implication is that the coffer in which Osiris is drowned is the first sarcophagus and Anubis presides over the first mummified body – Osiris's reassembled remains. Anubis is associated with mummification and embalming, and here we see him helping Isis attend to the body. It is also Anubis who performs the opening–of–the–mouth ceremony, necessary before Osiris can rise again.

It is this legend of Osiris's death and rebirth that underlies his role as god of the dead and the underworld. In the Book of the Dead and the Pyramid Texts, it is evident that the dead pharaoh is thought to become Osiris, with the king's son taking on the role of Horus. Through the process of mummification and the rituals of death such as the opening–of–the–mouth ceremony, the dead king was not resurrected like Osiris; instead, the rituals signified renewal in the underworld and the next life, as well as on earth through his heir, as Horus. From around 2000 BC, it becomes evident that not just deceased kings but every man believed that he would become associated with Osiris at the time of his death.

Representations of Osiris are unique among those of gods of the Ennead. Unlike, for example, Thoth, he does not have an animal head but is always shown in human form. He is almost always shown as immobile, either prone, sitting on his throne or standing. Quite often, he is shown as a mummified man, wearing white and occasionally sheathed in bandages so that only his hands and face are visible; his skin is either green to represent vegetation or black like the fertile Nile mud. He also carries the symbols of his rule as a king on earth: the *atef* crown – based on the tall, white crown of Upper Egypt, with red plumes on either side – together with a flail and a crook.

There are two major sanctuaries of Osiris in Egypt. The first is at Busiris in the Delta, where, according to the Osirian myth, the corpse of Osiris was trapped inside the tamarisk tree. Busiris is also known as Djedu and was a centre for the cult of Osiris. In the myth, the tree containing Osiris's body was cut down to form a pillar in a royal palace. The *djed*, a cult object in the form of a pillar or stick, had been associated with Osiris and revered in the area even before worship of him became widespread, so it is no coincidence that this town was at the centre of the myth.

The other sanctuary of Osiris was at Abydos. It was here that Seth is said to have left the head of Osiris when scattering his mortal remains. Furthermore, it was at Abydos that Osiris overthrew Khentyamentiu, a canine deity associated with the underworld, to become the 'Foremeost of the Westerners' in another strand of the myth. Here we have the magnificent Osireion, attached to the rear of the temple of Seti I. The Osireion was thought of as the tomb of Osiris, while Seti I's temple I was dedicated to the god and known as the Temple of Osiris. Episodes from the Osirian myth are well preserved on the walls of this shrine.

Osiris's role as the god of vegetation is linked to the story of his resurrection. At the height of the cult of Osiris, rituals were carried out across Egypt celebrating his powers of renewal and rebirth. Wooden moulds known as Osiris beds were formed in the shape of the god and filled with rich Nile silt and seeds and grain. As the mould overfilled with sprouting green vegetation, it became an image of the rejuvenating energies of Osiris.

It has been suggested that the cult of Osiris may have developed from that of a lesser-known local deity called Andjety, also from the region of Busiris. This god seems to have been worshipped since

Predynastic times and Osiris appears to have taken on many of his attributes. Andjety means 'of the djed', and it may have been in the process of the absorption of his cult into Osiris's that the djed first became associated with the backbone of Osiris. Some commentators believe that the djed was brought to Egypt, and in particular to Busiris, from Syria, where it had been a religious fetish. This is interesting because one version of the Osirian myth mentions that Isis found Osiris's lifeless body under a tree in Syria, and not in Busiris.

The theory postulates that Osiris was originally a corn deity from Syria, whose attributes were merged with those of Andjety in Predynastic times and that slowly the story of Osiris was developed and enlarged. Over time, the cult of Osiris spread, until he was the most important deity in the whole of Egypt.

Proof of Osiris's origins as a corn deity was still evident centuries later. After the yearly inundation of the Nile, Egyptian farmers would plough and sow their seeds in the Nile mud. There was much lamentation and mourning for Osiris at this point because the seeds they were burying were seen as parts of his body and it was as if his divine being was being interred in the fertile ground. Diodorus Siculus tells us that later in the year, at harvest time, the farmers would mourn again when they cut their crops. When the first sheaf of grain was cut, they would beat their chests in lamentation and call upon Isis. However, when finally all the sheaves had been harvested and safely gathered, there was great rejoicing. Osiris had died and been buried in the ground, yet through his powers of renewal he had brought forth an abundant crop.

We cannot end this section without mentioning that many historians have pointed out the similarity between the Osirian myth and that of the books of the New Testament. The story of the suffering of Osiris in human form, God's (Geb's) own son, who is resurrected (if only for a short time), bears a striking similarity to the Gospels. It would therefore seem that the central themes of the stories of Jesus Christ were already present in Egyptian religion over 2,000 years before Jesus was born.

SEE ALSO: Abydos, Atum, Ennead, Horus, Isis

PYRAMIDS

There are few things on this earth that have aroused as much interest, mystery, contradiction, intrigue and speculation as the pyramids of Egypt. For thousands of years, travellers to this far-off, distant land have gazed in wonder at these amazing monuments that dominate a landscape imbued with history.

According to J.P. Lepre, in his brilliant work *The Egyptian Pyramids: A Comprehensive Illustrated Reference*, there are 100 pyramids in Egypt. This figure might come as a shock to most readers, who will be familiar only with the pyramids of the 3rd and 4th dynasties, namely those of Saqqara in the south through to Dahshur in the north, in the region of Memphis, the ancient capital of the Old Kingdom. Standing head and shoulders above the others in the minds of most are the three great pyramids that sit upon the Giza Plateau, those of Khufu, Khafre and Menkaure. The Great Pyramid of Khufu is the last remaining Wonder of the Ancient World.

All of these 100 pyramids sit upon the west bank of the Nile, stretching some 600 miles from Elephantine in the south to Athribis in the north. As Lepre points out, two of these hundred – those of Shepseskaf at Saqqara and Queen Khentkawes at Giza – are actually more like sarcophagus-shaped tombs. These structures were, however, undoubtedly built along the same lines and in the same context as their more conventional counterparts, and therefore can undoubtedly be counted as pyramids in their own right.

Many people believe, and indeed are told, that Egypt's first pyramid was the Step Pyramid of Djoser at Saqqara, but, according to orthodox Egyptology, this is not the case. Several structures of pyramidal form date from the first two dynasties. The Step Pyramid was, however, the first stone-built pyramid of monumental size. Constructed during the 3rd Dynasty, with a base measuring 121 m by 109 m and a height of just over 60 m, the Step Pyramid resembles a series of flat-topped mastaba tombs set one above the other in descending order of size. There is no indication that this pyramid was ever clad in an outer layer of masonry, as was the convention in the architecture of the later, 4th-Dynasty structures.

One of the things that becomes evident to the researcher when looking at the history of pyramid construction is that while there are many similarities between the so-called great pyramids of the 3rd and 4th dynasties, each one is unique in its internal chambers and external construction. Orthodox Egyptology claims that the development of the architecture of these pyramids and their associated structures can be traced in a linear fashion through this relatively short period. However, alternative authors and researchers have pointed out that there seems to be an anomaly in this theory in that following the 4th Dynasty's colossal stone monuments, the pyramids constructed during the 5th Dynasty and beyond show little of the refinement and technological advancement of their predecessors. When one is confronted with the evidence on the ground, this seems a reasonable point to raise. Indeed the pyramids of Abusir, just a few miles to the south of the magnificent pyramids of Giza, are in a shambolic and decaying state in comparison with their imposing northern counterparts. It is this seeming confusion that has led many alternative historians to speculate that a group of people possessed of great technical skill built the great pyramids long before the 4th Dynasty.

Following the technological lead taken by Djoser in the construction of the Step Pyramid, the first great king of the 4th Dynasty, Sneferu, undertook a building programme that to this day seems astonishing and unbelievable. Most people reading about the pyramids will come to the conclusion that Khufu, builder of the Great Pyramid, was the supreme pyramid-builder of all the kings of Egypt. That honour, however, lies with his father, Sneferu, who, according to orthodox Egyptology, built three or possibly even four huge pyramids. The now mainly collapsed pyramid of Meidum in the south of the Memphis necropolis area has been ascribed to Sneferu, who may have finished the structure on behalf of his predecessor, Huni. This, along with the two colossal stone pyramids at Dahshur, must have been an incredibly taxing undertaking for the Egyptian kingdom at that time.

Probably the most striking pyramid in the whole of Egypt is the southern stone pyramid of Dahshur, now known as the Bent Pyramid. The conventional story goes that Sneferu started to build this pyramid at a 54-degree angle, until it reached around halfway up, when he changed his mind and reduced the angle of incline to 43 degrees to finish the structure, having realised that to continue building at the original angle would result in its collapse. This pyramid is unique not only in its two angles but also in its two separate entrances. Like all pyramids of this era, it had a northern entrance, in this case leading down to a chamber with a magnificent corbelled ceiling; but it also had a western entrance, the door of which was high up on the side of the pyramid. This opened onto a corridor which led down to a series of antechambers and another corbelled chamber. These two internal complexes, once separate, are now joined by a roughly carved robbers' tunnel. The Bent Pyramid of Dahshur remains one of the most enigmatic and mysterious structures in all of Egypt.

Not satisfied with this unique building, Sneferu decided to construct yet another pyramid to the north of the Bent Pyramid. The resultant monument now goes by the name of 'the Red Pyramid' due to the hue of the limestone blocks from which it was constructed. This time, a single northern entrance leads down to a set of beautifully corbelled chambers, two at the original ground level, which are nearly identical and are laid out on a north to south orientation. A third, larger chamber, which Egyptologists believe was the burial chamber, is situated higher up in the body of the pyramid and positioned on an east–west axis. The beauty and precision of the architecture of the Red Pyramid is sublime.

Why Sneferu should have decided to build so many monuments is an intriguing question, especially considering the 'pyramid as tomb' theory. Why would you need more than one tomb? Strangely, Egyptologists claim that Sneferu's probable final resting place was actually within the Bent Pyramid, implying that the Red Pyramid was never actually used, although it was completed. This is one 'mystery of the pyramids' that needs more research.

It is to Sneferu's son Khufu that we now turn. We know very

little about this king, but what we do know speaks for itself: his monument remains the most incredible, beautiful and talked-about structure on the planet. Aligned perfectly with the cardinal points of the compass, with an accuracy that would defy construction techniques of the modern age, the Great Pyramid of Giza stands as stark testimony to the power of this king. With a base of 230 m by 230 m and a height of over 146 m, this massive structure is reputed to contain more than 4 million blocks of stone. Napoleon Bonaparte is said to have calculated, gazing upon it, that a wall three metres high could have been built around the whole of France using these blocks. Legend also tells of Napoleon spending a night alone in the King's Chamber of the Great Pyramid, emerging the next day and refusing to talk about his experience.

Khufu followed convention in pyramid construction in building a northern entrance to the Great Pyramid. But he also created a set of internal chambers that have invited debate and speculation as to their significance and use ever since. In the late nineteenth century and early twentieth century, several researchers (including Charles Piazzi Smyth, John and Morton Edgar and Adam Rutherford) investigated the Great Pyramid inch by inch. These men came to the conclusion that the internal and external measurements of the Great Pyramid acted as a form of prophecy in stone, foretelling future events (even including various estimates for the date of the second coming of Christ) and acting as a kind of divination tool. Needless to say, these assertions have been heavily refuted by traditional Egyptology over the years.

The first major clearing and survey of the Great Pyramid took place in the late 1830s and early 1840s by Colonel Richard Howard Vyse and his engineer J.S. Perring. Vyse also employed the Italian adventurer Giovanni Caviglia at the pyramid site. The Great Pyramid has excited and mystified in equal measure, generating probably more column inches and book pages than any other subject, with the exception of the Bible. Uniquely, the Great Pyramid not only contains three very different internal chambers but also possesses two sets of so-called airshafts. The set of airshafts originating inside the King's Chamber lead directly to the outside of the pyramid, but the airshafts leading from the Queen's Chamber, which were only discovered in the 1830s, have no such exit points. Recent exploration has led to the discovery within these shafts of a series of small portcullis-like stone blocks, which have been investigated by remote-control robots. This investigation is still ongoing, arousing much speculation about what the outcome will be if a way can be found past the blocks. Theories have been put forward that these airshafts are in fact 'star shafts', aligned with various heavenly bodies and intended to assist the soul of the pharaoh on its journey to the stars. However, recent research, such as that set out in 2000 by Ian Lawton and Chris Ogilvie-Herald in *Giza: The Truth*, has shown this to be unlikely.

Following Khufu, Egyptology encounters a problem in that the next king, a son of Khufu called Djedefre, would be expected to build his structure on the Giza Plateau as well. In fact, Djedefre chose the high plateau of Abu Roash, some 8 km north of Giza, as the site of his monument. At first glance this is a puzzling choice, and it gets even more confusing if you explore the now mostly destroyed superstructure and substructure of Djedefre's pyramid. Djedefre seems to have decided to return to a much older technique of pyramid construction whereby a large pit is first dug into the bedrock and a superstructure then raised above it. This is a much simpler and more cost-effective technique than the incredibly complex process chosen by his father. So why did Djedefre build his pyramid some distance away from Khufu's and in this comparatively primitive manner?

The American archaeologist George Reisner provided an answer to this question in the first half of the twentieth century, proposing that there must have been a family dispute which led to Djedefre building his pyramid some distance to the north. There is, however, not a shred of evidence for this quarrel; in fact, we find Djedefre's name associated with some of the structures around the Great Pyramid itself (including the roof slabs which covered the now excavated boat pit), which seems to imply that Djedefre completed the project on behalf of his father. It could be that Djedefre wanted his pyramid to be nearer to the cult centre of Ra at Heliopolis. Djedefre was the first king to use the title 'Son of Ra', and his site at Abu Roash was further north, and hence closer to Heliopolis, than Giza.

After Djedefre's reign, two further imposing pyramids were constructed at Giza. First, Khafre, another son of Khufu, built his monumental structure on a high natural mound at the centre of the plateau. Although this pyramid is smaller than the Great Pyramid, it nonetheless dominates the scene because of its position. A single, simple chamber is found in Khafre's monument. This can be entered via two passageways, one beginning several courses up on the pyramid's northern face and the other on the bedrock in front of the northern base. Interestingly, many of the Tura limestone casing blocks are still *in situ* at the apex of this pyramid, giving us an interesting insight into how the pyramids of Giza would have looked in antiquity.

It is with these 4th-Dynasty structures, beginning with Sneferu's pyramid, that we start to see associated complexes comprising mortuary temples to the east of the pyramid and causeways leading down to a 'valley temple'. Valley temples were so called because they were usually built at the level of the Nile Valley; they are thought to have been used in the funerary rituals for the pharaohs. In the case of Khafre's monument, a huge eastern mortuary temple is still to be found, with a causeway leading to an almost megalithic-style valley temple clad in granite. This valley temple has in its turn aroused much debate concerning its construction and age.

The next king to build his pyramid at Giza was a son of Khafre and grandson of Khufu called Menkaure. This pyramid is substantially smaller than the other two on the plateau and has several layers of granite casing on its lower courses, which seems to be a unique feature. This structure, like the Great Pyramid of Khufu, has three smaller subsidiary pyramids associated with it. Menkaure's subsidiary pyramids are on the south side of his structure and Khufu's to the east of the Great Pyramid. This makes a total of nine pyramids at Giza, or ten if we include the pyramid-like tomb of Queen Khentkawes. The pyramids of Giza represent the zenith of Egyptian pyramid-building. The technology and skills involved in their construction were never to be equalled, and they have been considered great wonders of the world from ancient times through to the present day.

From the end of the 4th Dynasty, pyramid construction took a downward technological turn, and the last pyramids of any substance are the 5th-Dynasty efforts at Abusir, a few kilometres south of the Giza Plateau. These pyramids were built using inferior techniques and smaller blocks, on a much reduced scale, and their internal design is also much simpler. It is almost as if the techniques and technology had been lost to these kings; their pyramids seem like poor copies of the great stone edifices built just one dynasty earlier, and by the time of the 6th Dynasty, they are mere shadows of their predecessors.

Pyramid construction continued after a fashion through to the

7th Dynasty and, after an absence, reappeared during the 12th Dynasty when a 'pyramid revival', as Lepre terms it, seems to have occurred. Generally, the Middle Kingdom pharaohs built their mud-brick pyramids in the region known as the Faiyum, near their capital city of Itjtawy, which is now lost. After another break in construction, the last-known royal pyramid built in Egypt was that of Ahmose I, the founder of the 18th Dynasty, at Abydos, but this is also a very modest stucture.

Most Egyptologists are adamant that the pyramids of Egypt were intended as tombs, a theory that has been challenged and debated for the past 100 years. There are major problems with the 'pyramid as tomb' theory, not least of which is that no bodily remains have ever been found in the great pyramids of the 3rd and 4th dynasties. A mummified arm was found inside the Step Pyramid at Saqqara, but scholars speculate that this was from a much later period than that of Djoser.

There is also the strange incident of the sealed sarcophagus discovered inside the unfinished pyramid of Sekhemkhet in 1954. When the archaeologist Zakaria Goneim first entered the burial chamber, he was certain that no tomb robbers had entered before him. Inside the roughly hewn and unfinished burial chamber, he found a fully sealed sarcophagus, unique in that, instead of having a lid, it had a T-shaped end section designed to slide upwards. Goneim was excited by the find, noting that the sarcophagus was still sealed, and was determined to open it to reveal the owner of the pyramid. When the sarcophagus was finally opened, after elaborate preparations and in front of a distinguished audience, it was found to be completely empty. Similarly, in 1900, in the huge pit of an unfinished pyramid (possibly of the 3rd or 4th Dynasty) at Zawiyet el-Aryan, the archaeologist Alexandre Barsanti discovered a fully sealed, oval-shaped sarcophagus sunk into the floor. Again, when the lid was lifted, the sarcophagus was found to be empty.

The pyramids, especially those of the 3rd and 4th Dynasty, remain as symbols in the sand, riddles and mysteries to decode and decipher, but, above all, as icons of their age. These astonishing structures have baffled and excited explorers both ancient and modern, and will continue to do so until time itself ends.

SEE ALSO: Abydos, Djoser, Giza, Khufu, Sneferu

QUEENS REIGNING AS PHARAOH

Throughout Egyptian history, it was the norm for the ruling pharaoh to be male, and the succession passed, generally speaking, from father to son. Some Egyptologists believe that where the next in line to the throne was female, a male claimant was able to legitimise his accession through marriage to the 'heiress', which in many cases resulted in brother–sister marriages. Over the course of 3,000 years of pharaonic dynasties, it is perhaps not surprising that there were exceptions to this rule, where, instead of acting as a consort, a queen ascended the throne and took full responsibility for ruling Egypt as the Pharaoh.

The first examples of this situation are not well documented and are difficult to confirm. Merneith was a 1st-Dynasty queen – probably a daughter of King Djer – who had a magnificent tomb at Abydos, on a similar scale to those of the pharaohs, with 41 subsidiary burials around it. Her name is enclosed in a royal *serekh* (rectangular device) next to that of Djer, and she is mentioned in the tomb of King Den as a 'king'. It appears Merneith was Den's mother, and it is possible that if he inherited the throne as a minor, she may have ruled as a regent for him. Alternatively, given the clues present at the royal burial site at Abydos, she may have reigned independently. In the official king lists, Merneith is not recorded as a 1st-Dynasty ruler. However, when later king lists are compared with other documentary evidence, it can be seen that these records were sometimes manipulated to remove 'unsuitable' pharaohs.

Another female pharaoh may have ruled at the end of the 6th Dynasty, after the extremely long reign of the pharaoh Pepi II. This king was thought to have governed for 94 years, and was succeeded by Merenre II, probably a son of his. His wife, Queen Nitocris (a Greek name, Nitiqret in Egyptian), was then credited by the historians Herodotus and Manetho with an independent reign, making her the last ruler of the dynasty. If Nitocris did indeed rule Egypt, it was at a time of crisis for the country. Immediately after her reign, there followed an era known as the First Intermediate Period, during which the country became divided and no single ruler could control the whole of Egypt.

A female ruler for whom there is solid evidence came to the throne *c*.1790 BC, when Queen Sobeknefru became Pharaoh and adopted the throne name Sobekkare. Sobek was the crocodile god, associated with royal authority, and the name Sobekkare means 'Sobek is the soul of Ra'. Again, the circumstances in which she came to the throne involved the death of an elderly predecessor, in this case Amenemhat III, who reigned for 45 years. He was succeeded by Amenemhat IV, and after his death, presumably because there was no obvious male candidate, his sister Sobekkare became Pharaoh. This solution was short-lived, and after only three years of her reign, the 12th Dynasty came to an end as a new ruler, Khutawyre, founded the 13th Dynasty. Little is known about her rule, although it is believed that she completed the Labyrinth of Hawara, begun by her father, Amenemhat III.

At the beginning of the 18th Dynasty, Queen Ahhotep, the mother of Ahmose I, played a pivotal role at the time of the expulsion of the Hyksos and may have exercised power as Pharaoh during the minority of her son, or acted as his coregent. Hatshepsut, a later 18th-Dynasty ruler, differed from other women who assumed the double crown as Pharaoh in that she seized power at a time when the Egyptian Empire was at its height and the country was well run and stable. Her father was Tuthmosis I, who, despite ruling only for six years, conducted some brilliant military campaigns and left the empire wealthy and strong. Hatshepsut was the daughter of Tuthmosis I by his queen, Ahmose. She married her half-brother Tuthmosis II, whose mother was a minor wife. Tuthmosis II ruled for 14 years, again successfully, and he had a son, also called Tuthmosis, by a member of his harem, as well as a daughter, Neferure, with Hatshepsut. When Tuthmosis II died, his young son – now Tuthmosis III – became Pharaoh, with his aunt/

stepmother as regent. This arrangement appears to have lasted for only a short time before Hatshepsut promoted herself to Pharaoh alongside her nephew/stepson, taking the name Maatkare. From this point, instead of being depicted as a queen, she was portrayed wearing the kilt and royal beard of a pharaoh and with all the trappings of kingship. Hatshepsut began building a mortuary temple at Thebes that is now known as Deir el-Bahri and is still a hugely impressive monument.

To legitimise her accession as Pharaoh, Hatshepsut made a great deal of her 'divine' birth, claiming that the god Amun had visited her mother and that Queen Ahmose had conceived her daughter with the god. Images of this divine conception are carved onto the walls of the temple at Deir el-Bahri, which is dedicated to 'my father Amun'. While all pharaohs claimed divine descent, it was especially important for Hatshepsut to have her reign validated in this way. It should not be thought that Hatshepsut, in emphasising her divine parenthood, was seeking to undermine her earthly father, Tuthmosis I. He was posthumously recruited to the cause of legitimising her reign with an assertion that he had presented his daughter to the court and pronounced her his successor. Since Tuthmosis I had a son who was able to succeed him, this claim can be dismissed as a fabrication on the part of Hatshepsut.

The presumably uneasy shared rule continued for around 16 years, until Hatshepsut's death. It is impossible to say whether she died from natural causes or at the instigation of Tuthmosis III. He went on to rule for another 23 years, was remarkably successful as a general and is known as the 'Napoleon of Egypt'. Tuthmosis III tried to systematically remove all images of Hatshepsut from monuments, and her name was eliminated from the king lists. It is difficult to tell how her actions were viewed by the majority of her subjects, although a glimpse can be seen in some graffiti referring to her adviser Senenmut. As a tutor to Neferure and one of Hatshepsut's principal advisers, Senenmut became a powerful man, and he was wealthy enough to have two tombs prepared for himself, one of which was in close proximity to Deir el-Bahri. There are graffiti of an explicit sexual nature portraying Senenmut and a king (presumed to be Hatshepsut), from which we can assume that rumours were prevalent about how he had obtained his elevated status.

In the Valley of the Kings, a tomb was prepared for Hatshepsut as Pharaoh, to replace the one which had been built for her in a remote valley when she was Tuthmosis II's queen. The new royal tomb (now designated KV20) contained two sarcophagi, one for Tuthmosis I and the other for Hatshepsut. Both were empty when Howard Carter excavated the tomb in 1903, and the body of Hatshepsut has not been positively identified. Carter remarked that:

> She would have been better advised to hold to her original plan. In this secret spot her mummy would have had a reasonable chance of avoiding disturbance: In the Valley it had none. A king she would be, and a king's fate she shared.

At this time, of course, Howard Carter did not know that he would be the man to discover the body of one king, Tutankhamun, which had not been moved from its original tomb.

There may have been another female to take the throne during the 18th Dynasty, in the person of a shadowy figure who ruled after the 'heretic' pharaoh Akhenaten. This individual is Neferneferuaten Ankhkheperure, and speculation exists as to whether this could have been Akhenaten's chief wife, Queen Nefertiti, ruling as a coregent with her husband or taking on the reins of power after his death. Another suggestion is that it may have been Meritaten, the eldest daughter of Akhenaten. The lack of documentary evidence about this ruler makes it impossible to regard the proposal of either female candidate as more than speculation.

A young man called Siptah inherited the throne in approximately 1215 BC, and during his reign his stepmother Twosret – who managed to become regent in preference to Siptah's own mother, Tiaa – held power. After a six-year reign, Siptah died and was succeeded by Twosret, who ruled for two years as Sitre Meryamun, the last ruler of the 19th Dynasty. As with Nitocris and Sobeknefru before her, her rule proved to be the final act of a royal dynasty.

The next woman to take the throne of Egypt was from the Greek Ptolemy family, who had appropriated Egypt from the empire of Alexander the Great after his death in 323 BC. To describe the machinations of the Ptolemies as complex would be a huge understatement. They were a singularly ruthless, manipulative and deceitful family, who thought nothing of changing allegiances regularly and murdering each other in the pursuit of power. Euergetes II, for example, was reputed to have had his son murdered and the body sent to the child's mother, Euergetes' sister/wife Cleopatra II. Berenice IV became the heir to the throne after Ptolemy XII fled the country, and, when married to a cousin she despised, she had him strangled about a week after the wedding. Berenice effectively ruled for three years before Ptolemy XII returned to his throne with Roman assistance and Berenice and her second husband, Archelaus, were killed. This was the background to the accession of Ptolemy XII's daughter, Cleopatra VII, after his death in 51 BC.

It was agreed that Cleopatra would marry her elder brother Ptolemy XIII, but he was unwilling to share power and tried to have her killed. Cleopatra sought refuge in Syria, gathered an army and returned to confront her brother. The Roman general Caesar became involved in the conflict, and, as history and Shakespeare have noted, he preferred Cleopatra to her brother. Ptolemy XIII drowned in an attempt to reclaim the throne, and Cleopatra married her younger brother, Ptolemy XIV. It was Caesar, however, who was the father of her son Caesarion, and Cleopatra had an image of herself and her son making offerings to the gods carved onto the temple walls at Denderah.

Cleopatra VII was unusual among the Ptolemaic dynasty for her assimilation into Egyptian culture. While the rest of the family had spoken Greek and kept very separate from their Egyptian subjects, Cleopatra learnt the Egyptian language. After Caesar's death and the dispatch of Ptolemy XIV by poison, Cleopatra became the partner of Mark Antony, and they ruled Egypt together for six years. In 32 BC, Octavian, the heir to the Roman Empire and the brother of Antony's Roman wife (who was naturally unhappy at her husband's activities in Egypt), attacked Egypt. After a sea battle at Actium in 31 BC, in which the Roman fleet was victorious, Octavian began an invasion of Egypt and by August of the year 30 BC was approaching the capital city, Alexandria. In a scene depicted countless times in art, rather than face captivity, Cleopatra killed herself by causing a deadly snake to bite her. With Cleopatra's death, not only the Ptolemaic dynasty but also the rule of the pharaohs came to an end as Egypt was absorbed into the Roman Empire.

SEE ALSO: Abydos; Akhenaten; Carter, Howard; Nefertiti; Tutankhamun; Valley of the Kings

RA

One of the chief gods of Egyptian religion and mythology was Ra. He represented the sun and was the sun-god of Heliopolis. He personified the sun itself, and one aspect of him was that his eye was equated with the solar disc.

It was around the time of the 5th Dynasty that Ra became a god of national importance in Egypt, although his name appears in royal titulary from the 2nd Dynasty, so he was evidently worshipped and associated with kingship from an early date. The kings of this era began to erect sun temples to Ra at Abu Ghurab, large stone platforms that held obelisks in his honour. He was often depicted as a pharaoh with a sun disc on his head. It was also thought that the sun required a boat to traverse the waters of the heavens without having his fire extinguished, so we often see images of Ra in his solar barque. During the daytime, this boat was known as Madjet, which means 'becoming strong'. As the day progressed and Ra passed across the skies towards evening, he travelled in a boat known as Semektet, 'becoming weak'.

At night-time, Ra had to steer his boat through the underworld, as the solar barque was swallowed in the darkness. He had other gods to help him on his journey – Thoth, Maat and, later, Horus himself. It was Maat's job to plot the course for the boat because she represented balance and order. Thoth was invariably at the helm of the boat as the personification of the moon. Another variation on the story of Ra navigating the skies is tied in with the tale of the god Khepri, a deity often represented as a dung beetle. These beetles roll balls of dung, in which they then lay their eggs, across the ground. The Egyptians believed that the sun moved across the sky in a similar fashion because it was pushed by Khepri in his dung-beetle form. So it was that Khepri came to be considered an aspect of Ra – the rising sun.

Later in Egyptian history, as religious mythology developed, Ra became one with Atum, the god who had come into being on the mound of creation, to form Atum-Ra. The sun is connected strongly with the myth of creation – the sun rose as Atum stood on the primeval mound. So it was that the sun and Ra were closely tied to the concepts of the Benben stone and the Benu bird.

Later still, as the importance of Horus, the son of Osiris, grew, Ra was merged with Horus to become Ra-Herakhty, literally 'Ra who is Horus of the two horizons', a reference to the fact that the sun rose in the east and set in the west – the two horizons. During this period when Ra-Herakhty rose to prominence, it was thought that the sun travelled on wings, it being no coincidence that Horus was often depicted as a hawk, a bird which could fly to great heights. Yet another variant on the story of the passage of Ra across the sky was that the goddess Nut, representing the sky, formed an arch around the world with her body and that each night at sundown Ra was swallowed by Nut and spent the dark hours passing through her body to emerge at sunrise.

All of these separate aspects of Ra may make his cult seem somewhat incoherent, but it does not seem to have troubled the priests and kings of Egypt. As Egyptian theology expanded and grew more complex, the whole fabric of the mythology began to tear and holes appeared, yet it never completely fell apart; instead, it was patched up time and time again to form a new weave. The Egyptologist I.E.S. Edwards highlighted the complications involved in this:

> The Egyptians of the Pyramid Age clearly found little difficulty in regarding their sun-god not as a single indivisible being but rather as a composite deity whose various attributes were derived from local solar deities, originally separate and subsequently united, without proper co-ordination, with Re of Heliopolis. Some of the constituent deities can be identified by their special functions or by their epithets. One, for instance, was the sun-god with whom the King became integrated after his

death. Others, whose epithets are known, are 'Re in the *senut*-house', 'Re in the sanctuary of Upper Egypt' and 'Re on the roof' (of the temple of Heliopolis). In these circumstances it is not surprising that the sun-cult contains many inconsistencies as it is presented in the earliest body of religious texts in our possession.

Ra played an important part in the Pharaoh's life: while the King was considered ruler of the earth, Ra was thought of as reigning over the universe. The two were therefore interrelated and inseparable concepts, so much so that when the dead pharaoh travelled to the Duat to become one with Osiris, he travelled through the netherworld with Ra beside him.

As Egypt approached the time of the New Kingdom, Ra was merged yet again with another god, this time one from Upper Egypt, Amun. Together they formed one of the most important gods of Egypt, Amun-Ra. Where Ra-Khepri was seen as the sun at dawn, and Ra-Herakhty the sun at evening, now Amun-Ra became the invisible aspect of the sun, the sun as it made its secretive nightly journey to reach the point of sunrise on the following day.

Obviously, this complicated an already tangled theology, and it has been suggested that it was this that led Amenhotep IV to change his name to Akhenaten and start to worship a much simpler solar deity, one that did not require multiple forms, embracing a religion which revered the sun in its simplest form: as the sun disc, the Aten. This new religion did not persist for long, however, and Ra was reborn in his final incarnation, as Atum-Ra, when the priests reversed all of Akhenaten's radical changes after the pharaoh's death.

Ra continued to be a powerful force right up until the later stages of the Egyptian Empire. His cult gradually declined sometime during the Graeco-Roman period, until he became a minor god. This time, the light really had gone out for good; the sun-god was never worshipped again in the Middle East.

SEE ALSO: Akhenaten, Amun, Atum, Duat, Horus, Obelisks, Osiris, Thoth

SEKHMET

Sekhmet was the goddess of war and destruction, the fiercest of all the gods of Ancient Egypt. She was the daughter of the sun-god Ra, and sister and wife of Ptah. She is most often depicted as a standing woman with the head of a lioness, dressed in red, the colour of blood. Her head is adorned with a sun disc and a uraeus, the snake headdress. Her name translates as 'mighty one' or 'powerful one'.

It was said that Ra created Sekhmet in an act of vengeance after humankind failed to obey and worship him. He made Sekhmet literally in a blink of his fiery eye. She took her terrible form, as a lion falling upon her prey, and went out to wreak death and slaughter amongst those who had disobeyed her father. The Nile ran red with blood for many nights as she delighted in the carnage. All who had disobeyed Ra were dead, but still Sekhmet's lust for blood could not be sated.

Ra looked on the destruction about him and he repented, yet even he could not stop his daughter, and it was declared that Sekhmet would end the destruction only of her own free will; such was her power that none could force her. So Ra planned to trick her. He mixed a great quantity of beer with red ochre from Elephantine Island and left it at the place where Sekhmet was planning to attack at dawn. Sekhmet arrived as the sun rose to find 7,000 jars of the beer mixture, and, thinking it the blood of all those that she had slain, she drank it all with great delight. Incapacitated by the amount of alcohol she had consumed, her slaughter finally ended.

It was because of her powers of destruction that the Egyptians worshipped Sekhmet. Countless statues of the goddess have been found in Egypt, and these were once worshipped in the hope that such acts of devotion could prevent a recurrence of Sekhmet's devastating killing spree.

One statue amongst hundreds of Sekhmet sculptures found at Karnak, attributed to the reign of the 18th-Dynasty pharaoh Amenhotep III, was inscribed with the following:

> The good god, the lord of action, Neb-Maat-Ra [Amenhotep III], Beloved of Sekhmet, the Mistress of Dread, who gives life eternally. The son of the God Ra of His own body, Amenhotep, ruler of Waset [Thebes], Beloved of Sekhmet, the Mistress of Dread, who gives life eternally.

This inscription may seem strange given the extent of Sekhmet's destructive powers. However, there was another side to Sekhmet: just as she was able to spread destruction, death and disease, so she also had the ability to cure and heal. The priests of Sekhmet were renowned for their abilities in the field of medicine and were skilled surgeons.

Sekhmet was also said to protect the Pharaoh on the field of battle, and she was even believed to accompany him and launch fiery arrows ahead of his charge, felling his enemies. She would also cast plagues and diseases down on the Pharaoh's opponents.

Sekhmet was linked with another cat goddess, Bastet, and it is often said that the two were twins, although this was probably a comparatively late addition to the mythology. Together they represented the duality of good and evil, with Sekhmet taking on the darker role, although both aspects were often manifest in Sekhmet alone. Bastet was originally a goddess of Lower Egypt, while Sekhmet was a goddess of Upper Egypt. It has been suggested that this could be one of the origins of Sekhmet's legendary ferocity: that when Upper Egypt conquered Lower Egypt in battle, Sekhmet was seen thereafter as an aggressive and dominant goddess, and that from this her legend grew.

Today, many women see in Sekhmet a strong character with whom to identify, and she has become a focus for many people following new-age religions and alternative belief systems. Sekhmet ruled over menstruation in ancient times and this has also had an effect on her popularity as a pagan goddess in modern times. It is her powers of healing and nurturing that attract people now; yet there is always the knowledge that this is a goddess who wields great power, one to be worshipped with respect and caution.

SEE ALSO: Ra

SNEFERU

Sneferu was the first pharaoh of the 4th Dynasty. He ruled sometime around the year 2600 BC, and, according to the Turin King List, he sat on the throne for some 24 years; other sources, however, including the Ancient Egyptian scribe Manetho, suggest a longer reign. He is probably most famous for two things: he is remembered for the monuments he left behind; and he was the father of Khufu, the king to whom the Great Pyramid is attributed. There are many different spellings of his name, and we find Snofru, Snefru, Senefru and quite a few others, as well as the Greek, Soris. The name itself is said to mean 'he of beauty'.

Sneferu was married to Hetepheres, said to be his sister, or possibly half-sister. Their father is thought to have been Huni, the last king of the 3rd Dynasty. It is likely that Sneferu's mother was Meresankh, a woman not of royal blood. By marrying Hetepheres, he was strengthening his claim to the throne.

The earliest recorded mention of Egypt making contact with its neighbours dates from Sneferu's reign. The inscription on the Palermo Stone describes a mission that comprised 40 ships bringing wood into Egypt from a foreign land, probably cedar from Lebanon. Interestingly, some original cedar timbers survive inside the internal chambers of the pyramid of Meidum, which is attributed to Sneferu. While he was seen as a benign ruler within Egypt, Sneferu was also a strong king and carried out many campaigns abroad. Records detail military operations in

Nubia and Libya. From the latter, he was said to have brought back to Egypt 11,000 captives and some 13,000 cattle.

As the founder of the 4th Dynasty, he was responsible for some truly huge construction projects. Furthermore, the transition from step pyramid to true pyramid is believed to have occurred during his reign. However, this wasn't the only alteration that suddenly arose in the construction of these monuments. The axis of the buildings was switched from an orientation of north–south to an east–west design. Similarly, the mortuary temple was now positioned to the east where previously it had been to the north. Additionally, we see the introduction of monumental causeways and a second temple – the valley temple –linked to the mortuary complex via the causeway. These were radical changes that were not brought in over the course of several generations but in one lifetime. It is said that the reason for this massive shift in design was a move away from older star cults towards the sun cult of Heliopolis, with the new east–west axis of the pyramids following the course of the sun.

Four pyramids in total are attributed to Sneferu: two at Dashur, one at Sila and one at Meidum – although not all scholars are in agreement about this. The smallest and most difficult to attribute is that at Sila, a small step pyramid where a limestone stela was found inscribed with the name of Sneferu. Without any evidence to the contrary, this pyramid has been added to the list of those Sneferu commissioned.

Next is the ruined pyramid at Meidum. Some have raised the possibility that this pyramid was started by Huni and only finished by Sneferu. However, there is little evidence of kings finishing their predecessors' funerary monuments, so this should probably be disregarded. The name of Sneferu is found at Meidum, and the tombs of his sons Nefermaat and Rahotep have been found amongst the mastabas there. Mark Lehner, in his book *The Complete Pyramids*, deals with the issue of to whom we should assign this pyramid:

> Previously it was suggested that Huni was responsible for this pyramid, based solely on the need to identify a large royal tomb for this king. However, the ancient name of Meidum, *Djed Sneferu* ('Sneferu Endures'), and the fact that Sneferu's name, unlike Huni's, appears in texts at the site, all point to the former as the builder of Meidum from start to finish.

The final two pyramids associated with Sneferu are those at Dashur. The building that we know today as the Red Pyramid was in its day called the Shining Pyramid. The so-called Bent Pyramid was originally titled the Southern Shining Pyramid. These two constructions, like those at Giza, remain more or less intact today. In fact, the Bent Pyramid probably retains more of its casing blocks than any other Old Kingdom pyramid.

We don't know why Sneferu started work on the Dashur pyramids when he had already begun work at Meidum. However, it is said that in Year 15 of his reign he stopped work at Meidum and began work on the Bent Pyramid instead, creating a whole new necropolis at the same time. The story goes that faults developed during the construction of the Bent Pyramid and that Sneferu decided to move north and start work on another pyramid, the Red Pyramid, sometimes called the North Pyramid.

There is archaeological evidence which shows us that Sneferu was definitely building at Dashur. In the 1950s, the valley temple attached to the Bent Pyramid was discovered, containing elaborate reliefs depicting Sneferu, as well as six statues of the king. Furthermore, a block of stone was found inside the Bent Pyramid's upper chamber that contained red quarry marks bearing the name of Sneferu.

What is remarkable about these tales of construction and abandonment is that, despite the problems that many say developed and that led to the move first from Meidum to Dashur and then from the Bent to the Red Pyramid, Sneferu still chose to finish all these pyramids. Even once he had completed the Red Pyramid, he is supposed to have gone back to Meidum and finished the pyramid there, despite the fact that he must have known he would never need to use it.

Is there some vital piece of information that we have not yet discovered concerning the meaning and use of the pyramids? Why would Sneferu need three, perhaps even four, pyramids, while other kings seem to have built only one? He couldn't be entombed in all of them. So either there was some other reason for their construction or some doubt must be attached to the attribution of all three, possibly four, to Sneferu.

If these pyramids truly were all raised by Sneferu, then it makes him the greatest pyramid-builder of all the pharaohs. The total amount of material needed to build the three pyramids at Dashur and Meidum is estimated to come close to a staggering ten million tons of cut stone. As a comparison, Sneferu's son Khufu moved only six million tons when he constructed the Great Pyramid.

SEE ALSO: Heliopolis, Giza, Khufu, Pyramids

SOKAR

We know relatively little about this deity in comparison with some of the other Egyptian gods and goddesses. However, it would seem that Sokar had a far deeper and more important role than orthodox Egyptology would have us believe.

The name Sokar appears in the earliest surviving Egyptian texts (notably the Pyramid Texts of the 5th Dynasty and the Palermo Stone fragments dating from the latter part of that dynasty), where he is already associated with his cult centres and cultic objects. He seems at this early stage to have a long history and be a fully formed godhead. Sokar in his earliest form is depicted as a figure with a human body and a falcon's head, and this can lead to confusion because of the similarity with other hawk-headed deities such as Horus. Etymologically, the Ancient Egyptians tell us within the Pyramid Texts that the name Sokar (*'skr'*) is brought forth when the god Osiris cries out. This vague explanation, however, seems to intimate that, because of his long history, his origins were obscure even by the 5th Dynasty. The Greek version of this god's name was Sokaris. The Athenian dramatist Cratinus (*c.*520–423 BC) associated Sokaris with the figure of Pamylas, who in turn appears to be a Greek variation on the god Osiris.

So what do we know about this strange and enigmatic figure? According to the Palermo Stone, from the 1st Dynasty onwards there was a periodic festival of what was known as the Maaty barque, which seems to have been a celebration of Sokar, who is described as 'foremost of the Maaty barque'. In later dynasties, a fully fledged and very important Festival of Sokar would become one of the major events of the Ancient Egyptian calendar. The Maaty barque itself may well be an early version of one of the main cultic symbols of the god, namely the Henu barque with which Sokar became intimately associated. The Henu barque is unique in Ancient Egyptian iconography because of the animal fetishes which decorate it. Its appearance is more primitive than those of other Egyptian barque shrines; it resembles representations of boats dating from Predynastic times. It consists of a high-prowed boat resting on a sled. This boat in turn has a mound-shaped object placed amidships, which seems to represent the ancient shrine of Sokar called the *shetayet*. High on the prow is to be found either the head of an antelope or that of a bull (and in some depictions, both), along with several fish. In many images of the Henu barque, there is the figure of a hawk above the mound. Some of the ivory jar-sealings of the 1st-Dynasty king Hor-Aha, on which a ship of nearly identical description is shown, seem to indicate a very early dating for the Henu barque.

Beautiful depictions of this boat are to be found in the temple of Seti I at Abydos, in the corridor leading to the Osireion, where the young Prince Ramesses II, Seti's son and heir, is seen in glorious detail pulling the Henu barque on its sled. Other depictions can be found at the mortuary complex of Ramesses III, Medinet Habu, on the west bank of the Nile at modern day Luxor. Here, in the second hall of the mortuary temple, scenes showing the Festival of Sokar adorn the walls and the Henu barque is carried aloft upon its sled by a group of priests. Through the work of Egyptologists Kitchen and Gaballa, who studied these scenes and wrote about them in their 1969 paper 'The Festival of Sokar', we are able to understand the full importance of this significant occasion.

Sokar, it seems, was one of the original deities of the underworld before Osiris usurped this role at the end of the Old Kingdom. Echoes of Sokar's important status as a god of the underworld are to be found in the texts known as the Book of the Duat. In the Book of the Duat, the underworld is associated with the 12 hours of the night, through which the sun-god Ra must travel in his solar boat in order to be reborn in the new morning. In the fourth and fifth hours of this underworld journey, we find the realm of Sokar, depicted in unique and mysterious scenes. The best example of these is found in the tomb of the pharaoh Tuthmosis III in the Valley of the Kings, Luxor.

The fourth hour of the Duat marks a considerable change from the previous hours of Ra's journey. Suddenly, after a journey through water, the fourth hour presents Ra with a descent into a realm on land (indicated by the representation of sand). Most Egyptologists concur that this realm, called Rosetau, corresponds geographically to a location south of the pyramids at Giza. The 'road to Rosetau', shown in scenes depicting the fourth hour of the journey through the Duat, descends into the realm of Sokar itself, which is reached in the fifth hour. Representations of the fifth hour have generated little interest among orthodox Egyptologists but have excited and mystified alternative authors and researchers over the past 20 years. Here, in the fifth hour of the Duat, we see Sokar 'upon his sand', which is shown as an oval, sarcophagus-shaped area. Within this oval, we find Sokar in his anthropomorphic form, with a human body and a falcon's head – nearly identical in appearance to the god Horus. He clutches a strange, double-ended, winged serpent. The oval in which he appears rests on the backs of two sphinxes facing in opposite directions, and all of this in turn is enclosed within a mound which has the head of a woman. Above the female-headed mound, a strange, black, conical object is placed, upon either side of which two falcons sit, and from which a beetle is emerging. This scene remains one of the most enigmatic, mysterious and under-explained images of Ancient Egypt.

Many alternative theorists have written and speculated about this scene. Interestingly, though, it is a well-respected conventional historian, Erik Hornung, who has added the most intriguing explanation, stating that he believes that the fourth and fifth hours originally constituted a whole. In other words, it is Hornung's opinion that, at some distant period of Egyptian history, what we now know as the fourth and fifth hours of the Duat were seen as a complete cycle.

One other point to highlight is that depicted within the fourth hour of the Duat is a small, often overlooked vignette of a truly mysterious nature. This scene shows the ibis-headed god Thoth handing over the *wadjet* eye to a figure that could be either Sokar or Horus. The strange aspect of this encounter is that the wadjet eye itself in this context seems to be called Sokar. In other words, what is happening here is that Thoth is handing Sokar his own life, as symbolised by the eye, and therefore, potentially, power over life and death. During these two hours, we find the god Ra no longer sailing his boat through water but having it dragged over the sands of the fourth and fifth hours of the Duat, and it is also clear that within the realm of Sokar, Ra has no dominion, being able only to skirt the kingdom and not actually to enter it. This is made evident by the fact that the souls of the dead can only cry out forlornly to Ra but can receive no answer.

Along with the Henu barque, another cultic object associated with Sokar was his shrine, the shetayet. This was viewed as being both part of the Henu barque and a separate entity. As we have mentioned, Egyptologists believe that the geographical area of southern Giza was associated with Sokar's realm of Rosetau, and it is believed that the remains of a shetayet shrine are yet to be found there. The great Egyptologist I.E.S. Edwards wrote that in the area to the south of the Great Pyramid, on a hilly limestone outcrop, his illustrious predecessor Sir Flinders Petrie found 'many pieces of red granite, and some other stones scattered about the west side of the rocky ridge, as if some costly building had existed in this region'.

It is not unreasonable, therefore, to speculate that the shetayet of Sokar is yet to be discovered beneath the sands at the southern end of the Giza Plateau. It is our assertion that the shetayet may well be an underground crypt, not unlike depictions of the fifth hour of the Duat, and with a striking similarity to the Osireion at Abydos. The Roman historian Strabo mentions that the Osireion was originally covered with an earthen mound. In our opinion, a shetayet shrine could have taken a similar form, with a subterranean chamber beneath the mound representing the realm of Sokar as shown in representations of the fifth hour of the Duat.

Egyptology essentially sees Sokar as a chthonic deity, that is, a deity very much associated with the realm of the dead. This aspect of Sokar is certainly an important one, and it was also an area with which Osiris quickly became closely connected when he made his first recorded appearance at the end of the Old Kingdom. It is from this point that confusion sets in, with Sokar's identity becoming blurred with those both of Osiris and also the creator god Ptah, whose cult area, Memphis, was in close geographical proximity to Sokar's. It has traditionally been assumed that the Ancient Egyptian necropolis at Saqqara, close to Memphis, took its name from the god Sokar. However, it is now believed that the name Saqqara probably comes from that of a local Berber tribe, the Beni Saqqar.

By the Middle Kingdom, and very possibly from an earlier time, Sokar had assumed a significant role in the opening-of-the-mouth ceremony, in which the soul of a deceased person is transfigured and released from the mummy for rebirth. Also by the Middle Kingdom, a new deity known as Ptah-Sokar had appeared. He was associated with the wealth of the soil and its powers of growth and regeneration. This deity in turn became Ptah-Sokar-Osiris from the New Kingdom onwards, a deity of creation, metamorphosis and rebirth, who combined the attributes of the three gods. By the Late Period and in the Ptolemaic era, the figure of Sokar was almost fully subsumed by that of Osiris.

It appears clear to us that the figure of Sokar is one of the earliest deities known to the Ancient Egyptians. Even by the time of the 5th-Dynasty Pyramid Texts, his original history and character were somewhat lost in the mists of time. Sokar in his original form seems without a doubt to have been associated with the realm of the dead, although perhaps not in the purely chthonic role that orthodox Egyptology would have us believe he played. As a result of the assimilation of Sokar into Osiris, and hence many of the attributes which were originally Sokar's becoming associated instead with that god, the picture has been clouded from an early time. It is our opinion that many facets of Osiris – in particular his association with resurrection and renewal – originated with Sokar, and we believe that more in-depth study and a reappraisal of this much misunderstood deity are long overdue.

SEE ALSO: Abydos, Duat, Giza, Osiris, Thoth, Valley of the Kings, Wadjet Eye.

SPELLS

The wealth of diverse sources of information which have been preserved from Ancient Egypt allow us an extraordinary degree of insight into the lives of its people. One area that has always proved of interest to scholars and laymen alike is Egyptian magic. Within this vast topic, the power and magical force inherent in spells can be found throughout the fabric of everyday Egyptian life.

Spells are depicted and inscribed on tomb scenes, upon statues, written down on papyrus and other media, on artefacts left within tombs or on items intended for everyday use. Spells were used for protection against poisonous creatures or anything that could cause harm in this life or the next, in times of danger such as at childbirth, for medicinal reasons, for funerary purposes to allow the deceased to live in the afterlife and in love spells such as one from Deir el-Medina dated to c.1186–1069 BC, written on limestone and asking a god to make an individual 'run after me like a cow after grass, like a servant after her children, like a drover after his herd'!

In Ancient Egyptian literary texts, books of magic are often described as having extraordinary origins, which was a way of enhancing their aura and magical qualities. The actual existence of books of magical knowledge can be found within the Old Kingdom tomb of the vizier Washptah (c.2400 BC). From his tomb inscription, we learn of Washptah's collapse before King Neferirkare. In an attempt to revive him, the king called for books of magic and medicine to be consulted by his doctors and the lector-priests, although these magical spells were unfortunately unable to save Washptah.

Other hints at the existence of books of magic are contained within the 'Admonitions of Ipuwer' from the Middle Kingdom, a text that relates the disarray of the world during a period of civil war, urging: 'Behold the hidden chamber, its books are stolen. The secrets in it are revealed. Behold, magical spells are revealed.' Often, so-called books of magic consisted only partly of spells, which would be written on papyri along with accounts, myths or medical texts. A number of surviving papyri contain spells, including the London Medical Papyrus (c.1250 BC); a collection of gynaecological spells (c.1850 BC); and the Brooklyn Magical Papyrus, which deals almost exclusively with snakebites.

Spells often drew upon Egyptian mythology to explain their antecedence or state how a god suffered with a similar complaint, the point being that it is easier to solve a particular difficulty if its origin is understood. With this in mind, a spell to ease stomachache relates how Horus suffered a similar discomfort after eating fish. Isis was particularly famous for her magical powers and was often mentioned in spells against snakes and scorpions. These spells were very common, and the reason for this goes beyond the obvious need for protection. Mythology plays a significant part in their popularity. The god responsible for sending the poisonous creatures was invariably Seth, the god of chaos. Hence, by protecting yourself against snakes and scorpions, you were also protecting yourself against chaos and confusion as embodied by Seth.

Egyptian spells worked on three levels – word, action and medium. To distinguish them from normal speech, spells were meant to be chanted or spoken in an authoritative voice, using the correct tone and exact pronunciation. Because of the Egyptians' belief that the spoken word had sufficient power to create and destroy, it was extremely powerful when used in magic. Once uttered, a spell was active and influential, and had to be driven in the required direction by way of a hand held around the mouth to ensure the words of power reached their correct goal. The sound, rhythm and verbal form of a spell amplified the power of the word, with repetition a significant factor in ensuring the correct build up of magical energy, or *heka*. Both four and seven were particularly important repetitions.

Wordplay was a specific magical tool: puns, homophony, alliteration, meaningless words and names were used in order to amplify the inherent magical properties of language. The use of apparently meaningless words and names worked on the idea that power was contained in a sound and its hidden meaning. Their significance was in their very unintelligibility – their intrinsic sense was beyond the comprehension of mere mortals.

As Egyptian personal names were theophoric, derived from the names of gods (for example, Ptahhotep, 'Ptah is Content'; Meretamun, 'Beloved of Amun'), whenever a name was uttered, a god was glorified. A name had a specific magical potency and was an extension of a person's personality. In fact, the name *was* the person and so to know a person's name was to have power over them. This was used to great advantage by the goddess Isis, who tricked Ra into revealing his secret name and thereby furnishing her with great power.

The action part of the spell took many forms. It was as valid as the oral part and a major component in accomplishing the spell. As with cupping the hand around the mouth, pointing the spell at its intended recipient ensured it would reach the correct destination. Licking was a major practice within spells. The concept of using licking as part of healing probably arose from watching animals licking their wounds. Licking spells and images drawn on the hand for healing purposes is attested to from the time of the Old Kingdom (c.2687–2191 BC) in the form of the Pyramid Texts and was probably in use before that time as well. A later spell, against scorpion venom, states that the words of the Ra/Isis spell are to be said over a drawing of Ra, Isis and Horus, and the same image drawn on the hand of the person who has been bitten. The person was then to lick the image off, so that the three deities could magically fight the poison from within the body. The deities were also to be drawn on linen and worn around the neck. It was noted that this spell was 'truly effective, proved a million times'. Spells could also be swallowed. This might be done by writing the spell on papyrus, tearing it up and dissolving it in beer. The mixture was then drunk so that the magic would be absorbed.

Alternatively, healing stelae or cippi could be used. These depicted Horus standing on two crocodiles whilst holding poisonous creatures in his hands. Water was poured over the stela as the spell was spoken, and collected in an attached basin. This water, which had absorbed the efficacy of the words and image, was then drunk or poured over the wound, bringing the spell's potency into direct contact with the patient.

Spitting was also used in spells, but its use lay mainly in its destructive aspect, as in spitting on enemy statuettes as part of the execration ritual. However, it did hold some medicinal and protective power, not surprising bearing in mind spitting's integral role in the origination of the gods Shu and Tefnut in the Heliopolitan creation myth, a concept that finds expression in our idiom 'spitting image'. Thus, for the spell to heal the *wekhdu* disease, the practitioner spits on the diseased limb (Ebers Papyrus, recipe 131). An anti-scorpion spell from the Saite period (*c.*664–525 BC) notes: 'You should recite them to your finger while it is moistened with spittle. Then you should seal the opening of the wound with it.'

The last aspect of spells is the medium used, which included saliva, blood, sweat, urine, semen and excrement, which were all considered divine secretions and hence valid in spells. Clay, wax, dough and animal fats were also used, in particular to form models because of their malleability and because they were easily destroyed. They were therefore ideal for any type of destructive magic or curses. Interestingly, garlic was used in imitation of teeth in a spell against ghosts and demons, and this may be the antecedent of later vampire tales and garlic's place within these. Ivory boomerang-style wands were used by practitioners to form a protective circle around the patient, particularly necessary in childbirth, when both mother and child were susceptible to malevolent forces. Knots were often used in spells against snakes and scorpions, with the rubric specifying that, after the words were spoken, knots – usually seven – were to be made in linen to act as an obstruction against the poison.

Also important was the time at which spells were said, as some days were better suited than others and some times were not appropriate to certain spells. Dawn was the best time for a spell to work, bearing in mind the connection of dawn with rebirth and the creation of a new, unique day.

SEE ALSO: Curses, Magic, Symbolism

SPHINX

The Great Sphinx at Giza gazes eternally towards the east, a guardian of the plateau behind it. With its huge body carved from the limestone bedrock into the shape of a lion with the head of a man – a king adorned with the *nemes,* or pleated headdress, of Ancient Egypt – the Sphinx lies majestically in the landscape, a statue of unprecedented size.

This enduring image of Ancient Egypt has become an icon of a place and time in history. Mystery has surrounded the human-headed lion since antiquity, and speculation as to why and when it was carved has persisted right down to modern times. In Arabic, the Sphinx is known as Abu Hol, which translates as 'father of terrors'. So what secrets does this terrible father conceal?

Orthodox Egyptology dates the Sphinx to around 2500 BC. This would attribute its creation to the 4th-Dynasty pharaoh Khafre (Chephren to the Greeks), in whose image it is supposedly carved and at the end of whose pyramid causeway it is situated. In front of the Sphinx lies a large temple, known today as the Sphinx Temple, next to which, on its south side, lies the Valley Temple of Khafre. The eastern walls of the two temples are perfectly aligned. The Sphinx Temple was constructed from the blocks of limestone which were cleared from around the Sphinx during its carving, but very little else is known about this temple, as there are no surviving Old Kingdom texts that refer either to it or the Sphinx itself. The Sphinx Temple is unique in having both a western and an eastern sanctuary, which, Egyptologists speculate, represent the rising and setting of the sun.

Much theorising still surrounds the incredible piece of sculpture which is the Sphinx. Some alternative-history authors see in the Sphinx a representation of the constellation Leo. However, this theory assumes not only that the constellations were recognised by the early Egyptians but also that they saw in them the same symbols that we refer to today. In recent years, researcher John Anthony West and Boston University geologist Robert Schoch have proposed a new chronology for the Sphinx based upon their research. The theory goes that by looking into the water-weathering of the rocks which make up the Sphinx's body and enclosure, a date for the carving can be arrived at based on the known wet periods for the region. West also claims that there is evidence that the Sphinx was repaired in the 4th Dynasty and asks why, if the monument was only carved during this dynasty, repairs would be needed. West and Schoch disagree on the earliest possible date for the creation of the Sphinx, with West claiming a very early date of 10,500 BC or even before, and Schoch proposing a date between 7000 and 5000 BC. Needless to say, the established orthodox view is at odds with these findings, and other geologists have put forward data which refutes West and Schoch's findings.

British researcher Colin Reader also argues for a new chronology for the monument. Reader believes that the Sphinx could have been in place, along with the Sphinx Temple and the accompanying causeway of Khafre, before the pyramids appeared on the plateau at Giza.

Yet another theory on the origin of the Sphinx has been put forward by Dr Farouk El-Baz of Boston University, an expert on remote sensing – the use of methods such as satellite imaging and aerial photography to gather scientific data. He posits that the Sphinx was originally something known as a yardang. El-Baz explains that yardangs are wind-carved landforms that have been consistently eroded to form the shape of inverted boat hulls with their prows facing into the wind. He writes:

> As their aerodynamically shaped features are subjected to further erosion, the resulting landforms have sphinx-like shapes of reclining animals. The uppermost part of the Sphinx may have started as a wind-carved feature whose shape was completed by the Egyptian stone masons.

This theory was featured in the *Book of Proceedings* of the First International Symposium on the Great Sphinx, 1992, during which event he also showed many photographs to illustrate his thesis. However, this theory has been more or less discounted by the orthodox and the alternative camps alike, due to the evidence that seems to show that the body of the Sphinx was carved out of the surrounding bedrock by human hands.

The word 'sphinx' is of Greek origin and means 'strangler', a name which derives from the place of the sphinx in Greek mythology. To the Greeks, it was a murderous, riddling female monster. The Great Sphinx itself was known, certainly by the New Kingdom, as Horemakhet, which translates as 'Horus in the horizon'. A monumental work, the Sphinx measures 73.5 m in length and over 20 m in height, and stands to this day as the most immense piece of sculpture ever undertaken. As we have seen, much debate rages about the date when the Sphinx was carved, and even orthodox Egyptology is unsure of the king who was responsible for it.

For many years, Egyptologists viewed the so-called Dream Stela of Tuthmosis IV (a New Kingdom ruler) as conclusive evidence of the name of the king involved, that is, Khafre, a son of Khufu, the supposed builder of the Great Pyramid, and himself the assumed builder of the second pyramid at Giza. The Dream Stela recounts a story that sees the young Prince Tuthmosis out hunting for gazelle in the vicinity of Giza. As the midday sun reached its peak, the young prince fell asleep beneath the shadow of the Sphinx, which was already hundreds of years old and had become largely buried under the desert sands. The Sphinx appeared to Tuthmosis as he slept, proclaiming that if the prince removed the sand from around the body of the monument, he would become Pharaoh of Egypt. It seems that the prince carried out this request and, after ascending the throne as Tuthmosis IV, set up a great granite stela, the Dream Stela, between the forepaws of the Sphinx to commemorate the event. It is one line, no longer visible due to weathering, but previously copied and recorded, that Egyptologists have referred to when making the claim that Khafre built the Sphinx. On it, Tuthmosis asks the people of Egypt to praise 'Osiris of Rosetau, the goddess Bastet, and the gods and goddesses of the resting place or sanctuary of . . . khaef'. Egyptologists have interpreted 'khaef' as 'Khafre' and cite this as proof that he was responsible for the building of the Sphinx.

This evidence seems scant when one compares positively identified statues of the pharaoh Khafre with the face of the Great Sphinx. This problem is highlighted in the work of John Anthony West, who brought in Frank Domingo, former senior forensic artist with the New York City Police Department, to compare the two faces. Needless to say, they proved to be distinctly different.

Another piece of evidence for an earlier date for the construction of the Sphinx, or at least the carving of its head, is in the detail found on the nemes adorning the creature's head. This headdress bears no resemblance to 4th-Dynasty nemes headdresses but appears to more closely resemble those of the time of Djoser, a 3rd-Dynasty pharaoh.

American archaeologist Mark Lehner has carried out extensive work on the Sphinx, and in the Sphinx enclosure, and asserts that there is enough archaeological evidence to ascribe its construction to Khafre. In contrast, the French Egyptologist Vassil Dobrev claimed in 2004 that the image was actually the face of Khufu and that the Sphinx could be attributed to the little-known King Djedefre, a son of Khufu and brother of Khafre. He compared the face of the Sphinx to that on the small seated statue of Khufu in the Egyptian Museum in Cairo and found resemblances. He also noted that the angle of the causeway leading to Khafre's pyramid suggests that it was designed to go around the Sphinx, which he interprets as evidence that the Sphinx was built before Khafre's reign, by his older brother. However, in a twist to this theory, the Egyptologist and head of the Supreme Council of Antiquities Dr Zahi Hawass has written a paper in which he claims that the Khufu statuette dates from the 26th Dynasty (some 2,000 years after the reign of the pharaoh Khufu), which would negate its use by Dobrev as evidence for facial similarities. Such scant evidence survives from the time of the 4th Dynasty that a conclusive resolution to the identity crisis of the Sphinx would be unlikely even if the date of its contruction could be agreed upon.

SEE ALSO: Giza, Khufu

SYMBOLISM

Symbolism was the technique the Ancient Egyptians used to convey more information than the surface of a building, image or object otherwise could. The use of symbolism transcended the need for decoration and design, and created another reality beyond that which the eye could see. It was believed that everything depicted or made had its own potency and life force, as well as a symbolic meaning based upon a number of associations, such as mythology, antecedents, funerary beliefs, magic and status. Thus, symbols embodied many Ancient Egyptian ideas and beliefs concerning all aspects of life and death. Implicit in the use of symbols is the knowledge that individuals will read different things into the signs depending upon their knowledge, education and hence status.

Much Egyptian symbolism is ambiguous, with location and context vital to a full understanding of its meaning. Tomb scenes contain prime examples of this, with the funerary context adding to the potency and determining their interpretation. For example, fording scenes were very common in Old Kingdom tombs and appear to show the dangers faced by herdsmen and cattle as they cross the Nile. A particular worry was the threat from crocodiles, which could kill or wound men and their animals. These scenes often depict a man standing up in the boat pointing at a crocodile as he speaks a spell against the creature. However, whilst the scenes imitated everyday occurrences, they also metaphorically reflected Egyptian beliefs about the afterlife, symbolically portraying the deceased's journey through the underworld and the dangers to be met on that final voyage.

Throughout Egyptian history, crocodiles played a significant role in relation to fate and the individual. In later literature, the idea developed that crocodiles were created in order to act as an 'agent of pursuit and justice' (Westcar Papyrus). This concept had its genesis in the Old Kingdom period, when crocodiles were seen as instruments of retribution against tomb violators. To be eaten by a crocodile was to be devoured body and soul, so that a person died a second and permanent death, with no chance of reincarnating. With crocodiles associated with death and destruction, these scenes therefore depict the tomb owner's triumph over adversity, his successful journey and rebirth into everlasting life. To the Ancient Egyptians, the symbolic depiction in the tomb of the voyage into the afterlife influenced the reality of that journey and could help to protect the deceased.

A similar tomb scene, used by royalty, was the hunting of dangerous animals in the marshes and the spearing of fish by the King, whether depicted on the walls of the tomb or in sculpture. The Pharaoh might also be shown netting fish or fowl. Not just a means of showing the athleticism of the King or providing food for him in the afterlife, these depictions were connected to the concept of containment, be it of enemies or chaos. In fact, these seemingly tranquil scenes can be directly linked to the more violent temple scenes of the King killing the enemies of Egypt by smiting them over the head with a heavy implement. These scenes were very common and were symbolic of the Pharaoh's protection of Egypt and its people from chaos, and his power to defeat Egypt's enemies. The depiction of the scene perpetuated the act and guaranteed the King's eternal victory. The underlying symbolism of other tomb scenes or statues whereby the Pharaoh is spearing fish, firing a bow and arrow or pouring out water is to do with the word *seti*, which also means 'ejaculation' and so suggests rejuvenation and rebirth – an important concept for the deceased.

Symbolism enabled the Egyptians to convey a number of ideas at once, hieroglyphic signs often having several levels of meaning. Visual puns were frequently used in depictions, so that 'duck' (*sa*) could mean 'son', a young gazelle (*ina*) could represent the heir, and a mirror (*ankh*) could signify life. The ankh is a very important symbol and is often shown being held by royalty and gods, or used to represent water, the ankh sign emphasising its life-giving qualities.

Another way hieroglyphs were used was in rebuses, groups of symbols which together spelled out a word or name. The most famous example of this is the statue of Ramesses II as a child, which represents Ra with a sun disc worn on the king's head, '*mes*' with the depiction of the king as a child, and '*su*' with the plant shown at his left side, spelling Ramessu, his birth name. The use of hieroglyphs in the design of objects was also common. For example, bowls that were used to hold purified water were often shaped like an ankh, the sign of life, whilst a headrest could represent the *akhet* (horizon), equating the raising of the head and the desire to awaken with the sun rising at dawn to enjoy another day. Amulets utilising specific signs – ankh, *sa* (protection), *djed* (strength) and *ib* (heart), for example – called on the power of these symbols and all the mythology connected to them to protect the wearer.

The symbolism of amulets and objects depended upon context and similarity of shape. Cowrie shells, for example, are similar in shape to the vagina and hence symbolic of sexuality, but when strung together and worn about the hips, they were considered a protection to ensure fertility. An amulet representing a bunch of grapes was symbolic of life, as it had similarities to a heart because of its shape and the red colour of the juice. Many objects were symbolic on a number of levels. For example, a mirror was symbolic of the sun due to its ability to reflect sunlight, its shape and its brightness. To reinforce this, mirrors could be decorated with depictions of Hathor, shaped like lotus, a papyrus stem or a nubile girl. All these show a connection to Hathor and the solar cult, and hence to love, fertility and beauty.

It was not just the object itself that contained meaning; the material that it was made from also had a symbolic value. This usually stemmed from mythological associations or perceived magical properties. For example, gold was linked with the sun-god Ra, Hathor and Isis, as well as symbolising eternal life because it does not tarnish. Water was a symbol of purification, life, rebirth and fertility. Wax could symbolise both protection and destruction: because of its malleability and vulnerability, it was used in figurines that were meant to be ritually destroyed, usually by burial or burning; however, wax was also symbolic of *maat* (truth) and the sun-god Ra, underlining how one item can have two quite different meanings.

Colour, too, had specific associations, and, even linguistically, *iwen* meant 'colour', 'character' and 'disposition', in the same way we are 'in the pink', 'green with envy', 'feeling blue' or 'seeing red'. Red symbolised life and regeneration, as well as being symbolic of Seth, god of chaos, and hence representative of hostility, anger and death. Blue represented fertility and rebirth due to its link with the Nile; yellow was associated with the sun and so symbolic of eternity; green was the colour of plants and therefore symbolised fecundity, life, resurrection and healing. White was the symbol of ritual purity, whereas black evoked night, death and the underworld, although it could also represent fertility because of the extremely fertile black Nile silt.

Certain numbers were also considered significant. The most obvious examples are found in spells, with the rubric often stating that the spell is to be repeated four or seven times. The number four represents totality because of the four compass points, so that in magic the recitation of the spell four times ensured that the energy was sent throughout the world. Repetition itself had a magical, performative power, increasing the potency of a spell, but four-fold repetition further enhanced this effect. However, it was the number seven that was most important in magic. It was perceived as the healer of all ills and therefore equated with perfection. As the sum of three and four, it took on the qualities of both these numbers, with three representing plurality, as in the use of three strokes in hieroglyphs to represent 'many'. Gods were often grouped into trinities to show unity in plurality. It was also believed that the deceased took three forms – *ka*, *ba* and *akh*. So seven was an extremely powerful number. This is highlighted by the fact that Ra had seven souls; the tying of seven knots was a very powerful magical action, as were stamping on the ground seven times and turning to the north seven times. Its symbolic significance was further underpinned by the Ancient Egyptian concept, mentioned in the Coffin Texts, that the world was created by seven utterances. It was believed that the Seven Hathors visited every child on the seventh night after its birth in order to disclose its fate in life. The symbolic significance of the number seven is tied in with the Egyptian word for seven – *zefekh* – which is very similar to the word *sefekh*, which means 'to remove evil'. Although what it meant to them is obscure, the Fibonacci spiral must also have held a special significance for the Egyptians, bearing in mind its use in hieroglyphs to represent the number 100, as an element of the crown of Lower Egypt and as part of the design that makes up the Eye of Horus (representing $1/32$ in

213

the mathematical interpretation of the sign). The Fibonacci spiral, which appears frequently in nature, is one based on the Fibonacci series, a sequence of numbers in which each is the sum of the two preceding it (1+1=2+1=3+2=5+3=8+5=13+8=21 and so on).

As can be seen, just about everything had a symbolic value, including the location of a building, in the case of the orientation of some temples towards Heliopolis, the rising sun or the Nile, depending on the period or fashion. So too temple architecture sought to represent the universe and creation, and the desire to replicate and recreate perfection as experienced at *set tepi* – 'the first time', the time immediately following the Creation. Images on temple and tomb walls also deal in the symbolism of size, so that a pharaoh towers over everybody else, thereby indicating status. When such norms are broken, as in the case of the relative size of Nefertiti to Akhenaten, it becomes obvious that other concerns and concepts are meant to be revealed.

Gestures could also have a symbolic meaning, notably the reversal of a bow, which represented victory and dominance. However, whilst many gestures made by figures in amulets or on tomb scenes certainly convey an attitude (adoration, praise, protection), it is questionable whether these everyday actions have any more arcane meaning, as has sometimes been inferred.

The pyramids of Giza are probably the most famous symbolic objects, representing creation and the primordial mound out of which the Egyptians believed life began. It is thought by many modern researchers into Egypt (although not by Egyptologists) that the Great Pyramid held certain symbolic numerical values that were linked to astronomy, such as its base measurement, which equates to the time the earth takes to orbit the sun. Some say that the measurements of the Great Pyramid show that the Ancient Egyptians understood the principle of pi, although it has been pointed out that this ratio will naturally occur when a rotating drum is used for measurement.

Symbolism takes many forms and unfortunately, because we are so far removed from the original context, we are limited in our knowledge of Egyptian symbolism to what we can see. As the surviving evidence naturally concerns visual symbolism, there is little information regarding the part played by sound and smell, senses both evocative and provocative.

SEE ALSO: Giza, Pyramids

THOTH

Thoth was the Egyptian god of knowledge, wisdom, letters, writing and the recording of time. He was said to have invented writing and to be the teacher of man and the messenger of the gods, as well as a divine mediator. Thoth was the Greek name for this god. To the Egyptians, he was known as Tehuti, also spelled as Djehuty, Zehuti, Tetu and Techu amongst others.

In later times, Thoth was seen as a son of Ra, the sun-god, but he was originally a deity connected only with the moon. In early Egyptian mythology, the moon was one of the eyes of Horus. When Horus had his legendary battle with Seth and lost his eye, it was Thoth who restored it. The German scholar René Schwaller de Lubicz comments on this event: 'Later, Thoth, symbolised by the ibis, miraculously "filled" or "completed" the eye, bringing together its parts so that the eye reacquired its title "the whole eye", or "the healthy eye".' After this, over time, the moon came to be seen as a separate deity and not just one of the eyes of Horus. Thoth took on a more important role in Egyptian mythology, and although he was still considered to be connected with the moon, he became more closely associated with knowledge, wisdom, magic and writing.

Thoth was usually represented as a man with the head of an ibis, holding a wax writing tablet. He wore a crescent moon on his head because of his position as a lunar deity. It has been suggested that the curved beak of the ibis was symbolic of the crescent moon to the Ancient Egyptians and that this is why this particular creature was associated with Thoth.

Another animal connected to Thoth was the baboon. The Egyptians noted that these animals were nocturnal and thus allied with the moon in mythology. There are reliefs and statues of Thoth as a baboon, with and without a moon above his head. Because of this animal's association with Thoth, baboons were also shown in Egyptian art assisting scribes in their work.

In many Egyptian myths, Thoth's counsel is sought and he is shown as a resourceful mediator and peacemaker. It is probably for this very reason that Thoth was always present during the extremely important weighing-of-the-heart ceremony. It was his role to question the souls of the dead and then to record the answers on his wax tablet.

Tehuti, Thoth's name when spelt in hieroglyphics, translates as 'he who balances'. We can see the significance of this when we discover that Thoth was associated with Maat, whose name also means 'balance' and 'truth' in the context of certain funerary rituals. Maat was actually depicted with a feather protruding from her head, and sometimes simply as a feather, and it was against her that Thoth weighed the deceased's heart. Together, they brought balance and wisdom, justice and truth to the ceremony, and the two were intrinsically linked.

Although he was seen as a god, there are Ancient Egyptian sources which seem to be stating that Thoth once ruled Egypt as a king. In the Museo Egizio in Turin, Italy, there is a document known as the Turin King List, or Turin Canon, which dates to the rule of Ramesses II. It is a comprehensive list of the rulers of Egypt, and all the accepted kings of Egypt, however minor or short-lived, are noted. Even the Hyksos kings are listed, although they were not thought to merit royal cartouches in which the names of the other kings of Egypt are enclosed. The first King of Egypt was Menes; however, on the Turin King List there is a record of deities who were thought to have ruled Egypt before Menes. Barry J. Kemp, in his 1993 book *Ancient Eygpt: Anatomy of a Civilzation*, describes how the document appears to show that Thoth had once ruled Egypt for a very long period of time:

> Immediately before Menes came several lines which summarize the collective reigns of 'spirits', not given individual names, and before these, and heading the whole compilation, a list of deities. The name of each is written in a cartouche, as if a king, and followed by a

precise length of reign. In the case of the god Thoth, for
example, this is 7,726 years.

Thoth's importance grew as Ancient Egypt reached its late period.
The main centre of the cult of Thoth was at Hermopolis, where
thousands of mummified ibis have been found buried in his
honour. Hermopolis became the capital of Egypt, and as the city
grew to prominence, so did Thoth. During this period of Egyptian
history, Thoth was so revered that he was even believed to have
given birth to Ra, laying an ibis egg from which the sun-god
hatched. This can be seen as a variant of the Heliopolitan creation
myth, one in which the ibis egg laid by Thoth takes the place of
the primeval mound.

The Greeks identified Thoth with Hermes, and the two were
eventually combined (probably during the period when the
Ptolemaic kings ruled Egypt) to become Hermes Trismegistus. It is
said that much of the knowledge and wisdom of Thoth passed into
the writings attributed to Hermes Trismegistus, a body of work
that is today termed hermetic literature. Works said to have been
written by Hermes Trismegistus include the *Corpus Hermiticum*, a
very important body of knowledge that was influential in the birth
of the hermetic tradition, which flourished during the Middle
Ages and the Renaissance and covered such esoteric subjects as
alchemy, magic, philosophy and astrology – all of which we can
trace back to Thoth.

According to Egyptian mythology, Thoth himself possessed a
book, written by his own hand and called simply the Book of
Thoth, that contained all the knowledge that he had acquired.
The famous occultist Aleister Crowley drew on this legend when
he created his own version of the tarot deck, the Thoth Tarot. The
volume he wrote to accompany and explain the deck was even
called *The Book of Thoth*.

Finally, Schwaller de Lubicz probably did as good a job as
anyone in summing up the mystical, esoteric aspects of Thoth.
In his seminal book *The Temple of Man*, he discusses what Thoth
encompassed and what he didn't:

> Some of the titles given to Thoth, chosen from among his
> numerous names, make it easier to understand the power
> of this *neter* [aspect of God]: 'thrice great', and also 'twice
> great'; 'master of truth' (justice, balance); 'power that

casts the deciding vote'; 'judge of the two combatants'; '*neter* of the *neter-medu*' (sacred writing); 'scribe of the Ennead of the *neters*'; 'Thoth-moon'; 'master of the Eight'; 'master of the city of Eight, in Hesert, at the heart of the temple of the net'.

Thoth is 'master of . . .'; he is not the thing itself. He is not that which 'comes and goes', but that which 'causes to come and then go back to its source'. He is the creator of the cycles of that which renders apparent, but he is not writing, Seshat. Thoth is that which creates alternation, but he is not the weaving, Neith, who makes things tangible; Thoth can nevertheless become visible and perceptible – Thoth-mes – which is to say that he can be revealed: Her-mes, the secret.

SEE ALSO: Ennead, Horus, Ra

TUTANKHAMUN

Although only a relatively insignificant pharaoh in his time, Tutankhamun is probably the most well-known king of Ancient Egypt, thanks to the discovery in 1922 of his intact tomb in the Valley of the Kings, near modern Luxor. Since this discovery, a great deal of interest and intrigue has surrounded Tutankhamun, focusing on the fabulous wealth of the tomb, the Tutankhamun 'curse' and the reason for the early death of the king.

Tutankhamun belonged to the long line of 18th-Dynasty pharaohs and ruled Egypt for approximately nine years around 1355–1346 BC, although estimated dates for his reign vary considerably. He was born during the reign of the 'heretic king' Akhenaten and was at that time known as Tutankhaten – 'Living Image of the Aten'. No doubt born and certainly raised at Amarna, the new capital of Egypt after Akhenaten moved his court there, Tutankhamun grew up in this time of upheaval and uncertainty, surrounded by all the trappings of Aten worship.

After the demise of Akhenaten, Egypt was ruled for three years by the enigmatic Neferneferuaten Ankhkheperure, followed by the short-lived Smenkhkare. On Smenkhkare's death, Tutankhamun became Pharaoh. Aged only nine, he seems a rather lonely figure, without grandparents or parents to guide him, instead at the mercy of aged officials. He was, however, married to Ankhesenpaaten, a daughter of Akhenaten and Nefertiti, and although she herself was barely an adult, being only three years older than Tutankhamun, it would appear from

219

the various depictions of the couple that their relationship grew into a loving and supportive one.

Unusually, there is no hard evidence as to the identity of Tutankhamun's parents. We have no depictions of his childhood, although we do know that he was a member of the royal household. This is confirmed by the many blue ceramic royal rings found in the palace rubbish heaps bearing his Tutankhaten name, along with other rings bearing the names of Akhenaten, Nefertiti and the royal daughters. An inscription states that he was a 'king's son, of his body, his beloved Tutankhaten' but we do not know to which king this refers. A number of candidates have been put forward, notably Amenhotep III and his Great Wife Tiye, parents of Akhenaten. Indeed, on a colonnade at the Luxor temple, Tutankhamun calls Amenhotep III his 'father', but this was a very loose term and often carried the sense of ancestor. Bearing in mind the seventeen-year reign of Akhenaten and the three-plus years of Neferneferuaten Ankhkheperure and Smenkhkare, the possibility that Amenhotep III fathered Tutankhamun from beyond the grave is remote, unless Tutankhamun was older at his death than the 19 years usually attributed to him.

Queen Tiye does, however, appear to have a special affinity with Tutankhamun. Within his tomb is buried a small box containing a plait of hair – the 'sidelock of youth' cut off when a child reaches maturity. The box was inscribed with Tiye's name and placed within another box containing a small gold statuette of the king. This box carried the name of Tutankhamun, thus linking the two individuals. Whether grandmother and grandson or mother and son cannot be determined, but this cherished keepsake suggests a strong bond between the two.

Other candidates for the parentage of Tutankhamun are Akhenaten and Kiya, his secondary wife. If they were his parents, it would account for why Tutankhamun was not depicted within the Akhenaten/Nefertiti family group, even supposing that Akhenaten was his father. If Akhenaten and Kiya were his parents, though, why was neither of them mentioned in Tutankhamun's tomb and why is there no personal memento from them? It is known that Akhenaten had sisters, and it has even been suggested that he fathered Tutankhamun by one of these. Again, no evidence has been found to support this, and the lack of any mention of maternal connections is puzzling, unless his mother died in childbirth and he never knew her. In the two small burial chambers in the royal tomb at Amarna, there are depictions of the deaths of two women, each mourned by Akhenaten and Nefertiti. One is stated to be their daughter Meketaten, but the other has lost the vital information that would confirm who the woman was. However, a babe in arms is being carried by a nursemaid and it is fascinating to wonder if this is a depiction of Tutankhaten/amun.

By the time Tutankhamun became King, the popularity of the Aten cult was waning, no doubt due to the death of its main instigator three to four years previously. In order to distance himself from the old Aten cult, and at the same time appease the once powerful Amun cult, he changed his name from Tutankhaten to Tutankhamun, while his wife changed hers to Ankhesenamun. Undoubtedly on the advice of his officials, he moved his court to Memphis in the north of Egypt, thus cutting all ties to his recent past. A couple of years into his reign, Tutankhamun issued a proclamation which is documented on the Restoration Stela he set up in the temple to Amun at Thebes. In this, he expresses his grief at how the gods and goddesses of Egypt had been neglected, a situation that had left the land 'in confusion'. He states, however, that he is to restore the god Amun to his rightful place and that offerings can once more be made in the temples in order to restore the land to 'a state of jubilation'.

At some point in his ninth year as King, Tutankhamun unexpectedly died. The state of his tomb (now designated KV62) highlights his sudden death. It is apparent that the tomb was not meant for a king, being a small private tomb obviously appropriated from somebody else and prepared in haste. The tomb was so small that the funerary items were literally packed into the four chambers, covering the rooms from top to bottom. Due to lack of time, only the burial chamber was painted, and many of the objects found within had originally been made for other members of the royal family. For example, of the ten main burial items, five had been meant for someone else, including the second coffin, which has the same facial features as the Canopic jars that bear the name of Smenkhkare, and mummy bands originally inscribed for Neferneferuaten. Other items bear the names of Akhenaten, Nefertiti and Tiye, and it is thought that, because the king had not had enough time to piece together sufficient funerary equipment, items had to be 'borrowed' from the tombs of his relatives. There were a number of personal items, however, such as his chariot, weaponry and golden shrine, but most poignant of all were the mummified remains of his two stillborn daughters, the larger of whom was suffering from spina bifida.

But how did Tutankhamun die? Was it due to natural causes or something more menacing? Various sources have suggested that Tutankhamun's death was the result of lung disease, a brain tumour, a hunting accident or poison. Estimates of Tutankhamun's age at death range from 16 to 25 years, but in 1969 Tutankhamun's mummy was X-rayed by a team from the University of Liverpool and it was reckoned that he was 19 years old when he died. On examination of the king's skull, the team noticed a detached bone fragment suggesting that a blow to the back of the head was the cause of Tutankhamun's death. However, it is now believed that the bone fragment resulted from damage caused at the time of embalming or from rough handling by Douglas Derry and Howard Carter, who, during the initial examination of the mummy, literally chiselled out Tutankhamun's head from the back of the burial mask. The re-examination of the 1969 X-rays by the Egyptologist Bob Brier called attention to a blood clot at the base of the skull over which a calcified membrane had formed. Such a trauma would have caused the young king a lingering end, falling in and out of consciousness and finally slipping into a coma over a period of two months before the arrival of death. Brier suggested that this kind of trauma is not usually received accidentally, pointing to intentional killing of the king.

With murder a possibility for the death of Tutankhamun, who are the candidates for such a deed? The chief suspect in any crime is invariably the one who has the most to gain by a person's death, and in this case that person is Ay, successor to Tutankhamun. Although he has been put forward as a possible brother of Queen Tiye, his family origins are unspecified. Indeed, in order to uphold his claim to the throne of Egypt, Ay had to marry Ankhesenamun, the only surviving heiress to the royal house. A letter from the Hittite archives from a widowed queen of Egypt pleads for the king, Suppiluliuma, to send her a son to marry, because 'never shall I pick out a servant of mine and make him my husband . . . I am afraid'. Another letter from this woman – tentatively identified as Ankhesenamun – asks: 'give me one of your sons . . . to me he will be a husband, but in Egypt he will be king.' Eventually, Suppiluliuma sent Prince Zannanza, but, despite an Egyptian escort, he was murdered before he could reach the widowed queen. Once again, the finger points to Ay – perhaps unjustly. Another candidate put forward for Tutankhamun's murder is Ankhesenamun herself, but what she would gain from this is uncertain.

Whatever the circumstances surrounding Tutankhamun's death, his tomb and the treasures contained within have ensured the survival of his name, and hence his *akh*-spirit, for eternity – a concept he surely would have delighted in. Tutankhamun rests still within his tomb in the Valley of the Kings; he is the only pharaoh who has been discovered and examined still to lie in his original burial place.

SEE ALSO: Akhenaten; Carter, Howard; Nefertiti

USHABTIS

While for the majority of Ancient Egyptians an elaborate funeral and tomb were luxuries only to be dreamed of, they believed that the goal of happy immortality was achievable by those with sufficient wealth and power. The whole burial ceremony, preparation of the tomb and mummification of the body were accompanied at all stages by magic rituals. Sacred and meaningful prayers and spells were said, necessary objects were placed correctly, everything calculated to revivify the dead person so that they might live in eternity in a paradise which, they imagined, would be very much like their own beautiful homeland.

Among all the magic artefacts produced by the Ancient Egyptians, none today inspire a shiver of excitement greater than the *ushabti*. These figures, also known as *shawabti* in the Theban area, or *shabti*, represent the deceased, usually in mummified form, carrying agricultural implements. They were usually found inside tombs and are a tangible point of contact with the long dead.

Those Egyptians fortunate enough to be able to plan for their life beyond death tried to ensure that they would be as comfortable in the next world as they were in this one. Loving their pleasant, narrow stretch of agricultural land bordering the River Nile, these people envisaged that, once they had made it through the barriers and perils of the journey which all must follow at death, they would emerge into a wonderful land much like that which they had known in their earthly lives. But there was a problem. Who was to do the work in the fields of this paradise? The god of the afterlife, Osiris, would demand service, just as Pharaoh did in his kingdom. Chapter Six of the Book of the Dead provided the answer.

The Shabti Formula is a piece of magic designed to spare a tomb owner from the backbreaking, sweaty, wearisome toil to which he or she might be called. 'If any one of you [ushabtis] is called on to carry out a task in the other world, you will reply, "Here I am. I will do it."' A more elaborate version specifies that when essential ploughing of the fields, irrigation or carrying of sand was ordered, the ushabti should jump to it and perform the task, while, presumably, the deceased would lie back in the shade in a leisurely fashion.

The ushabtis, or 'answerers', would then go out and work in their owner's place. They sometimes carried a hoe or mattock and a basket or sack. Over the shoulder, a pouch for seeds might be carried. Often packed in boxes of hundreds, one for each day of the year, with overseers who sometimes carry whips to supervise them, these workers would supernaturally come to life and perform their tasks. They became particularly popular in the New Kingdom period and were still being manufactured in Greek and Roman times. During the New Kingdom, the ushabtis were not depicted as mummies but were shown in everyday dress.

Ideally, the figures were inscribed with the names of their owners as well as the magic words from the Book of the Dead, and they sometimes even had their own individual miniature coffin to rest in, just like the dead person. In size, they varied from just a few centimetres long to over 30 centimetres or more. Some are beautifully detailed and of great artistic merit, while many are mass-produced lumps of pottery bearing little resemblance to human figures, even mummified ones. They were of particularly poor quality in the 17th Dynasty and some examples dating from this period are little more than old-fashioned clothes-pegs in shape. Yet, from the 26th Dynasty to the Ptolemaic Period, some very fine examples were produced. Materials used for the manufacture of ushabti figures included faience, stone, wood, bronze, glass and wax (for the very earliest). Faience consists of quantities of fine quartz, with the addition of a little lime and natron salt or plant ash, mixed with water. Shaped, often in a mould, it could then, when partially dry, be given a coat of alkaline glaze, which bonds with the inner core when fired. When well done, it can give a beautiful effect, occasionally polychrome, but more normally blue and green, matching the lapis lazuli and turquoise colours so beloved by the Egyptians, who used the word *tjehenet*, meaning 'shining' or 'brilliant', for it.

During the Old Kingdom period, it had been usual for models

to be placed in the tombs of rich nobles. These were often of wooden manufacture and represented male and female servants, brewing, baking and performing those many household tasks which had been performed for their masters and mistresses during their lifetimes. Generally, these seem to have revolved around the essential, but pleasurable, activities of eating and drinking. The burial rituals would have activated these figures in eternity and ensured that, even should the depictions of food offerings which often decorated a tomb be obliterated and those real offerings which for a generation or two the deceased's family might provide fail to arrive, the soul would still be provided for. Put in the context of placing flowers on a memorial or grave in our modern world, the rationale behind the practice is readily understandable.

In Predynastic and early Dynastic times, it appears that great lords and kings had their servants killed at the time of their own deaths to perform their duties in eternity. More humane practices began to prevail, and the use of ritual magic and models superseded the human sacrifice, though the need for servants still remained. The ever-resourceful Egyptians created ushabtis to at least partly fulfil that need. Model stone statuettes of workers in many professions first began to appear in tombs during the Middle Kingdom, around 2000 BC, though not in particularly large numbers.

It has been said, perhaps rather pedantically, that the term 'ushabti' should only be used for those figures which are inscribed with the instruction to go and do the labour. Those which are merely labelled with the titles and name of their owner are technically not being commanded to answer, therefore they are not 'answerers' or ushabti. It might be argued, though, that models placed in a tomb which are specifically labelled as belonging to the tomb owner are there to serve the deceased in some way, and consequently they do indeed answer.

At most of the ancient sites in Egypt that are open to tourists, it is difficult to escape being offered souvenirs for a 'very good price'. Most are of indifferent quality. But it is not really necessary to visit Luxor or the Khan el-Khalili bazaar in Cairo to pick up a passable modern imitation of an ushabti. Over the Internet, ersatz conversation pieces that look almost as good as the real thing are readily available. Those who fancy taking out insurance guaranteeing that they will never need to labour after they have passed on might do worse than take an answerer with them to the grave.

SEE ALSO: Cannibalism and Human Sacrifice

VALLEY OF THE KINGS

The bustling valley that is visited by countless tourists today as 'the Valley of the Kings' takes its name from the Arabic description of the site, Wadi Biban el-Muluk, which actually translates as 'The Valley of the Gates of the Kings'. It forms part of the Theban necropolis, and the majority of pharaohs from the 18th to the 20th Dynasty were buried in the East Valley of the Kings. There is another valley, the West Valley, which contains only a few royal burials, and the Valley of the Queens, which holds the tombs of around 80 wives and children of the royal family. The most beautiful example of the tombs in the Queens' Valley is that of Nefertari (QV66), the Great Royal Wife of Ramesses II. On the walls of the chambers, the queen is represented in exquisite detail, and she is shown passing into the underworld. Extensive conservation and restoration of these wall paintings has been undertaken to try to preserve this treasure for future generations.

The tombs in the valleys are numbered according to a system devised by John Gardner Wilkinson in 1827. Each has a number preceded by the designation KV for those in the eastern Valley of the Kings, WV for those in the West Valley, or QV for those in the Valley of the Queens.

Several of the tombs in the Valley of the Kings, for example those of Ramesses IX (KV6) and Merenptah (KV8), have been open since antiquity, and visitors have left graffiti since Greek and Roman times. One, however, has only very recently been discovered. On 10 February 2006, Dr Zahi Hawass, the Secretary General of the Supreme Council of Antiquities, officially designated a new discovery in the valley KV63. The small, single-chambered tomb was discovered by the team from the University of Memphis, led by Dr Otto Schaden, who have been working on KV10 since 1992. An initial examination of the tomb has revealed seven wooden coffins and a number of storage jars, which are being conserved and will then be studied in order to try to identify the burials. The entrance to the tomb is around 14 m from that of Tutankhamun (KV62), and the excavators have estimated that the tomb dates from around the same time, that is, the late 18th Dynasty.

TOMBS AND THEIR OWNERS IN THE VALLEY OF THE KINGS

Tomb	Built for	Location of Body	Excavated by
KV1	Ramesses VII		Edwin Brock, 1983
KV2	Ramesses IV	Tomb of Amenhotep II	Edward Russell Ayrton, 1905; Howard Carter 1920
KV3	Unknown son of Ramesses III		Harry Burton, 1912
KV4	Ramesses XI		John Romer, 1978–80
KV5	Sons of Ramesses II		James Burton, 1825; Howard Carter, 1902; Kent Weeks, from 1987
KV6	Ramesses IX	Deir el-Bahri cache	Georges Daressy, 1888
KV7	Ramesses II	Deir el-Bahri cache	Harry Burton, 1913; Christian Leblanc, from 1995
KV8	Merenptah	Tomb of Amenhotep II	Howard Carter, 1903; Edwin Brock, 1987
KV9	Ramesses V and VI	Both in the tomb of Amenhotep II	James Burton, 1820s; Georges Daressy, 1888
KV10	Amenmesse		Edward Russell Ayrton, 1907; Otto Schaden, from 1992
KV11	Sethnakhte; appropriated by Ramesses III	Ramesses III in Deir el-Bahri cache	Jacques de Morgan, 1895; Howard Carter, 1901
KV13	Chancellor Bay		Hartwig Altenmüller, 1987–94

KV14	Twosret; appropriated by Sethnakhte	Two of the bodies in the tomb of Amenhotep II have been tentatively identified as Sethnakhte and Twosret	Hartwig Altenmüller, 1983–7
KV15	Seti II	Tomb of Amenhotep II	Howard Carter, 1902–4
KV16	Ramesses I	Deir el-Bahri cache	Giovanni Belzoni, 1817
KV17	Seti I	Deir el-Bahri cache	Giovanni Belzoni, 1817
KV18	Ramesses X		John Romer, 1978–80
KV19	Montuherkhepeshef (son of Ramesses IX)		Giovanni Belzoni, 1817; Edward Russell Ayrton, 1905
KV20	Tuthmosis I and Hatshepsut		James Burton, 1824; Howard Carter, 1903–4
WV22	Amenhotep III	Tomb of Amenhotep II	Howard Carter, 1915
WV23	Ay		Giovanni Belzoni 1816; Otto Schaden, 1972
KV34	Tuthmosis III	Deir el-Bahri cache	Victor Loret, 1898
KV35	Amenhotep II	His own tomb	Victor Loret, 1898
KV36	Maiherpri (official of Hatshepsut)	His own tomb	Victor Loret, 1899
KV38	Tuthmosis I		Victor Loret, 1899
KV39	Uncertain. Possibly Amenhotep I	Amenhotep I in Deir el-Bahri cache	Victor Loret, 1899; John Rose, 1989–92
KV42	Hatshepsut-Merytre (wife of Tuthmosis III) or Tuthmosis II	Tuthmosis II in Deir el-Bahri cache	Victor Loret, 1898; Howard Carter, 1900
KV43	Tuthmosis IV	Tomb of Amenhotep II	Howard Carter, 1903
KV45	Userhat (official)		Howard Carter, 1902; Donald P. Ryan, 1991
KV46	Yuya and Thuya (parents of Queen Tiye)	Their own tomb	James E. Quibell, 1905
KV47	Siptah	Tomb of Amenhotep II	Edward Russell Ayrton, 1905; Harry Burton, 1912
KV48	Amenemopet (vizier of Amenhotep II)		Edward Russell Ayrton, 1905

KV55	Uncertain. Possibly Smenkhare or Akhenaten	A body was found in the tomb but its identity could not be confirmed	Edward Russell Ayrton, 1907
KV56	Unknown; designated 'the Golden Tomb'		Edward Russell Ayrton, 1908
KV57	Horemheb		Edward Russell Ayrton, 1908
KV62	Tutankhamun	His own tomb	Howard Carter, 1922–32
KV63	Under investigation		Otto Schaden, from 2006

Note: The tomb numbers missing from the table are those for which no conclusive details have been obtained.

An examination of the column in the table above showing the locations of burials discovered in the Valley of the Kings shows that many of the bodies have been found in so-called caches. One example of this is the Deir el-Bahri cache (designated DB320), discovered by the authorities in 1881. At some stage prior to this, a local family called Abd el-Rassul had discovered a tomb filled with coffins, ushabtis and funeral papyri. Artefacts began to appear on the antiquities market and eventually the rumours of a great discovery reached the Egyptian Antiquities Service. The local governor questioned two of the Abd el-Rassul brothers and torture was used to try to uncover the location of the tomb. Despite their treatment, the two men refused to reveal where their treasure was coming from; but their elder brother, Mohammed Abd el-Rassul, intervened and confessed that the family had been plundering a tomb at Deir el-Bahri.

It is possible to visit this remote tomb, in the cliffs overlooking the temple of Deir el-Bahri, but it requires a head for heights and an expert guide. From the paths below, there is nothing to suggest that a tomb is located high among the jagged cliffs, and the fact that it was discovered at all seems incredible. When the deputy head of the Antiquities Service, Emile Brugsch, visited the tomb, he was amazed at the number of mummies it contained. In the May 1887 edition of *Century Illustrated Monthly Magazine*, he wrote:

> Collecting my senses, I made the best examination of them
> I could by the light of my torch, and at once saw that they
> contained the mummies of royal personages of both sexes;

and yet that was not all. Plunging on ahead of my guide, I came to the [end] chamber . . . and there standing against the walls or here lying on the floor, I found even a greater number of mummy-cases of stupendous size and weight.

To prevent any further theft or damage to the burials, there was a very hurried clearance of the tomb and the bodies were placed on a boat and transported to Cairo. It is said that as the coffins were carried to the boat, and as they made their way up the Nile to Cairo, villagers came to the banks of the river wailing and paying their respects to the long-dead pharaohs. Once the bodies reached the Egyptian Museum at Bulaq (the predecessor to the current Cairo Museum), Gaston Maspero, the head of the Antiquities Service, was able to examine them. A complicated picture began to emerge from inscriptions on the mummies and papyrus dockets that accompanied them, suggesting that as the royal tombs were plundered, the bodies had been recovered and grouped together for safety. Several locations were used as intermediate resting places for the mummies, including the tombs of Seti I and of Queen Inhapi. DB320, the eventual resting place, was the tomb of a high priest of Amun, Pinudjem II of the 22nd Dynasty.

When Victor Loret excavated the tomb of Amenhotep II in 1898, another cache of royal bodies was found. Several of these have been identified, including Amenhotep II, Amenhotep III and Merenptah. Some of the mummies in the tomb, however, were discovered largely unwrapped and their identities are the subject of much speculation. In particular, two female bodies designated 'Elder Lady' and 'Younger Woman' have attracted suggestions that they may be from the family of Akhenaten. Theories have been put forward that the Elder Lady is Amenhotep III's wife Tiye or Ankhesenamun, the wife of Tutankhamun. Dr Joann Fletcher has recently identified the Younger Woman as Nefertiti, based on the positioning of the arms of the mummy, the double-pierced ears and the shaved head. Until a detailed DNA database is created from the royal bodies whose identity is more certain, there will remain controversy over many of these mummies.

Despite the discovery of the Deir el-Bahri cache, and the extra burials in the tomb of Amenhotep II, there are still a number of important pharaohs 'missing'. As the recent discovery of KV63 shows, the Valley of the Kings has not yet given up all its secrets – is there another cache waiting to be discovered?

The largest tomb in the Valley of the Kings has so far yielded over 120 rooms and is the massive burial complex for the sons of Ramesses II. When it was originally excavated, by James Burton in 1825, and again by Howard Carter in 1902, only the first few rooms were accessible, so the scale of the structure was not appreciated. Even when the current team, led by Kent Weeks, began to work in the tomb, they were confined to the outer chambers. Once these were cleared, long corridors became accessible which led to further rooms and pillared halls running further into the mountainside.

Despite being one of the smaller and less visually impressive burial places in the Valley of the Kings, the tomb of Tutankhamun is usually the one with the most visitors queuing up outside it. The story of Howard Carter's discovery of the tomb, the wonderful array of treasures that emerged from these few small rooms, and the opportunity of looking at the gilded face of the pharaoh himself, add to the allure of this tomb. It seems that originally Tutankhamun had planned his final resting place to be sited in the Western Valley, now known as WV23. Perhaps because at the time of his early death this tomb was unfinished, alternative arrangements were hastily made, and KV62 was used instead. Work continued on WV23, and Tutankhamun's successor, Ay, was eventually buried there.

Above the Valley of the Kings looms a distinctive pyramid-shaped mountain, which may have acted as a physical reminder of earlier traditions of pyramid-building. The peak was regarded as the personification of a snake goddess of the Theban area called Meretseger, which meant, appropriately, 'she who loves silence'. Whereas in the mortuary temple and pyramid complexes of the Old and Middle Kingdom the burial place and the temple dedicated to the deceased were close together, the mortuary temples of the pharaohs buried in the Valley of the Kings were situated on the cultivated strip of land by the west bank of the Nile. Today they are in varying states of repair. At Medinet Habu, the temple dedicated to Ramesses III is still largely intact, but the much larger temple built for Amenhotep III has virtually disappeared, leaving only two large statues, now known as the Colossi of Memnon. The tombs themselves, in the dusty valleys, consist of corridors that descend into the hillsides, excavated in the hope of creating a resting place where their occupants would not be disturbed. As we have seen, this was almost always a forlorn hope; most of the royal bodies are now in the Egyptian Museum in Cairo. Almost uniquely, Tutankhamun enjoys his own tomb – albeit in the daily company of tourists.

In 1979, UNESCO designated the Valley of the Kings, along with the Valley of the Queens, part of the World Heritage Site of Thebes. Work is currently being done to try to minimise the impact visitors have on the valley, in order to preserve the delicate wall paintings for future generations to enjoy.

SEE ALSO: Carter, Howard; Carnarvon, Lord; Mummies; Nefertiti; Tutankhamun

WADJET EYE

The *wadjet* eye is another name for the Eye of Ra, which evolved to become the Eye of Horus. It was a powerful symbol of protection, and people and objects which bore the emblem were shielded from harm by Ra or Horus. The Eye of Horus was used as an amulet, and pharaohs had this emblem interred with them when they were mummified and entombed. For example, an Eye of Horus amulet was found deep inside Tutankhamun's wrappings, just below the 12th layer of bandages. Often, this amulet was placed over the exact spot where an incision had been made in the dead king's body during embalming, and in such a position the Eye of Horus protected and symbolically healed the damaged area.

Early in the development of Egyptian theology, before Horus was incorporated into the Osirian myth, he was a powerful god in his own right and was known as a god of the sky. In those times, his eyes were thought of as the sun and the moon. Over time, Horus's association with the sun came to the fore; he was transformed into a sun-god and even came to be thought of as Ra, in his form as Ra-Herakhty. This translated literally as 'Ra who is Horus of the two horizons'.

Later still, after the Osirian myth had spread right across Egypt and Horus took his place in the pantheon as the son of Osiris, this earlier understanding of Horus – and especially the link between his eyes and the sun and moon – was not lost; rather, it was woven into the legend.

The term 'the Eye of Horus' traditionally refers to his right eye. This was the eye that was not damaged in his battle with his uncle Seth. It was Horus's left eye that was lost in that legendary clash. This eye was said to have been restored to Horus by Thoth, and consequently the left eye of Horus became known as the Eye of Thoth and represented the moon.

The two eyes of Horus were seen as together symbolising the whole universe, much in the same manner as the yin-and-yang symbol does to cultures of the East. The right eye of Horus represented the sun, as well as masculine energies, and also symbolised mathematics and logic. The left eye, the Eye of Thoth, was seen as an emblem of the moon and represented the feminine, as well as symbolising creativity and magic.

This is very interesting, as we have all heard of 'right-brained' and 'left-brained' people. However, the attribution of concepts to the two eyes of Egyptian mythology seems to be a reversal of our modern understanding of what the left and right brains, or hemispheres of the brain, are responsible for. It becomes a little clearer when we realise that the right hemisphere of the brain actually controls the left eye: in other words, what is seen by the left eye is transmitted to the right hemisphere of the brain. This then means that the right eye, the Eye of Horus associated with reason and logic, is connected to the left hemisphere of the brain, the side of our brain that is linked with these qualities. The Egyptians, quite remarkably, seem to have been fully aware of this concept.

Another fascinating aspect of the Eye of Horus is that it also represented a mathematical formula, a way of expressing fractions of a whole. It was said that Seth broke Horus's eye into six parts, and each of those six components of the Eye of Horus – the pupil, eyebrow and so on – represented a fraction. These were said to comprise one *hekat* (a hekat being a unit of measurement of volume) when all put together. The fractions were $\frac{1}{2}$, $\frac{1}{4}$, $\frac{1}{8}$, $\frac{1}{16}$, $\frac{1}{32}$ and $\frac{1}{64}$.

When we add these up, we find that they do not actually equal one hekat; instead they comprise $\frac{63}{64}$. This is what is referred to as the 'missing $\frac{1}{64}$'. Scholars have pointed out that, within the Ancient Egyptian frame of reference, nothing except the Absolute – as exemplified by Osiris, who was thought of as representing perfection itself – could equal 'one'. This concept may have been incorporated into the Great Pyramid of Giza, said to have been left unfinished in deference to this idea.

The connection between the sun and the Eye of Horus can be seen in the figure which represents it. It has been suggested that the Eye of Horus bears a strong resemblance to the sun at the time of a full solar eclipse. This phenomenon was not unknown in ancient times. It could even be suggested that the Egyptians believed that, during an eclipse the sun, Ra himself had been covered over by the appearance of such an eye in the sky. It is possible, then, that the Egyptians, fascinated by this rare – and surely sacred – event, incorporated this magical moment into the symbol of the Eye of Ra, later to become the Eye of Horus.

The Eye of Horus appears many times in the Pyramid Texts, and other funerary texts, and seems to play a very important role in the spells and procedures carried out around the dead king during his interment. The rituals and spells are extremely complex and hard to fathom over a distance of 5,000 years; however, the importance of the Eye of Horus is unmistakable. Here are two phrases taken from the texts:

> O Horus who is this Osiris the King, take the uninjured Eye of Horus. O Horus who is this Osiris the King, I paint it on your face for you, for Horus painted his uninjured eye. O King, I attach your eyes to your face for you intact, so that you may see with them.
>
> Pyramid Texts, Utterance 80

> The Eye of Horus has made me holy. . . I will hide myself among you, O you stars which are imperishable. My brow is the brow of Ra.
>
> The Papyrus of Ani, 'The Chapter of Not Dying a Second Time in Khert-Neter'

In more recent times, Freemasons have embraced the emblem and used the symbolism of the wadjet eye to create their own 'Eye of Providence', the all-seeing eye. In this variation, the eye is surrounded by rays of sunshine and is often inside a triangle. The eye in this form is most famously found on the United States dollar bill, where it floats above an unfinished pyramid.

SEE ALSO: Horus, Mummies, Ra, Symbolism, Thoth

APPENDIX - TIMELINE

There is much debate about the chronology of Ancient Egypt, and many different versions have been proposed. For the purposes of this book, we have taken as a guide one of the more orthodox dating sequences, detailed here.

Predynastic Period 5500–3050 BC

Early Dynastic Period 3050–2687 BC
1st Dynasty 3050–2850 BC
   includes: Djer
2nd Dynasty 2850–2687 BC
   includes: Khasekhemwy

Old Kingdom 2687–2191 BC
3rd Dynasty 2687–2649 BC
   includes: Djoser 2687–2668 BC
4th Dynasty 2649–2513 BC
   Sneferu 2649–2609 BC
   Khufu 2609–2584 BC
   Djedefre 2584–2576 BC
   Khafre 2576–2551 BC
   Menkaure 2551–2523 BC
5th Dynasty 2513–2374 BC
6th Dynasty 2374–2191 BC

First Intermediate Period 2191–2061 BC
7th to early 11th dynasties

Middle Kingdom 2061–1786 BC
late 11th Dynasty 2061 – 1991 BC
12th Dynasty 1991–1786 BC
   includes: Amenemhet III 1843–1797 BC
   Sobeknefru 1790–1786 BC

Second Intermediate Period 1786 – 1569 BC
13th and 14th dynasties 1786–1664 BC
15th Dynasty 1664–1555 BC
16th Dynasty 1664–1555 BC*
   Hyksos
17th Dynasty 1664–1569 BC

New Kingdom 1569–1081 BC
18th Dynasty 1569–1315 BC
   includes: Tuthmosis III 1504–1452 BC
   Hatshepsut 1502–1482 BC
   Amenhotep III 1410–1372 BC
   Akhenaten 1372–1355 BC
   Smenkhkare 1355 BC
   Tutankhamun 1355–1346 BC
   Ay 1346–1343 BC
   Horemheb 1343–1315 BC
19th Dynasty 1315–1201 BC
   includes: Seti I 1314–1304 BC
   Ramesses II 1304–1237 BC
   Merenptah 1237–1226 BC
   Twosret 1209–1201 BC
20th Dynasty 1200–1081 BC

Third Intermediate Period 1081–724 BC
21st to 23rd dynasties

Late Period 724–333 BC
24th to 31st dynasties

Graeco-Roman Period 332 BC–AD 337
Macedonian Dynasty 332–305 BC
   includes: Alexander the Great 332–323 BC
Ptolemaic Dynasty 305–31 BC
   includes: Cleopatra VII 51–31 BC
Roman Era 30 BC–AD 337

*NB the 15th and 16th dynasties were concurrent

BIBLIOGRAPHY

Abo el Ela, Ahmed M., *Prophets and Pharaohs: Egypt and the Old Testament*, Studio 33, 2003

Bauval, Robert, and Gilbert, Adrian, *Orion Mystery: Unlocking the Secrets of the Pyramids*, Arrow, 1994

Bauval, Robert, and Hancock, Graham, *Keeper of Genesis: A Quest for the Hidden Legacy of Mankind*, Arrow, 2001

Baines, John, and Málek, Jaromir, *Atlas of Ancient Egypt*, Andromeda Oxford Ltd, 1980

Budge, E.A. Wallis, *Egyptian Ideas of the Afterlife*, Dover Publications, 1995

Clayton, Peter A., *Chronicle of the Pharaohs*, Thames & Hudson, 1994

Dodson, Aidan, and Hilton, Dyan, *The Complete Royal Families of Ancient Egypt*, The American University in Cairo Press, 2004

Edwards, I.E.S., *The Pyramids of Egypt*, Penguin, 1991

Ellis, Ralph, *Tempest & Exodus*, Edfu Books, 2000

Fakhry, Ahmed, *The Pyramids*, University of Chicago Press, 1974

Faulkner, R.O., trans., *The Ancient Egyptian Coffin Texts* Vols I–III, Aris & Phillips, 1973

Faulkner, R.O., trans., *The Ancient Egyptian Pyramid Texts*, Aris & Phillips, 1985

Faulkner, R.O., trans., *The Egyptian Book of the Dead: The Book of Going Forth by Day*, Chronicle Books, 1994

Hornung, Erik, *Conceptions of God in Ancient Egypt* (trans. John Baines), Cornell University Press, 1982

Kitchen, K.A., *Pharaoh Triumphant: The Life and Times of Ramesses II*, The American University in Cairo Press, 1990

Lawton, Ian, and Ogilvie-Herald, Chris, *Giza: The Truth*, Virgin Books, 2000

Lehner, Mark, *The Complete Pyramids*, Thames & Hudson, 1997

Lepre, J.P., *The Egyptian Pyramids: A Comprehensive Illustrated Reference*, McFarland & Company, 1991

Murray, Margaret A., *The Splendour that was Egypt*, Four Square Books, 1962

Oakes, Lorna, and Gahlin, Lucia, *Ancient Egypt: An Illustrated Reference to the Myths, Religions, Pyramids and Temples of the Land of the Pharaohs*, Barnes & Noble, 2003

Omm Sety and El Zeini, Hanny, *Abydos: Holy City of Ancient Egypt*, LL Company, 1981

Redford, Donald B., ed., *The Oxford Encyclopedia of Ancient Egypt*, Oxford University Press, 2001

Reeves, Nicholas, *The Complete Tutankhamun*, Thames & Hudson, 1990

Reeves, Nicholas, and Wilkinson, Richard H., *The Complete Valley of the Kings*, Thames & Hudson, 1996

Rohl, David, *A Test of Time: The Bible – From Myth to History*, Arrow, 1996

Schoch, Robert, and McNally, Robert Aquinas, *Pyramid Quest: Secrets of the Great Pyramid and the Dawn of Civilization*, Jeremy P. Tarcher/Penguin, 2005

Shaw, Ian, and Nicholson, Paul, *The British Museum Dictionary of Ancient Egypt*, British Museum Press, 1995

Siliotti, Alberto, *Guide to the Valley of the Kings*, A.A. Gaddis & Sons, 1996

Watterson, Barbara, *Gods of Ancient Egypt*, Bramley Books, 1999

West, John Anthony, *Serpent in the Sky: The High Wisdom of Ancient Egypt*, Quest Books, 1996

Note on translations: Quotations from Ancient Egyptian texts are by R.O. Faulkner, from *The Ancient Egyptian Pyramid Texts* (pp. 40, 42, 57, 78, 79, 236), *The Ancient Egyptian Coffin Texts* (pp. 44–5) and *The Egyptian Book of the Dead* (pp. 50, 236).